THE CASE FOR SOUTH WEST AFRICA

THE
CASE
FOR
SOUTH WEST
AFRICA

Compiled by Anthony Lejeune

TOM STACEY LTD.

Tom Stacey Ltd., 28-29 Maiden Lane,
London, WC2E 7JP

First published 1971

ISBN   Case o 85468 112 4
            Paper o 85468 113 2

Printed in Great Britain

Set and Photo-composed by
T. Bailey Forman Ltd., of Nottingham
and printed by
A. W. Wheaton & Co., Exeter

CONTENTS PAGE

A NOTE TO THE READER

by Anthony Lejeune

This book is not my own analysis of the South West Africa question, nor does it purport to set out every side of the argument. It presents, as its title implies, the case for South West Africa; that is, it expresses South Africa's point of view, and, perhaps more importantly, it includes the complete text of the two dissenting judgments given in the so-called "World Court."

I agreed to collate the chapters which follow, and to help with their publication, not because I necessarily agree with everything in them (though I do in fact agree with most of it) but for two reasons which go far beyond the rights and wrongs of this particular, rather technical, case.

The first is my dislike of the blatant prejudice (prejudice in the literal sense that crucial questions are begged, the answers taken for granted) with which the affairs of southern Africa are generally discussed in the newspapers, on the wireless and on television, very often in private conversation and *a fortiori* in the United Nations.

The assumption seems to be that the white peoples of southern Africa were born with an extra dose of original sin, or, at the very least, that they are stupider and more selfish than other people. This is not only a misleading, but a very dangerous, idea to disseminate. Its effect on the minds both of the white Africans and of their critics is cumulatively poisonous.

In reality, of course, the problems of southern Africa are unique, complicated and intractable. The Government of

South Africa, where these problems are most acute, is trying to find ways of solving them or at least living with them. Whether these are the best ways, whether they are fair or in the long run even workable, how they should be developed, or modified, are proper subjects for debate: and they are being debated, honestly and rationally, by many South Africans. It is the outside world which refuses to debate them, refuses to believe that there is such a thing as an honest and rational South African point of view. Any book which may help to correct this imbalance, however slightly, seems to me useful.

What was so depressing about the International Court's treatment of the South West Africa case was that, instead of being manifestly and magisterially unaffected by such prejudices, it seemed positively to embody them.

Here we come to my second, and more important, reason. A politically biased trial anywhere is obnoxious (obnoxious, that is, to Western ideas of justice, though not of course to Communist theory). Even the belief that trials are politically biased is harmful. The damage extends far beyond the parties directly involved. The very concept of law, on which any civilization must be founded, is brought into disrepute. A politically biased international trial, or an international trial which is believed, rightly or wrongly, to have been politically biased, perpetrates this evil on a global scale. The points raised in this book — not only the arguments of the South African Government but the worries expressed in the dissenting judgments — deserve, therefore, to be considered very seriously indeed.

The South West Africa case is not just about South West Africa. It raises inescapably the question whether, in the present state of the world, any international court which has to deal with politically or morally controversial questions could function tolerably — let alone whether such a court can function under the aegis of the United Nations.

Anybody interested in international affairs must be concerned about the issues raised in this book, for they epitomize a great deal which has been going on and they hold the seeds of much peril in the future.

PREFACE

by Sir Colin Coote

Managing Editor of

The Daily Telegraph 1950-64

BETWEEN JANUARY and June 1971 the World Court at The Hague succumbed to the renewed pressure of the Afro-Asian bloc of the United Nations, and ranged itself among the dismal throng of snarlers against South Africa. It is not my purpose nor that of this book to counter-snarl against International Organizations as such. I was actually on the Executive Committee of the League of Nations Union under Lord Robert Cecil after the First World War, and shared his hopes that the League could save future generations from a holocaust like that which had bled mine white. But the League perished of debility; and it must be confessed that the title of its successor, the United Nations, is becoming a contradiction in terms. The UN is in danger of deserving Gibbon's label of "a scandal to the pious and a laughing-stock to the profane". Fifty years ago, I was taught to describe the Crusades as "Corruptio Optimi Pessima" ("When the best goes bad, it becomes the worst"). The verdict of the Court can only increase the applicability of this maxim to the United Nations.

The verdict, in the form of an Advisory Opinion, found that South Africa was acting illegally in continuing, after the demise of the League, the administration of South West Africa entrusted to her under Mandate in 1920. The Court went far beyond calling on South Africa to hand over to the United Nations. In a tone appropriate to the declaration of a Jehad or Holy War, it even called upon non-UN members to help the UN in terminating a situation illegal in every respect; and

9

hinted that the Security Council ought soon to take further action. It is not the Court's fault that, luckily, the South Africans are unlikely to take any notice of its verdict, particularly because, out of 15 Judges, the British and French Judges dissented on principle, two others on points of detail, and the personal opinions of several more showed traces of uneasiness. I must leave to the book to show in detail whether justice has been done and seen to have been done, but here certain key facts and odd episodes can be underlined.

The first is that the American State Department sent its legal Representative to argue in Court that the UN should take over South West Africa, and that South Africa's offer of a plebiscite was irrelevant. This is another instance of the obsession of the American Government against South Africa. It refuses to do itself and world liquidity a restorative service by increasing the price of gold, because that would suit South Africa and Russia. It belabours so-called racialist policies, when it has utterly failed to solve its own racial problems, and when the streets of New York are notoriously more dangerous after dark than those of Pretoria — not to mention Windhoek. This bias persists. One of the charges in the 1966 offensive of the Afro-Asian bloc (which was supported by the United States) was that South West Africa was being turned into a military base, and a special American envoy, General S. L. Marshall, reported that the territory was "less militarized and more underarmed" than any other spot in the world. Why the Court and the Americans should have treated today's charges as less questionable passes understanding.

American persistence in following red herrings owes much to suspicion of "colonialism" everywhere outside territories administered by the Americans themselves. No doubt the preference for self-government over good government is fashionable and irresistible. But too often, particularly in Africa, it has resulted in no government at all. Egypt today is a serf of the Soviets, directly because Washington ganged up with Moscow and the Afro-Asian bloc to frustrate the Suez operation in 1956. The second key point is that the two dissenting Judges, the British and French, represent two different legal systems. The British assume innocence until guilt is proved; the French guilt until innocence is proved. Nevertheless neither could stomach the procedure followed by the Court.

Monsieur André Gros, supported on this point even by an *African* colleague, was specially revolted by the fact that one at least of the Judges was a notorious partisan of the ejection of South Africa [1] , and yet the Court rejected South Africa's request for the appointment of an *ad hoc* Judge as is normal in controversial cases. Sir Gerald Fitzmaurice, who was more comprehensively scathing even than his French colleague, held that mandatory supervision by the League was not inherited by the UN. "The proceedings," he said, "represented an attempt to use the Court for a purely political end." Such a purpose would never have been condoned by the League, as I knew it, and seems to reflect a thirst more for force than for peace. Surely it is damning to the verdict that these two Judges, associated with different legal systems, should both dissent for different reasons. For the deduction is that from whatever angle the verdict is viewed, it is nonsensical.

A third point is that the reader might find relevant the case of another international court with which I was well acquainted — the Nuremberg Court which tried the Nazi war criminals. There, too, prejudice against the defendants was unavoidable, the the Judges spent several preliminary months in drawing up a Charter which gave the alleged monsters unquestionable fair play. It occurred to me that the Nuremberg Court was fairer to Goering than the Hague Court has been to South Africa! A last point. Surely the interests of the inhabitants are more important than legalities? Yet the Court blandly, and, as Sir Gerald Fitzmaurice contends, without proper examination, assumed that apartheid was oppressing the non-Europeans in South West Africa. It is the basic principle of sound journalism to "verify your references". Should not that also be the basis of sound law?

Did any judge personally know South West Africa? Did the Court send anyone to check what was happening there? Did any judge recall the record of the UN in the Congo? Is Dr. Connor Cruse O'Brien to be considered an impeccable author-

---

1 Not one only but three are reported to have taken sides before being appointed to the Court.

ity on African problems, and Field Marshal Smuts negligible? Perhaps the reader will allow a modest slice of my own recent and first-hand evidence of events and conditions. It is at least as good as the evidence of the Rev. Michael Scott whom the UN, relying, as so often, on inspiration rather than information, accepted as an expert in 1949 on the strength of a three-weeks' stay in the territory — incidentally nearly twice as big as France.

Even study on the spot cannot guarantee the complete absence of discontent; but the South Africans are entirely confident that the main tribes, without any outside pressure, would vote for their continued administration. The system is, indeed, more Lugardism than apartheid — *i.e.* indirect rule with meticulous respect for the tribal traditions — except for the tradition of tribal warfare. Oddly enough, the dissatisfaction I found was more among Europeans who were tired of being cursed for oppression when by far the greater proportion of what they pay in taxation is spent on non-Europeans. Only a few years ago the most common epithet for South West Africa was "arid". In a few years the vast irrigation projects — such as that in conjunction with the Portuguese on the Cunene River — will make it the best watered area in all South Africa. And who was it that discovered the huge mineral deposits of uranium, copper, lead and zinc which seem a certain guarantee of a brilliant economic future? Not the Ovambos, nor the Hereros, nor the United Nations.

Therefore I hope this book will help in substituting objectivity and facts for hysteria and ignorance. South Africa has sometimes disconcerted the impartial by doing apparently silly things. But in any competition for silliness the first prize would be easily won by her critics.

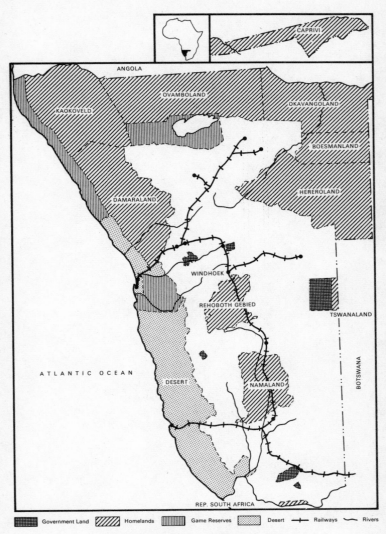

ANGOLA

CAPRIVI

KAOKOVELD

OVAMBOLAND

OKAVANGOLAND

BOESMANLAND

DAMARALAND

HEREROLAND

WINDHOEK

REHOBOTH GEBIED

TSWANALAND

ATLANTIC OCEAN

DESERT

NAMALAND

BOTSWANA

REP. SOUTH AFRICA

■ Government Land ▨ Homelands ▥ Game Reserves ▨ Desert ┼ Railways ～ Rivers

SOUTH WEST AFRICA   1971

1

RESULTS OF THE
1971 WORLD COURT ACTION

IN 1920 SOUTH AFRICA accepted in respect of her administration of the former German colony, South West Africa —
a vast, sparsely populated, desert-like territory, then still finan-
cially bankrupt — a Mandate from the League of Nations.
This authorized her continued administration of the territory
as an integral part of her own and "under her own laws".
South Africa pledged herself to promote to the utmost the
moral and material well-being and social progress of the inhabitants. This was the so-called "sacred trust for civilization".

Today, after half a century, the foundations have been laid
for a modern, capital-intensive economy. Millions are provided annually for the large scale development of the homelands of the various non-White population groups as well as
for the territory's overall development. In fact, South Africa's
assistance constitutes the highest per capita foreign aid ever
provided by one country to the people of another territory.
International agreements have been concluded for the development of hydro-electric schemes and water supplies and, as
reported in internationally known newspapers such as the
New York Times, impressive progress has been made in the
construction of numerous additional dams, roads, airfields,
hospitals, schools and housing projects. Telecommunications
and railway services have been greatly expanded.

The progress which is everywhere apparent has arisen from
the close links which South West Africa has enjoyed with the
advanced industrial and technological economy of South

Africa and from South Africa's determination to develop the area along well-conceived political and socio-economic lines. On 27 October 1966, however, the General Assembly resolved that since South Africa had not carried out its pledge, the Mandate was terminated and that henceforth South West Africa came under the responsibility of the United Nations (resolution 2145 (XXI).

Subsequently the General Assembly confirmed this resolution by various other resolutions, in which it proclaimed, *inter alia,* "that, in accordance with the desires of its people, South West Africa shall henceforth be known as 'namibia'.", and on three occasions the Security Council has called upon the Government of South Africa to withdraw its administration from the Territory (resolutions 264 and 269 (1969) and 276 (1970)). South Africa refused on legal, historical and practical grounds to do so.[a] On 29 July 1970 the United Nations Security Council requested the International Court of Justice to furnish it with an Advisory Opinion. The question put to the Court was:

"What are the legal consequences for States of the continued presence of South Africa in Namibia (i.e. South West Africa) notwithstanding Security Council resolution 276 (1970)?"

This was but the latest in a long chain of political moves on the part of certain members of the United Nations in an attempt to engineer the removal of South Africa from the territory of South West Africa. The Council's request had its genesis in the disappointment of a number of states with the International Court's Judgment of 1966 rejecting the claims of Ethiopia and Liberia in the contentious proceedings initiated by them against South Africa.[b]

In the United Nations the reaction of many of the States concerned was one of near-hysteria. The Court was reviled and ridiculed and its motives and impartiality violently attacked. Repeated calls were made for the Assembly to terminate the Mandate forthwith. It was in this atmosphere and

a South Africa's reasons were set out in several hundred pages in its pleadings before the World Court during 1971. The necessary documentation can be obtained from city libraries or the World Court in The Hague. See also Chapter 9.

b See Chapter 3.

14

ignoring the legal and factual issues involved that the Assembly purported to revoke the Mandate in its resolution 2145 (XXI) of 27 October 1966. Warnings from certain countries that the Assembly was exceeding its powers under the Charter were brushed aside. Suggestions that the Assembly should ask the Court for an advisory opinion on the matter were similarly treated.

Since that time both the General Assembly and the Security Council have repeatedly demanded that South Africa withdraw from the territory. They have also adopted a series of resolutions aimed at applying tangible pressures to force South Africa to withdraw. South Africa has consistently denied the legal validity of resolution 2145 (XXI) as well as the existence of any factual justification for it.

Her position has led to attempts by certain African and Asian States in the Security Council to brand the situation in the territory as a threat to international peace and security so that coercive measures may be applied against South Africa under Chapter VII of the United Nations Charter. These attempts have so far been unavailing because some of the Western Powers on the Council recognize that the situation in South West Africa does not at all constitute a threat to international peace and security and have accordingly declined to proceed upon the basis that it does. This situation of near-stalemate led the Afro-Asian members of the Council to support a compromise resolution requesting the Court for its Opinion.

As a result of subsequent elections the composition of the Court has changed substantially since the Assembly adopted resolution 2145 (XXI). And the Afro-Asian states were frankly confident that this factor would result in an Opinion which would support their political position and so enable them to bring further pressure to bear on the Western States concerned. On the other hand, all the members of the Court had for the first time the opportunity of pronouncing themselves judicially on the validity of the action taken by the Assembly and the Council. The Court which heard the pleadings on South West Africa were:

> Sir Muhammad Zafrulla Khan (President)
> Mr. Ammoun (Vice-President)
> Sir Gerald Fitzmaurice

Messrs Padilla Nervo
Forster
Gros
Bengzon
Petren
Lachs
Onyeama
Dillard
Ignacio-Pinto
de Castro
Morozov
Jimenez de Arechaga (Judges)
Aquarone (Registrar)

Following the Security Council's request for an Advisory Opinion, the States entitled to appear before the Court were notified that the Court was prepared to receive from them written statements furnishing information on the question. Written statements were received from the following twelve States: Czechoslovakia, Finland, France, Hungary, India, Netherlands, Nigeria, Pakistan, Poland, South Africa, United States of America, Yugoslavia. In addition, the Secretary-General of the United Nations transmitted to the Court documents likely to throw light upon the question and a written statement. (The latter arrived after the deadline set by the Court to all parties concerned but was nonetheless accepted).

The Government of South Africa took objection to the participation of President Sir Muhammad Zafrulla Khan and Judges Padilla Nervo and Morozov in the proceedings; and applied for leave to choose a judge *ad hoc* to sit upon the Bench. After deliberation, the Court decided not to accede to the objections raised against the three. After hearing *in camera* the submissions of South Africa on the appointment of a judge *ad hoc*, it decided to reject the application presented with that object.

The States entitled to appear before the Court, and also the Organization of African Unity (from whose member states three judges sat in the Court), were informed that the Court was prepared to hear oral statements. Such statements were made, in the course of 23 public sittings held between 8 February and 17 March 1971, by representatives of the Secretary-General of the United Nations, the Organization of African

Unity, Finland, India, Netherlands, Nigeria, Pakistan, the Republic of Vietnam, South Africa and the United States of America.

At the opening of the sittings, the President announced that the Court had decided not to entertain the observations which the Government of South Africa had made, in its written statement and elsewhere, in support of its submission that the Court should have declined to give the Advisory Opinion requested. At the close of the sittings, the President announced that the Court had decided to defer its reply to the requests of the Government of South Africa, presented before and during the sittings, concerning the possibility of holding a plebiscite in Namibia (South West Africa) and the supply of further factual material concerning the situation in that territory.

In a letter dated 14 May 1971 to the representatives of the States and organizations which had participated in the oral proceedings, the President stated that the Court had decided to refuse both of those requests. On 21 June 1971 the Court delivered its Advisory Opinion in which it replied to the question put to it by the Security Council, by 13 votes to two:

1) that, the continued presence of South Africa in Namibia being illegal, South Africa is under obligation to withdraw its administration from Namibia immediately and thus put an end to its occupation of the territory; c by eleven votes to four,

2) that States Members of the United Nations are under obligation to recognize the illegality of South Africa's presence in Namibia and the invalidity of its acts on behalf of or concerning Namibia, and to refrain from any acts and in particular any dealings with the Government of South Africa implying recognition of the legality of or lending support or assistance to, such presence and administration;

---

c It should be noted that an Advisory Opinion has no legally binding force and thus no State is obliged to give effect to it. It can at most serve as a guide, the persuasive force of which must necessarily depend on such factors as the cogency of the Court's legal reasoning, the presence or absence of political motivation, and the extent and strength of dissenting opinions.

3) that it is incumbent upon States which are not Members of the United Nations to give assistance, within the scope of subparagraph (2) above, in the action which has been taken by the United Nations with regard to Namibia.

Judges Sir Gerald Fitzmaurice and Gros appended dissenting opinions to the Advisory Opinion.[d] Judges Petren and Onyeama appended separate opinions in which they stated that they voted for the above subparagraph (1) but against subparagraphs (2) and (3). The President, the Vice-President and three other Members of the Court each appended either a declaration or a separate opinion in which he stated his agreement with the Court's reply. In its Advisory Opinion the Court explained why it had earlier rejected requests by South Africa concerning:

the participation of three Members of the Court in the proceedings, the appointment by South Africa of a judge *ad hoc,* its submission that the Court should refuse to give an advisory opinion on the question on account of political pressures to which, it contended, the Court had been or might be submitted, the supply of further factual material, the possibility of holding a plebiscite in South West Africa under the joint supervision of the Court and the South African Government.

In the Opinion itself:

(a) The Court recalled that the Government of South Africa had advanced several other reasons why, in its view, the Court was not competent or, alternatively, should decline to give an advisory opinion. After "due consideration", the Court saw no reason to refuse the opinion requested.

(b) The court recapitulated the history of the Mandate for South West Africa, rejecting the contentions of South Africa in that respect and recalling its own pronouncements on the subject in its Advisory Opinions of 1950, 1955 and 1956 and its Judgment of 1962. (But not in that of 1966).

(c) Objections having been raised against the validity of the General Assembly and Security Council decisions declaring the continued presence of South Africa in Namibia illegal

d See Chapter 5b: Appendix E.

(General Assembly resolution 2145 (XXI) and Security Council resolution 276 (1970)), the Court examined these objections and held them to be without foundation.

(d) The Court expounded its conclusions as to the legal consequences for States of the illegal presence of South Africa in "Namibia" (see points (1), (2) and (3) above).

(e) The Court declared that it viewed the policy of apartheid now applied in Namibia as a flagrant violation of the purposes and principles of the United Nations Charter.

This book was compiled from various South African, United Nations and private legal sources for the purpose of showing that the Opinion expressed by the World Court was not only political in character but also based on the most dubious legal reasoning while at the same time openly shying away from the examination of factual evidence; and that the Opinion thus endangered the status of international law and would seriously damage the prestige of the World Court. Because of the nature of the call made upon Member States of the United Nations and other countries (see operative clauses (2) and (3) of the Opinion), it is essential for people who care for what is right and who are involved in law and politics to study seriously the material here presented.

In this way they will be armed with facts to obviate any imprudent decision concerning South West Africa on the part of those who still (incredibly) cling to the belief that the General Assembly of the United Nations are solely interested in the welfare of the people of "Namibia". The major part of the book consists of the dissenting opinions of Judges Sir Gerald Fitzmaurice (England) and Gros (France) who alone among the judges chose to deal with the South West Africa issue on purely legal grounds and with proper regard to previous findings of the Court. In fact they alone could be seen as having acted in the best tradition of Western jurisprudence. (The reader is referred to Appendix D which contains an excellent index to the various points made by Judge Fitzmaurice.)

The voice of reason is not often heard when South African issues are ventilated in the press or in Parliament. However, the points of view published in this book *are* the voices of reason and they *do* need to be heard. The fact that a cogent case was made out by South Africa's very able legal team at The Hague will be drowned in the clamour of the Afro-Asian majority at the United Nations for Western "action" against South Africa, and this clamour will be dutifully reported by a large segment of the press in this country, who stubbornly cling to the assumption that a majority opinion is necessarily both objective and correct. The publication of the views of Judges Fitzmaurice and Gros in this book is designed to ensure that the voice of reason is heard.

Should the Afro-Asian majority tactics eventually lead to a disastrous military confrontation with South Africa over "Namibia", there will be no possible basis for saying that the politicians and those responsible for informing the public were themselves ill-informed. This book is for students, specialists in international law, editors, officials, parliamentarians — all who have a rôle to play in influencing and formulating foreign policy. Quite apart from the issues concerning South West Africa the dissenting opinions of Judges Fitzmaurice and Gros contain most illuminating analyses of the role of the Security Council, the powers of the General Assembly of the United Nations, and the dangers inherent in any abuse of these powers.

The Case for South West Africa is no easy book. In view of the long history of legal battles over South West Africa it was impossible that it should be. The issues are not simple. Nor are the possible implications. Even so, the layman who is concerned as to whether his taxes will be used to finance some illogical, illegal and potentially disastrous action against South Africa, or the businessman who is advised to get out of South West Africa (only to see someone else better informed, step into his place), should find here enough material to persuade even the least easily persuaded that this country should reject the majority opinion of the World Court, and should view the incidental attempt by the Court and the Secretary General of the United Nations to transmute the General Assembly into a world legislature with the gravest misgivings.

The ultimate result of the political manoeuvres at The Hague has been exactly in accord with the wishes of the United Nations majorities, and those wishes bear no resemblance to justice or reality. In their eyes the Court has, by

means of its newly-constituted majority, indeed "rehabilitated" itself and "redeem(ed) its impaired image". The majority has ruled that South Africa's title to administer South West
Africa has been validly revoked by the General Assembly of
the United Nations, by unilateral action which is binding on
South Africa and all other dissentients (despite the fact that,
with irrelevant exceptions, the Charter of the United Nations
confers on the General Assembly only powers of discussion
and recommendation). In the process the majority has ignored
the 1966 Judgment of the Court and the various important
findings upon which it was based; yet the majority opinion
does not so much as mention what was said in that Judgment!
As regards the majority of 13 to two, the two minority judges
are the only survivors of the 1966 majority.

The actions of the majority of the judges of the World
Court during the preliminary stages of the latest proceedings
were more like those of a steamroller than of a court in which
matters of international law (and of life and death) are appre-
ciated. There was an unseemly and undignified haste on the
part of the majority to say "no" to every request made by
South Africa, irrespective of its merits and importance. Of
some members of the Court this was indeed to be expected.
Take the case of Judge Morozov. It was he who led the Soviet
delegation at the United Nations until 1969, and had on various occasions condemned South Africa's administration and
actions in South West Africa at length and in unbridled terms,
of which the following extract is typical:

"the South African racists have extended to South West
Africa the régime of repression and terror against the
indigenous population that prevails in Pretoria. The
South West African patriots who stand up for the libera-
tion of their fatherland are subject to savage persecu-
tion, arrest and torture".[e]

e During the 1962-66 case the same allegations had at first been made in the World
Court but had significantly been withdrawn in the face of evidence to the contrary
effect. Just before the 1971 World Court opinion a team of top journalists from the
major news agencies of the world and such newspapers as the *New York Times* and
news magazines such as *Time* and *Newsweek*, toured South West Africa. In view of
what these men reported the conclusion must be that either they must have been
inventing things or else Mr. Morozov must merely have been handing out Soviet pro-
paganda for the pleasure of the Afro-Asian public.

In addition, in regard to one of those Security Council Resolutions which formed the subject-matter of the Court proceedings, this man was in 1968 thanked by the co-sponsors for his "constructive co-operation . . . and the great contribution (he) made to the formulation of the draft resolution." Yet, despite South Africa's objection, he had no compunction in sitting on the Court and was permitted by the majority to do so. This is one of the matters on which judges Fitzmaurice and Gros expressed great concern. And not these only. Their Swedish colleague in particular was firmly with them on this. The rejection of South Africa's request to be allowed to appoint a Judge *ad hoc* is another example. Certain passages from the dissenting Opinion of Sir Gerald Fitzmaurice should suffice:

"In my opinion this rejection was wrong in law, and also unjustified as a matter of equity and fair dealing, — for it was obvious, and could not indeed be denied by the Court, that South Africa has a direct, distinctive and concrete special interest to protect in this case, quite different in kind from the general and common interest that other States had as Members of the United Nations. In short, South Africa had, and was alone in having, precisely the same type of interest in the whole matter that a litigant defendant has — and should therefore have been granted the same right that any litigant before the Court possesses, namely that, if there is not already a judge of its own nationality amongst the regular judges of the Court, it can, under Article 31 of the Statute of the Court, appoint a judge *ad hoc* to sit for the purposes of the case. The Court's refusal to allow this was thrown into particular relief by the almost simultaneous rejection, in the three Orders of the Court dated 26 January 1971, of the South African challenge concerning the propriety of three regular judges of the Court sitting in the case . . . it is clear that the Court in no way lacked the power to grant the South African request, but was simply unwilling to do so. In fact, if ever there was a case for allowing the appointment of a judge *ad hoc* in advisory proceedings, that case was this one."

The above highlights the impression created at the time by *the Court's insistence upon hearing the South African applica-*

tion behind closed doors, and by its giving no reasons for its decision. The implications of the Court's action for Western States such as Britain and France and for the future outlook are thus of great importance. Part of the implications are those suggested for all members of the United Nations, including the United Kingdom, by the wide powers of binding decision attributed by the Court to the Security Council. More immediately, it seems highly likely that South Africa's adversaries will take the matter back to the Security Council and urge them that drastic action be taken in order to get South Africa out of the Territory. There are various points which will no doubt be relied upon by any Western government wishing to avoid involvement in any such action. For instance:

(a) The Opinion lacks persuasive force as a legal or factual basis for action.

(b) Whatever the legal position, it is clear on the majority's own showing that they did not make any such investigation into the present factual situation in South West Africa as could be of any assistance to the Security Council in determining its further course of action.

(c) The United Kingdom's, and also France's, view that there is no threat to international peace and security is fortified in particular by:

  i) The South African offer to join in arranging a plebiscite, and to invite for the purpose a committee of independent experts.

  ii) The articles of the international journalists who participated in the recent (June 1971) tour.

d) South Africa's methods in the administration of the territory were developed in concurrence with the Permanent Mandates Commission of the League of Nations: and their alleged incompatibility with the Mandate has never even now been judicially established, or properly inquired into. To this last point the United States judge himself drew attention.

2

SOUTH WEST AFRICA'S BIRTH — AND THE U.N.

ALTHOUGH Portuguese navigators went ashore on their voyages along the coast of the present South West Africa during the fifteenth and sixteenth centuries, European interest in this part of the African Continent was stimulated only after the settlement of the Dutch at the Cape of Good Hope in 1652. Between then and the end of the century the Governor at the Cape dispatched sailing vessels to explore the coast of South West Africa, and at the beginning of the eighteenth century, hunters and explorers, travelling overland from the Cape, started making periodic expeditions into the southern part of the Territory.

The beginning of the nineteenth century saw missionaries settling in the area, followed by traders and by explorers who gradually penetrated further and further northwards into the interior. At the same time important developments were taking place along the coast. In 1793 the Government at the Cape proclaimed Dutch sovereignty over Angra Pequena (later renamed Luderitzbucht), Halifax Island and Walvis Bay, so that when the Cape passed into British hands in 1795 these possessions came under British control. Certain islands along the coast were annexed by Great Britain in 1867 and incorporated in the Colony of the Cape of Good Hope in 1874. In 1878 followed the British annexation of the area surrounding Walvis Bay, known as the Port and Settlement of Walvis Bay, which was incorporated in the Cape of Good Hope in 1884.

German interest in South West Africa arose out of a business enterprise established there by a German merchant, F. A. E. Luderitz. In 1883 Luderitz purchased from a Nama Chief the Bay of Angra Pequena and an adjacent strip of land along the coast, and appealed to the German Government for protection of his interests, which led to diplomatic exchanges between Germany and Great Britain. The outcome was a German Protectorate, proclaimed in 1884 over the area surrounding Angra Pequena, renamed Luderitzbucht. The British Government "decided to acquiesce in the action of the German Government," thereby leaving the way open for Germany to establish her authority over the Territory of South West Africa, with the exclusion of Walvis Bay and certain islands off the coast, which were recognized as British territory. German authority in the Territory was thereafter gradually extended by the conclusion of treaties of friendship and protection with various indigenous chiefs.

The boundaries of the Territory, which eventually became known as German South West Africa, were laid down in broad outline by agreements, concluded in 1886 with Portugal, then already in possession of Angola, and in 1890 with Britain, which had earlier proclaimed a protectorate over Bechuanaland. Within these boundaries lay the regions formerly known as Namaland and Damaland, as well as the northern areas of the Kaokoveld, Ovamboland, the Okavango and the Caprivi. The advent of the Germans did not in itself bring hostilities to and end between the indigenous groups in South West Africa, which continued for quite some time, in particular between the Herero and certain Nama tribes.

The Germans brought troops from Germany and established military posts in different parts of the Territory in an effort to secure peace and order. In 1897 the total strength of the German forces in the Protectorate was 700 men, and by 1898 the whole of the southern part of the Territory had been temporarily pacified. The German authorities could then turn their attention to the economic development of the country. First priority was given to communications, and in 1898 a start was made with the construction of a railway line between Swakopmund on the coast and Windhoek. By 1901 Windhoek was in telegraphic communication with Germany and in 1902 the first train steamed into Windhoek station. At the same time, the harbour at Swakopmund was improved and a regular steamship service instituted to and from Europe. Improved communications paved the way for further development. Germans were encouraged to settle in the Territory, and by 1903 the White civilian population numbered 3,701.

Peace in the Territory, however, was shortlived. In 1903 trouble broke out among the Bondelswarts, a Nama tribe in the South. While the German forces were engaged there, a general Herero uprising flared up in the central part of the Territory, giving rise to the Herero-German war in which a number of Nama tribes also participated. Peace was not restored until the end of 1906. Between the years 1907 and 1914 German rule was firmly established. The construction of further internal railway lines, commenced during the wars, was completed after the termination of hostilities, while the discovery of diamonds near Luderitzbucht in 1908 acted as a stimulus to investment. During the last years of the German period, the White population, which numbered 14,830 in 1913, was engaged in farming, mining, commerce and other activities. The majority of them were Germans, but a considerable number, particularly of the farming community were South Africans who had settled in the Territory.

While much had been done by the German authorities to widen the economic structure of the Territory, the central problem of opening up the interior and developing its resources still remained unsolved. Indeed, effective German administration never extended beyond the southern and central parts of the Territory, in the area then known as the Police Zone. The northern areas outside the Police Zone, comprising the Kaokoveld, Ovamboland and the Okavango, were left untouched, while in the Caprivi only a very sketchy form of administration existed from 1910. South West Africa remained under German rule until after the outbreak of the First World War. The South African Government undertook the conquest of the Territory. A military campaign followed, and the German troops surrendered to the South African Forces on July 9, 1915. From that date until the inception of the Mandate for South West Africa, the Territory was under South African military government.

The Mandate System originated, together with the League of Nations, from the peace settlements after the First World

War. Its application provided a solution to a clash of views and aspirations within the ranks of the Allied and associated powers concerning the future of territories and colonies conquered from enemy powers during the War. On the one hand, certain states strongly pressed for the annexation of the territories occupied by them. On the other hand, there had been proposals, made during the war years, for international control of conquered territories, proposals which were in due course linked with others, also then current, for the establishment of a League of Nations. Thus arose the idea of a mandate system under which administering states would act as mandatories on behalf of the League. Two distinguished early protagonists of this idea, G. L. Beer, American historian and adviser to President Wilson of the United States of America, and General J. C. Smuts, both excluded South West Africa from their proposals and favoured incorporation of the Territory in the Union of South Africa.

President Wilson, however, advocated an unequivocal policy of "no annexation" and sought to secure the application of a mandate system in an extreme form to all ex-enemy colonies and possessions, without exception. According to his proposals, complete authority and control would be vested in the League of Nations, and mandatories (who could be states or "organized agencies") would be mere agents, appointable and changeable at the League's discretion; further the expenses of mandatory government would, if necessary, be borne by all the Members of the League. The conflict to which these divergent views gave rise at the Paris Peace Conference was eventually resolved by the adoption of a compromise by which President Wilson abandoned certain of the more extreme aspects of his proposals on League supremacy and control, in return for the inclusion of all the former German colonial possessions in the Mandate System.

In particular all the mandatories were to be States, not "organized agencies"; the mandates were to be allocated by the principal Allied and associated powers, not by the League; in some instances, including South West Africa, the Mandatory would have to be the neighbouring power then occupying the Territory, and would be authorized to govern the Territory as an integral part of its own territory; the relationship between the League and the Mandatories was in each case to be regulated by a mandate instrument, the terms of which had to be agreed to by the Mandatory; and there was to be no question of all League Members paying administrative expenses. This compromise arrangement was embodied in Article 22 of the Covenant of the League of Nations which was incorporated in the Treaty of Versailles. The Treaty was signed in June, 1919, and came into force on January 10, 1920. In anticipation of the signing of the Treaty, the principal Powers decided in May, 1919, on the allocation of the former German Colonies. This included a decision that the Mandate for South West Africa was to be held by the Union of South Africa. On December 17, 1920, the Council of the League confirmed the Mandate and defined its terms.

The functions of the League of Nations in respect of Mandates were exercised by the Council, the Assembly and the Permanent Mandates Commission. It was to the Council, specifically, that the Mandatories were to render reports to its satisfaction, and it was to the Council that they were ultimately accountable. The Council alone had power to take decisions about Mandates and to address recommendations to the Mandatories. While the Assembly had powers to deal at its meetings with any matter within the sphere of action of the League, a "working basis" was decided on at the first Assembly, according to which neither the Council nor the Assembly would have jurisdiction to render a *decision* in a matter which, by the Treaties of the Covenant, had been expressly committed to the other organ of the League. Either body could, however, *discuss* and *examine* any matter within the competence of the League. The Assembly's role in respect of Mandates was therefore a very limited one. It was described in an official League publication as confined to the function of maintaining touch between public opinion and the Council.

The role of the Permanent Mandates Commission in the Mandate System was to receive and examine the annual reports of the Mandatories and to advise the Council on all matters relating to the observance of the Mandates. The members of the Commission were independent experts selected for personal merit and competence, who, in the language of the Commission, were to exercise their authority "less as judges from whom critical pronouncements are expected, than as collaborators who are resolved to devote their experience and their energies to a joint endeavour." Supervision of the administration of the various Mandates by the Council of the League, acting with the assistance of the Permanent Mandates Commission, continued from the inception of the Mandate System until the outbreak of the Second World War when meetings of the Commission ceased. Throughout this period South Africa regularly submitted annual reports concerning South West Africa to the League and accounted to the Council for its administration of the Territory.

The Charter of the United Nations was drafted, unanimously agreed upon, and signed by the representatives of all the nations, fifty in number, attending the San Francisco Conference in 1945. The Charter came into force on October 24, 1945. At that time the League of Nations was still in existence and, although its dissolution was imminent, it continued to exist side by side with the new organization until April, 1946. There was no suggestion that the United Nations was to be the League under a new name, or an automatic successor in law to League assets, obligations, functions or activities. The two organizations differed not only in membership but also in the composition and procedures of their respective organs.

The Charter made no provision for the continuation of the Mandate System of the League under the United Nations Organization. It provided, instead, for the establishment of United Nations Trusteeship System for the administration and supervision of such territories, including former Mandated Territories, as might be placed under it by agreement. This was, however, to be on purely voluntary basis, an individual agreement being required in respect of each territory admitted to trusteeship. In the case of South West Africa, the South African Government, from the very outset, at the San Francisco Conference, declared that it had no intention of placing the Territory under the United Nations Trusteeship System. Similar declarations were repeatedly made thereafter.

The United Nations commenced functioning in January, 1946. At the first session of the General Assembly the different Mandatory Powers declared their intentions concerning the future of the territories administered by them respectively. The South African Representative drew attention to the special position occupied by South West Africa in relation to the Union of South Africa. He intimated that arrangements were being made for the consultation of the people of the Territory regarding the form which their future government should take, and he formally reserved the position of his Government concerning the future of the Mandate. The League of Nations Assembly held its last session on April 18, 1946. Its final resolution provided that the League should cease to exist as from the following day. Previously, several other Resolutions had been adopted in contemplation of the League's dissolution, one of which was concerned with Mandates. This Resolution was preceded by statements in which the Mandatory Powers again declared their intentions regarding their respective Mandates.

Certain mandatories declared that they were prepared to negotiate trusteeship agreements while others made reservations concerning their position. Among the latter was South Africa, whose Representative informed the Assembly of the League that South Africa intended to put to the General Assembly of the United Nations a case of the incorporation of South West Africa into the Union of South Africa. In making their declarations in the League Assembly some of the representatives mentioned the fact that upon the dissolution of the League and the disappearance of the League Council and the Permanent Mandates Commission, it would be impossible to comply fully with the provisions of the Mandates.

In general, however, the tenor of each of the statements was that until a trusteeship agreement was concluded, or some other arrangement was made regarding a particular mandated territory, the Mandatory concerned would continue to *administer* the territory for the well-being and development of the inhabitants thereof, in accordance with the provisions of general principles of the Mandate. In none of these statements did the Mandatory Powers acknowledge or even suggest that, pending the conclusion of a trusteeship agreement or any other arrangement, they would be obliged to report and account under their respective Mandates to the United Nations as they had previously done to the League Council. The League Assembly's Resolution on Mandates merely noted the declared intentions of the Mandatory Powers, and no provision was made for any transfer of the League's supervisory functions in respect of Mandates to the United Nations or for

31

B

reporting and accounting by Mandatories to that organization.

South Africa's proposal concerning the incorporation of South West Africa was submitted to the General Assembly of the United Nations in 1946. A written memorandum was lodged, setting forth reasons for the proposed step, among which was the fact that an overwhelming majority of the inhabitants of the Territory, both white and non-White, were in favour of incorporation. The General Assembly rejected the proposal and recommended instead, that South West Africa be placed under the Trusteeship of the United Nations. South Africa's attitude, however, was that it was not obliged to conclude a trusteeship agreement, and that it was not prepared to do so as such a step would not be in accordance with the wishes of the vast majority of the inhabitants concerned. South Africa informed the General Assembly that it would therefore continue to administer the Territory in the spirit of the principles laid down in the Mandate. And it would transmit regularly to the United Nations, but only for purposes of information, statistical and other information of a technical nature relating to economic, social and educational conditions in South West Africa.

It was explained in communications to the United Nations during 1947 and 1948 that such reports would be submitted on a purely voluntary basis; that they would be limited to the same type of information as was required for Non-Self-Governing Territories under Article 73 of the Charter; that they were intended merely for information purposes; and that they should not be treated as if the United Nations were vested with supervisory powers in respect of South West Africa. In particular, it was stressed that, outside of a trusteeship agreement, the United Nations would, in the view of the South African Government, have no supervisory jurisdiction over the Territory. In 1947, and again in 1948 and 1949, the General Assembly repeated its earlier request that a trusteeship agreement be submitted for South West Africa, but, for the reasons previously advanced, South Africa refused to accede to the request.

In 1949 South Africa withdrew its undertaking to submit reports for information purposes to the United Nations, on the ground that the organization had used the one report which had by then been submitted (for the year 1946) as if it were vested with supervisory powers over South West Africa, and had thus failed to observe the conditions on which South Africa had voluntarily undertaken to furnish reports. The situation in regard to South West Africa formed the subject of frequent debates in the United Nations over the years 1947-1949. The attitude of Member States to various aspects of the matter differed. These differences related mainly to the questions as to whether the Mandate was still in force, whether South Africa was under a legal obligation to enter into a trusteeship agreement, and whether, outside of trusteeship, South West Africa was to be regarded as a Non-Self-Governing Territory falling under the provisions of Chapter XI of the Charter. In view of these differences the General Assembly decided in December, 1949, to request the International Court of Justice for an Advisory Opinion concerning the international status of South West Africa.

The Advisory Opinion of the International Court was delivered on July 11, 1959. The fourteen members of the Court who participated were unanimous in the view that the Mandate for South West Africa was still in force. Further, in answer to certain specific questions of the General Assembly, the Court expressed the following views:

(a) that Article 6 of the Mandate had survived the dissolution of the League; the supervisory functions formerly exercised by the League were to be exercised by the United Nations, to which the annual reports and petitions were to be submitted. Two judges dissented on this part of the opinion;

(b) that the adjudication clause in Article 7 of the Mandate was still in force and therefore that South Africa, as Mandatory, was under obligation to accept the jurisdiction of the International Court of Justice with regard to disputes concerning the interpretation or application of the provisions of the Mandate;

(c) that South Africa was not under a legal obligation to conclude a trusteeship agreement in respect of South West Africa. Six judges dissented on this part of the opinion;

(d) that the competence to determine and modify the international status of the Territory rested with South Africa acting with the consent of the United Nations.

33

The General Assembly of the United Nations accepted the 1950 Advisory Opinion and proceeded to act thereon. Difficulties were, however, experienced by the Organization in attempting to apply the Opinion in practice, and a result the Court was asked in 1955 and 1956 for further Advisory Opinions interpreting the 1950 Opinion. The 1955 Opinion concerned voting procedures on questions relating to reports and petitions in connection with South West Africa, and the 1956 Opinion dealt with the admissibility of oral hearings of petitioners by the United Nations organs. As these Opinions were advisory only, they were not binding on South Africa, which stated its reasons for not accepting as correct at least some of the views expressed.

In particular, South African Representatives at the United Nations drew attention to important facts which had come to light since the Court had given its 1950 Opinion and which, it was submitted, had a direct bearing on the reasoning and conclusions of the Court with regard to certain material points. It was contended that if these facts had been placed before the Court in 1950, it would probably not have come to the same conclusion regarding transfer to the United Nations of the League's supervisory functions in respect of the Mandate. Under these circumstances a situation arose and developed over the years in which the General Assembly, acting on the majority vote of the Members of the United Nations, repeatedly requested South Africa to submit a trusteeship agreement in respect of South West Africa, while it sought, at the same time, to exercise supervisory functions in respect of the Territory in implementation of the Court's Opinion.

In the process the General Assembly appointed various Committees for the purpose, *inter alia*, of studying, and reporting on, the administration of South West Africa. These reports regularly contained critical and condemnatory statements concerning South Africa's policies and practices in South West Africa. South Africa, for its part, consistently refused to accede to the repeated requests to submit South West Africa to the Trusteeship System. Relying on its contention that the United Nations had no supervisory powers in respect of the Territory, the South African Government also refused to cooperate in attempts by the United Nations to exercise supervisory functions. In conformity with this attitude, South Africa's representatives refrained from dealing systematically with complaints contained in the reports of the various Committees concerning policies and practices in South West Africa, although they did on occasion, for purposes of illustration, demonstrate the factual inaccuracy of certain of the complaints.

Over the years, efforts were made to find a solution to the impasse. These took the form of negotiations between South Africa and organs and agencies of the United Nations appointed for that purpose. The negotiations showed, however, that the majority of the Members of the United Nations would not be satisfied with any arrangement unless its effect was to bring South West Africa under the control and supervision of the United Nations, a solution which was not acceptable to South Africa. While negotiations were still proceeding, the General Assembly in February, 1957, requested the Commitee on South West Africa to study what legal action could be taken

".... To ensure that the Union of South Africa fulfils the obligations assumed by it under the Mandate, pending the placing of the Territory of South West Africa under the International Trusteeship System."

The Committee thereupon prepared and submitted to the General Assembly several reports on matters which it considered could be raised for adjudication by the Court, either by a request for an advisory opinion or by contentious proceedings instituted by individual Members of the United Nations. The conclusions of the Committee concerning possible legal action were noted in Resolutions of the General Assembly and specially commended to the attention of Member States. In June, 1960, at a Conference of Independent African States, held at Addis Ababa, the Governments of Ethiopia and Liberia signified their intention of instituting contentious proceedings against South Africa in the International Court of Justice. The proceedings were in fact instituted on November 4, 1960.

CHAPTER

3

SOUTH AFRICA'S RIGHTS CHALLENGED
Legal Proceedings on
South West Africa 1960-66

ONE OF THE objects of the contentious proceedings instituted by Ethiopia and Liberia was to obtain declarations from
the Court that the Mandate was still in existence, and that the
General Assembly of the United Nations had succeeded to
the supervisory functions formerly exercised in respect of
Mandates by the Council of the League of Nations. If declarations to this effect could be obtained in contentious proceedings, they would be binding and enforceable, which is not the
position with advisory opinions. But the applicants did not
limit their charges to these aspects — they also contended that
South Africa had been guilty of a number of violations of the
Mandate. The most important of these related to Article 2 (2)
of the Mandate which read:
"The Mandatory shall promote to the utmost the
material and moral well-being and the social progress of
the inhabitants of the territory subject to the present
Mandate."
It was alleged that South Africa had violated this Article by
the policies it applied in the Territory, in the political,
economic, social and educational fields. It was further alleged
that South Africa had, in contravention of the Mandate, established military bases in the Territory, and had also pursued a
deliberate process of unilateral, piecemeal incorporation of the
Territory into the then Union of South Africa. The first stage
of the proceedings was devoted to the matter of jurisdiction.
South Africa's attitude was that, even assuming for the sake of

argument that the Mandate was still in existence, the applicants had not shown that the requirements for jurisdiction, as prescribed in the adjudication clause in the Mandate, had been satisfied. Briefly, South Africa relied in this regard on the following four contentions (the success of any one of which would have been sufficient to unsuit the Applicants):

"First Objection:
The Mandate for South West Africa — either as regards all its provisions or in any event as regards Article 7 — never was a treaty or convention within the meaning of Article 37 of the Statute of the Court or, at any rate, was no longer in force as such after the dissolution of the League of Nations.

Second Objection:
Even if the Mandate could be said still to exist as a 'treaty or convention in force,' the dispute disclosed in the Memorials was not between South Africa and 'another Member of the League of Nations' (as required by Article 7 of the Mandate) inasmuch as both Applicants had ceased to be Members of the League of Nations at its dissolution.

Third Objection:
In any event the conflict or disagreement alleged by the Applicants to exist between them and South Africa was not a 'dispute' as envisaged in Article 7 of the Mandate, inasmuch as this conflict or disagreement did not affect any material interests of the Applicant States or their nationals.

Fourth Objection:
Furthermore, in any event, the alleged conflict or disagreement was not a dispute which could not be settled by negotiation within the meaning of Article 7."

After written and oral argument, the objections to jurisdiction were overruled in December, 1962, by the Court by eight votes to seven. In view of the issue as to the correctness or otherwise of the 1950 Opinion on the question of United Nations supervision of the Mandate, the Court's attitude towards the second of the above objections was highly significant. The Applicants had strenuously invited the Court to find that the answer to the second objection lay in a *succession,* whereby the United Nations had succeeded to the supervisory powers of the League, and the Members of the United Nations had succeeded to the competence of the Members of the League to activate the Court. But the Court declined the invitation: it found, on the contrary, that the competence to invoke the Court's jurisdiction was retained by the States which had been Members of the League at the date of its dissolution.

On the associated question whether the United Nations as an organization had succeeded to the supervisory powers of the League, seven of the Judges on the majority side made no express finding; but their finding on competence to invoke the Court's jurisdiction, as well as their reasoning in support of that finding, was logically opposed to any idea of such succession. The eighth Judge on the majority side, and three of the minority Judges, explicitly found that no such succession had occurred. Their reasoning in support of this finding was strongly influenced by the facts which had come to light subsequent to the 1950 Opinion, and which had been specially stressed by Respondent during argument.[1] The opinions of the remaining four Judges had no bearing on this question.

After the dismissal of the Preliminary Objections, the case proceeded on the merits. The question of United Nations supervision was again extensively debated. At this stage the Applicants were eventually constrained to concede that some

---

1 These facts (as amplified during the Oral Proceedings on the Merits) included the following:

    (a) In the Preparatory Commission of the United Nations there were proposals (part of those concerning a Temporary Trusteeship Committee) to make express provision for United Nations supervision of Mandates not converted into Trusteeships. But some of these proposals were rejected, and the others were abandoned, probably because of opposition.

    (b) At the final session of the League Assembly, there was again a proposal (referred to in Court as the "first Chinese proposal") for the League's supervisory powers in respect of Mandates to be transferred to the United Nations. Again the proposal was abandoned, this time clearly because of opposition to it.

    (c) Statements made by States at the United Nations during the years 1947, 1948 and 1949 overwhelmingly showed a general understanding that unless a Trusteeship agreement were concluded, a Mandatory would not be obliged to report and account to the United Nations regarding compliance with its Mandate obligations.

South Africa contended that these facts, singly and cumulatively and in conjunction with other relevant facts, conclusively refuted the proposition on which the 1950 Opinion concerning accountability seemed to rest, viz., that a substitution of supervisory organs had occurred through a general, tacit agreement or understanding between all interested parties.

of the reasoning of the 1950 Opinion in that regard was unten-able, but they contended that the result was nevertheless correct. The main issue on the merits revolved round the alleged contraventions of Article 2 (2) of the Mandate quoted above. Applicants' case in their pleadings was that the politi-cal, educational, economic and social policies applied in the Territory (which policies were jointly called *apartheid*) were oppressive in nature, and were designed for the specific pur-pose of subordinating the interests of the Native population to those of the Europeans. In making this charge the Applicants were merely repeating accusations which had been bandied about in the United Nations for years, and had regularly been reflected in Resolutions of committees and organs of the Organization.

In very comprehensive pleadings South Africa refuted this charge. This was done not only by correcting false and dis-torted versions of fact in the Applicants' pleadings but also by providing the proper perspective in which different policies and measures should be seen. In addition South Africa gave notice of its intention to call 38 witnesses to testify in Court, and also invited the Court to visit the Territory so as to acquaint itself with the true circumstances. It is not proposed to provide at this stage a resume of the South African exposition in the pleadings. Suffice it to say that it demon-strated in detail that the policies in question were designed for the benefit of all population groups in the Territory, and in fact served the best interests of them all.

The important point for present purposes is that the Appli-cants apparently felt unable to controvert these expositions. The result was that in the course of the Oral Proceedings they admitted as true all the facts presented by South Africa, and amended their formal Submissions so as to delete all earlier references to allegations of oppressive intent or deleterious effects adhering to the South African policies. They also vigorously opposed the proposal for an inspection and, indeed, the calling of any witnesses. Applicants then limited them-selves to the contention that certain admitted features of the South African policies contravened an alleged "international human rights norm of non-discrimination or non-separation," or alleged "standards" of the same content. These concepts were described as follows:

". . . the terms 'non-discrimination' or 'non-separation'
are used in their prevalent and customary sense: stated
negatively, the terms refer to the absence of governmental policies or actions which allot status, rights, duties,
privileges or burdens on the basis of membership in a
group, class or race rather than on the basis of individual
merit, capacity or potential: stated affirmatively, the
terms refer to governmental policies and actions the
objective of which is to protect equality of opportunity
and equal protection of the laws to individual persons as
such."

It is important to note that the suggested norm or standards
were unqualified in their terms: they were not limited to discrimination which was oppressive in intent or harmful in
effect. Indeed, in argument Applicants, *inter alia*, expressly
and emphatically endorsed the following passage in the South
African pleadings:

"If indeed Article 2 of the Mandate must be read as containing an absolute prohibition on 'the allotment, by
governmental policy and action, of rights and burdens on
the basis of membership in a group', Applicants would
sufficiently establish a violation of the article by proving
such an allotment, irrespective of whether it was
intended to operate, or does in fact operate, for the
benefit of the inhabitants of the Territory."

After this change in Applicants' case, the rest of the proceedings concerning alleged violations of Article 2 (2) of the
Mandate was confined to the question whether or not a norm
or standards of this content existed. Applicants contended that
such a rule had been created primarily by the activities of the
United Nations, and should be applied in "interpreting"
Article 2 (2) of the Mandate. South Africa disputed the existence of any such rule, or its applicability to Article 2 (2). In
support of its denial it, *inter alia*, presented oral testimony by
13 expert witnesses, showing, *firstly,* that such a rule was not
observed in the laws and official practices of at least 50 states
and territories in the world, including both the Applicant
States and 38 other Members of the United Nations, and,
secondly, that in many parts of the world, including South
Africa and South West Africa, enforcement of such a rule

41

would cause bloodshed and chaos. This testimony is again referred to later, in another context.

The significance of the Applicants' *volte face* can hardly be overrated. It must be kept in mind that the Applicants, in instituting and conducting the proceedings against South Africa, in fact acted as representatives of the Organization of African Unity, which sponsored the proceedings. In their original charge of oppression Applicants presented a case of undoubted *legal* foundation, the success of which depended only on convincing the Court of the truth of the *factual* allegations of oppression which had virtually been treated as axiomatic before the United Nations. Moreover, the emotional impact of a finding by the International Court that South Africa's policies were intentionally oppressive, would obviously have been much greater than a finding merely to the effect that a somewhat colourless norm or standards had been violated — a finding which, in addition, required a revolutionary approach by the Court to the law-making processes in International Law.

Despite all these considerations, the Applicants abandoned the charges of oppression in favour of the case based on the norm and standards. The only possible explanation is that they realized their inability to substantiate the charges. By their admissions of fact they in effect conceded that the basis upon which South Africa's policies had been condemned at the United Nations over many years, was false. Possibly because of belated realization of the far-reaching impact of these dramatic events, representatives of the Applicant States have more recently been issuing rather astonishing denials that the substance of their case had been altered or that they had accepted as true all the facts presented in South Africa's pleadings. In answer to such denials made during debates at the 21st Session of the General Assembly of the United Nations, the South African delegation submitted a Memorandum which was circulated as United Nations Document A/6480 of 20 October, 1966, showing, *inter alia*, with detailed reference to the record of the Court proceedings, how unfounded the denials were.

The further issues in the Court proceedings, viz., those concerning alleged piecemeal incorporation of the Territory and the establishment of military bases, were also covered by the

Applicants' admission of the facts presented by South Africa, which virtually disposed of these complaints. However, South Africa went further to put the issue of militarization beyond doubt: for it was largely on the basis of alleged militarization that majorities at the United Nations had resolved that the situation in South West Africa constituted "a threat to international peace and security". An American military expert of recognised standing and renown, Gen. S. L. A. Marshall, was called as a witness. He told the Court that he had twice during 1965 visited the Territory, and that it contained no military bases whatsoever. Indeed, he said, "the Territory is less militarized and more underarmed than any territory of its size I have ever seen in the world."

In July 1966, the Court gave Judgment rejecting all the Applicants' claims. This decision was reached by the casting vote of the President after the Court had divided 7-7. Without deciding whether the Mandate was still in existence, the Court held that, even if it was, the Applicant States had no legal right or interest to question the Mandatory's performance of those obligations to which their complaints related. A decision on this antecedent point rendered it unnecessary for the Court to express itself on the further issues on the merits referred to above. However, certain inferences can be drawn as to the Court's views on some of them. Thus there are passages in the reasoning in the Judgment which strongly suggest that the authors were of opinion that there was no longer any entity vested with supervisory powers in respect of the Mandate. [1] Moreover, the Court's views, expressed in the Judgment regarding the legal principles of interpretation, were entirely

---

1 Of particular significance is a passage at p. 36 of the Judgment of 18 July, 1966, reading as follows:

"Another argument which requires consideration is that. *in so far as the Court's view leads to the conclusion that there is now no entity entitled to claim the due performance of the Mandate,* it must be unacceptable. Without attempting in any way to pronounce on the various implications involved in this argument, the Court thinks the inference sought to be drawn from it is inadmissible. If, on a correct legal reading of a given situation, certain alleged rights are found to be non-existent, the consequences of this must be accepted. The Court cannot properly postulate the existence of such rights in order to avert those consequences. This would be to engage in an essentially legislative task, in the service of political ends the promotion of which, however desirable in itself, lies outside the function of a court-of-law". (Italics added)

It will be noted that the Court nowhere says that the conclusion mentioned in the italicised words would not be justified.

opposed to those whereby the Applicants sought to read a recently-arisen norm or standard into the Mandate instrument — a document executed in 1920.

Some light was also cast on these issues by certain of the separate Opinions of individual Judges. Thus it is significant that Applicants' contention of an unqualified norm or standard of non-discrimination or non-separation was not accepted by any of the Judges. And the charges of militarization were emphatically rejected by the three Judges who referred to this topic — two of whom were in the minority in respect of the Judgment itself. It will therefore be evident, even from this extremely brief account, that the Court proceedings as a whole brought about a set-back for the cause of the Applicants and their associates, extending very far beyond the mere legal conclusion that they had no legal right or interest in the subject matter of their complaints.

4

THE MAJORITY AT THE HAGUE PREJUDGE THE CASE

IN THE 1970-71 CASE fourteen States as well as the Secretary-General of the United Nations and the Organization of African Unity participated in the written and oral proceedings before the Court. The proceedings embraced a very wide range of important legal issues and were the longest ever held in an advisory case. Before the start of the oral proceedings the Court decided against South Africa on three preliminary matters. Firstly, it rejected South Africa's application for the recusal of three of the Judges on the ground of their previous political involvement in the issues in dispute. It heard no argument on the matter and gave no reasons for its decision.

Secondly, by a majority of 10 to 5 it rejected an application by South Africa for the appointment of a Judge *ad hoc*. Although South Africa objected strongly, the Court heard this application in closed session. But having rejected the application it decided for some unknown reason to release the record of the hearing to the public. Thirdly, the Court refused to entertain South Africa's submission that there were compelling reasons why the Court should decline to give the Opinion requested of it. South Africa contended in its written statement that the United Nations had so embroiled the Court in the political issues surrounding the question that the Court would be unable to exercise its judicial function properly. South Africa pointed to the violent abuse and threats to which the Court has been subjected for its Judgment of 1966;

to the accusations of corruption, ulterior political motives and underhand dealings levelled against various Judges; and to the thinly-veiled warnings by members of the Security Council that in the present case the Court must "rehabilitate" itself and "redeem its impaired image." In these circumstances, South Africa said, it would be extremely difficult for the Court to give an Opinion which to an objective observer would appear to be free from political bias. It should therefore decline jurisdiction. To this the Court replied, without hearing oral argument, that in the exercise of its judicial function under the Charter and its Statute, it acts only on the basis of the law — independently of any outside influences whatsoever.

The merits of the question put to the Court involve both factual and legal issues. The former concern principally the question of whether there was any justification in fact for the Assembly's decision purporting to terminate the Mandate. The latter are concerned with the scope of the question put to the Court and whether the General Assembly and the Security Council were legally empowered to take the action they did. South Africa contended that apart from all other considerations, the purported revocation of the Mandate by the General Assembly was illegal because there was no factual basis for it. The Assembly's action was based on allegations that South Africa's practices and policies in South West Africa oppressed and repressed the peoples of the Territory and denied to them fundamental human rights and self-determination.

These allegations are still regularly repeated in the United Nations. South Africa's expositions of the real facts are contemptuously brushed aside. On the other hand, fantastic assertions of genocide and slavery, of murder and massacre, of militarization, terrorism and landgrabbing are apparently accepted as the absolute truth. They were seized upon as a basis for violent attacks upon South Africa and as justification for the revocation of the Mandate. The written statement of South Africa demonstrated the falsity of these allegations. Supplemented by a photographic presentation, it showed the impressive progress and development of the peoples of the Territory. It contrasted this with the far slower growth rates in a number of other African countries. And it illustrated why it is necessary for South Africa to continue to administer the

Territory while the inhabitants are still progressing towards self-determination.

All the participants in the proceedings adverted to the factual basis of the Assembly's action. Where South Africa's statement was not completely ignored it was simply dismissed out of hand on the ground that the real facts were common knowledge and could not be denied. Once again numerous allegations of oppression and the denial of self-determination were levelled at South Africa. But they were raised in the form of vague generalities and they indicated no specific ground of complaint. Moreover, they were either completely unsupported or else supported by a mere reference to a vast body of U.N. documentation. This bristled with contradictions and inconsistencies.

It was thus impossible to establish the precise nature of the charges made or the grounds on which they were based. A formal application by South Africa that the Court cause the factual issues to be properly defined and delimited was rejected. And there was no response to a subsequent invitation to the other participants to indicate in their oral statements exactly what their allegations were. South Africa was consequently faced with the task of investigating a field of factual issues that was vast in its ambit. She demonstrated to the Court the relevance and scope of such an enquiry. She indicated that should the Court so require, she would in due course present it with further factual material in refutation of the charges made against her. The Court decided to defer its decision on the matter.

It was important to South Africa that she be allowed to present further factual material should the Court not find in her favour on the legal issues. In her written statement she had refuted the more extravagant allegations made against her in the United Nations. But she contended that she was also entitled to reply to the mass of further allegations raised in the oral proceedings. The Court could not properly find that resolution 2145(XXI) was valid without allowing her that opportunity. But South Africa went still further. In an effort to place evidence before the Court she proposed that a plebiscite be held in South West Africa. The object of the plebiscite would be to determine once and for all whether it was the wish of the inhabitants that they continue to be administered by the

South African Government or whether they would henceforth rather be administered by the United Nations.

In this way the allegations of oppression, repression and denial of self-determination would be put to the most fundamental test of all — that of the expressed will of the inhabitants themselves. And the ambit of the factual enquiry could be greatly reduced. The plebiscite would be jointly supervised by the Court and the South African Government. Detailed arrangements would be as agreed upon by the Court and that Government. South Africa stated categorically that she was not opposed in principle to any fair and practical method of ascertaining the wishes of the inhabitants. She also made it quite clear that acceptance or support of the proposal by the Court or any participant would be entirely without prejudice to their legal position on the status of South West Africa.

Now if the other participants had really believed in the truth of their various allegations they would surely have seized upon the plebiscite proposal as an excellent means of proving them. For if South Africa was in fact oppressing the peoples of the Territory and denying them self-determination, those peoples would surely jump at any opportunity of voicing their distress and dissatisfaction. Yet the reaction of the participants was to reject the proposal completely. The flimsiest of pretexts were invoked. Vague and unspecified objections were raised as to the competence of the Court. Despite all the U.N. declarations to the contrary it was suggested that the peoples of the Territory were not yet ready to determine their own future.

Although the very issue before the Court was whether South Africa was in the Territory legally or illegally, it was said that she had no standing to make the proposal because she was there illegally! Some participants even denied the relevance or value of a plebiscite. The Secretary-General of the United Nations went so far as to say that a vote in favour of South Africa would not be evidence that South Africa had complied with her obligations under the Mandate. On the contrary, it could be interpreted to mean that South Africa had not promoted the welfare of the inhabitants — because it would only show their lack of political development under the South African administration.

The attitude of the Secretary-General would seem to be that the inhabitants might still vote in favour of South Africa even though they were being massacred and exterminated, terrorized and enslaved and robbed of their land!

As in the case of South Africa's request to furnish additional factual material, the Court decided to defer its decision on the plebiscite proposal as well. But on 14 May 1971 the Court advised South Africa that it did not find itself in need of further arguments or information. It had accordingly decided to reject both applications. The first of the legal issues concerned the scope of the question put to the Court. It was argued by several participants that that question concerned only the consequences of South Africa's presence in South West Africa. Therefore, it was said, the Court was precluded from going into the underlying question of whether the General Assembly's decision to revoke the Mandate and assume control of the Territory was valid or invalid. The Court must simply assume its validity.

South Africa showed that the Council did not intend to restrict the question in this way. The Assembly's decision was the very basis of all the issues before the Court. And an Opinion based upon an assumption regarding the fundamental issue in dispute would be altogether ridiculous and meaningless. The reluctance of participants that the Court should go into the matter only served to emphasize their realization that the decision had no basis in law. South Africa went on to demonstrate why the Assembly's decision was invalid. The Assembly had purported to act as successor to the League of Nations — which had exercised powers of supervision over the Mandate. But those powers did not include a power to revoke the Mandate unilaterally or to assume direct control over the Territory. And in any event no succession to the League had taken place.

Whatever the position, the Charter of the United Nations conferred no such powers upon the General Assembly. For apart from some irrelevant exceptions, the Charter provides unequivocally that the only powers which the Assembly has are those of discussion and recommendation. It cannot make binding decisions or itself take direct action. It was therefore not surprising to find that no single participant was able to show that any specific provision of the Charter empowered the Assembly to act as it did. Most participants evaded this

49

vital issue. The few who raised it did so very perfunctorily — usually by way of bare and unsupported statements. And all the participants failed even to try to meet any of the arguments of France and South Africa regarding the absence of any specific Charter basis.

Instead they suggested more than a dozen possible alternative bases for the alleged powers of the Assembly. This illustrates not only the disagreement and confusion of thought which reigned among them but also the insuperable difficulties with which they were faced. One participant frankly acknowledged that the Assembly's action could not be justified by the ordinary rules of international law. However, most participants recognized that the Assembly cannot act outside the Charter. Being unable to justify the Assembly's action under any specific provision thereof, they were forced to argue that the Assembly had very wide *implied* powers under the Charter. But in response to questions by the Court, they were totally unable to indicate the limits of these powers.

South Africa proceeded to show that implied powers can be admitted only in exceptional cases after certain strict requirements of law and logic have been satisfied. These requirements had certainly not been satisfied in the case of the General Assembly. She showed this by reference to the text of the Charter, the jurisprudence of the Court and the writings of publicists. And she demonstrated that the framers of the Charter had very carefully restricted the powers of the Assembly to discussion and recommendation. They had done this deliberately because they realized that States would not accept a Charter which curtailed their sovereign rights too far.

South Africa also pointed out the startling implications of a doctrine of virtually unlimited implied powers in favour of the Assembly. As some participants indeed argued, it would mean that the Assembly could make findings of fact and law which would bind even non-consenting States. If the Charter confers these powers in the case of South West Africa it must confer it in all cases. The Assembly could thus, for example, prescribe a socialistic economic policy for the U.S.A. or a capitalistic one for the U.S.S.R. It could prohibit space flights or state religions. It could enforce equal rights for women in Islamic countries or monogamy in African countries. It could prescribe a governmental system for Cyprus or independence for Northern Ireland. It could order the opening of the Suez Canal. And in all these cases the States concerned would be legally bound to obey.

The various attempts which were made to invest the Assembly with powers which it clearly does not have under the Charter goes to underline that the whole basis of Assembly resolution 2145 (XXI) was political — not legal. South Africa showed that the various resolutions of the Security Council were also invalid — both formally and intrinsically. They were *formally* invalid in several important respects. These related to the composition of the Council, non-compliance with the voting requirements and procedures laid down in the Charter, and the failure of the Council to invite South Africa to participate in its discussions.

They were *intrinsically* invalid because, firstly, they were based entirely upon the invalid decision of the General Assembly to terminate the Mandate. And, secondly, when the Council adopted them, it acted altogether beyond its powers as laid down in the Charter. They therefore had no legal effect whatsoever. The question put to the Court concerns the legal consequences for States of South Africa's continued presence in South West Africa, notwithstanding Security Council resolution 276 (1970). That resolution condemns South Africa's refusal to comply with various United Nations resolutions on South West Africa. It also "declares" South Africa's presence in the Territory to be illegal and calls upon all States to refrain from any dealings with South Africa in regard to the Territory.

Of all the participants in the proceedings, only four made any attempt to indicate what specific provision of the Charter empowered the Council to act as it did. And they suggested four different alternatives. The rest ignored this basic issue altogether. As in the case of the General Assembly, their confusion of thought is not surprising. For in terms of the Charter it is only under Chapter VII that the Security Council can take decisions which are binding upon States. And although one participant argued to the contrary, it is abundantly clear, and was indeed conceded by others, that in adopting resolution 276 (1970) the Council did not even purport to act under that Chapter.

Two participants saw Chapter VI of the Charter as the

source of the Council's authority. And indeed it is only under that Chapter that the Council *could* have purported to act. But in terms of Chapter VI the Council can only make recommendations — which can never have obligatory force. Thus, even if resolution 276 (1970) were to be regarded as valid, the only parts of it which could have any legal consequence would be those paragraphs which may be regarded as recommendations calling upon States to refrain from dealings with South Africa. And the only consequence would be that States should consider these recommendations and decide for themselves whether to carry them out or not.

However, South Africa showed that the resolution was *not* valid because the Council did not comply with the requirements of Chapter VI. For that Chapter can only be invoked in order to maintain international peace and security. And the Council must first make a proper determination that a particular situation is likely to endanger that peace and security. The Council made no such determination. Moreover its real purpose was not to maintain peace and security. It was to secure South Africa's withdrawal from the Territory so that the United Nations could assume control of it. That is manifest from all its debates and resolutions. For these reasons too, resolution 276 (1970) is invalid and without legal consequences.

These arguments were virtually ignored by the other participants who made no attempt to substantiate their claims that the Council had acted validly under Chapter VI. Other participants invoked Article 24 and Article 80(1) of the Charter in order to justify the Council's action. But since neither of those Articles confer any powers on the Council whatsoever, these participants were again forced to fall back on a vague theory of wide implied powers. In the result, South Africa demonstrated that the resolutions of the Council were invalid in a number of respects. They can therefore have no legal consequences for States at all.

The proceedings before the Court were remarkable for two things. One was the deliberate evasion by the other participants of the legal issues in dispute and the political basis of their statements. The other was the way in which they refused throughout to meet the arguments of South Africa. It was no doubt an awareness of this which prompted the Secretary-

General of the United Nations at the very end of the proceedings to request a special opportunity to address the Court. Upon being permitted to do so, he asked that his failure to reply to any of the points presented in the proceedings should not be construed by the Court as an admission on his part of their correctness or completeness or relevance!

SOUTH WEST AFRICA CASE
1970-1971

THE MAIN POINTS of interest in the proceedings may be briefly summarized as follows.

1. The Court rejected South Africa's applications and submissions —

(i) for the recusal of three judges of the Court;

(ii) for the appointment of a judge *ad hoc;*

(iii) that compelling political reasons existed why the Court should decline to give the Opinion;

(iv) that a plebiscite be held to test the wishes of the inhabitants of the Territory;

(v) that the factual issues be properly defined and that further factual material be laid before the Court.

2. The statements of the other participants were characterized by:

(i) the vague and unsubstantiated nature of the factual allegations made against South Africa's administration of the Territory;

(ii) their negative reactions to the holding of a plebiscite;

53

(iii) their inability to indicate any specific basis in the Charter for the action taken by the General Assembly and the Security Council;

(iv) their consequent forced reliance upon the doctrine of virtually unlimited implied powers;

(v) their reluctance that the Court should examine the validity of General Assembly resolution 2145 (XXI);

(vi) more generally, their deliberate evasion of most of the crisp legal issues in dispute and their failure to try to meet South Africa's arguments on these issues.

3. By contrast, South Africa's case was inherently strong and carefully prepared. She had no difficulty in showing that the Assembly and the Council acted *ultra vires* the Charter and that their resolutions were therefore void and of no effect.

5

SIR GERALD FITZMAURICE (UK)
DISSENTS

SIR GERALD FITZMAURICE — one of the world's leading international legal experts — felt he had to dissent from the opinion of the World Court on South West Africa. As his dissent unfurls in this chapter, it is worth remembering that Sir Gerald has tremendous weight in this field. Sir Gerald was legal adviser to the United Kingdom delegations at the San Francisco conference founding the UN in 1945. He was member and later President of the International Law Commission of the UN and has been a Judge at the International Court of Justice since 1960.

1. Although I respect the humanitarian sentiments and the avowed concern for the welfare of the peoples of SW. Africa which so clearly underlie the Opinion of the Court in this case, I cannot as a jurist accept the reasoning on which it is based. Moreover, the Opinion seems to me insufficiently directed to those aspects of the matter which really require to be established in order to warrant the conclusion that South Africa's mandate in respect of SW. Africa stands validly revoked. Much of the substance of the Opinion (i.e., that part of it which does not deal with formal, preliminary or incidental matters) is taken up with demonstrating that League of Nations mandates, as an international institution, survived the dissolution of the league — whereas what is really in issue in this case is not the survival of the Mandate for SW. Africa but

its purported revocation. Whether or not South Africa still disputes the survival of the Mandate, it certainly disputes its survival in the form of an obligation *owed to the United Nations* (this is the basic issue in the case); and denies that the organs of the United Nations have any competence or power to revoke it.

2. As regards the Court's conclusion that the Mandate has been validly revoked, this can be seen to rest almost exclusively on two assumptions — or rather, in the final analysis, on one only. I speak of assumptions advisedly, — and indeed, concerning the second and more far-reaching of the two (which in one form or another really underlies and entirely motivates the whole Opinion of the Court), there is an open admission that nothing more is needed — the matter being "self-evident." These two assumptions are *first* that there was, or there must have been, an inherent right, vested in the United Nations, unilaterally to revoke the Mandate in the event of fundamental breaches of it (unilaterally determined to exist), — and *secondly,* that there have in fact been such breaches. Since it is clear that the supposed inherent right of revocation, even if it exists, could never be invoked *except* on a basis of fundamental breaches (several passages in the Opinion specifically recognize that only a material breach could justify revocation), it follows that the whole Opinion, or at least its central conclusion, depends on the existence of such breaches. How then does the Opinion deal with this essential matter? — essential because, if there is insufficient justification *in law* for the assumption, the whole Opinion must fall to the ground, as also (though not only for that reason) must the General Assembly's Resolution 2145 of 1966 purporting to revoke, or declare the termination of the Mandate, which was predicated on a similar assumption.

3. The charges of breaches of the Mandate are of two main kinds. The first relates to the failure to carry out, *in relation to the United Nations* an obligation which, in the relevant provision of the Mandate itself (Article 6), is described as an obligation to make an annual report "to the Council of the League of Nations". At the critical date however, at which the legal situation has to be assessed, namely in October 1966 when the Assembly's resolution 2145 purporting to revoke the Mandate, or declare its termination, was adopted, the view that the

failure to report to the Assembly of the United Nations constituted a breach of it — let alone a fundamental one — rested
basically (not on a judgment but) on an Advisory Opinion
given by this Court in 1950 which, being advisory only, and
rendered to the United Nations, not South Africa, *was not
binding on the latter* and, as regards this particular matter, was
highly controversial in character, attracted important dissents,
and was the subject of much subsequent serious professional
criticism. This could not be considered an adequate basis in
law for the exercise of a power of unilateral revocation, even
if such a power existed. There cannot be a fundamental breach
of something that has never — *in a manner binding upon the
entity supposed to be subject to it* — been established as being
an obligation at all, — which has indeed always been, as it still
is, the subject of genuine legal contestation. That South Africa
denied the existence of the obligation is of course quite a different matter, and in no way a sufficient ground for predicat-
ing a breach of it.

4. The second category of charges relates to conduct, said to
be detrimental to "the material and moral well-being and the
social progress" of the inhabitants of the mandated territory,
and thus contrary to Article 2 of the Mandate. *These charges
had never, at the critical date of the adoption of Assembly
resolution 2145, been the subject of any judicial determination
at all,* — and in the present proceedings the Court has specifically refused to investigate them, having rejected the South
African application to be allowed to present further factual
evidence and connected argument on the matter. The justification for this rejection is said to be that practices of "apartheid", or separate development, are self-evidently detrimental
to the welfare of the inhabitants of the mandated territory, and
that since these practices are evidence by laws and decrees of
the Mandatory which are matters of public record there is no
need for any proof of them. This is an easy line to take, and
clearly saves much trouble. But is it becoming to a court of
law? — for the ellipsis in the reasoning is manifest. Certainly
the authenticity of the laws and decrees themselves does not
need to be established, and can be regarded as a matter of
which, to use the common law phrase, "judicial notice" would
be taken without specific proof. But the *deductions* to be
drawn from such laws and decrees, as to the effect they would

57

produce in the particular local circumstances, must obviously be at least *open* to argument, — and there are few, if any, mature systems of private law, the courts of which, whatever conclusions they might ultimately come to, would refuse to hear it. Yet it was on the very question of the alleged self-evidently detrimental effect of its policies of apartheid *in SW. Africa*, that the Mandatory wanted to adduce further factual evidence. Thus the Court, while availing itself of principles of contractual law when it is a question of seeking to establish a right of unilateral revocation for fundamental breaches, fails to apply those corresponding safeguards which private law itself institutes, directed to ensuring that there have indeed *been* such breaches. It is not by postulations that this can be done.

5. In consequence, since the whole Opinion of the Court turns, in the final analysis, on the view that fundamental breaches of the Mandate have occurred, it must (regrettably) be concluded that, in the circumstances above described, this finding has been reached on a basis that must endanger its authority on account of failure to conduct any adequate investigation into the ultimate foundation on which it professes to rest.

6. What, in truth, the present proceedings are or should properly speaking, and primarily, be concerned with, is not any of this, but issues of competence and powers, — for unless the necessary competence and power to revoke South Africa's mandate duly resided in the organs of the United Nations, — unless the Mandatory, upon the dissolution of the League of Nations, became accountable to such an organ, — no infringements of the Mandate, however serious, could operate in law to validate an act of revocation by the United Nations, or impart to it any legal effect. Here the fallacy, based on yet another unsubstantiated assumption underlying the whole Opinion of the Court, namely that the survival of the Mandate *necessarily* entailed the supervisory role of the United Nations, becomes prominent.

7. As to unilateral revocability itself, the Opinion proceeds according to a conception of the position of the various League of Nations mandatories, in relation to their mandates, which would have been considered unrecognizable in the time of the League, and unacceptable if recognized. My reading of the situation is based — in orthodox fashion — on what

appears to have been the intentions of those concerned at the time. The Court's view, the outcome of a different, and to me alien philosophy, is based on what has become the intentions of new and different entities and organs fifty years later. This is not a legally valid criterion, and those thinking of having recourse to the international judicial process at the present time must pay close attention to the elaborate explanation of its attitude on this kind of matter which the Court itself gives in its Opinion.

8. Under both heads, — the competence of the United Nations to supervise, and the liability of the Mandate to (unilateral) revocation, — the findings of the Court involve formidable legal difficulties which the Opinion turns rather than meets, and sometimes hardly seems to notice at all. Inferences based on the desirability or, as the case may be, the undesirability, of certain results or consequences, do not, as my colleague Judge Gros points out, form a satisfactory foundation for legal conclusions, — no more than would such an oversimplification of the issue as that involved in the assertion that South Africa administered its mandate on behalf of the United Nations which, therefore, had the right to revoke it, — a view which quietly begs virtually every question in the case. Here again, statements to the effect that certain results cannot be accepted because this would be tantamount to admitting that given rights were in their nature imperfect and unenforceable, do not carry conviction as a matter of international law since, at the present stage of its development, this is precisely what that system itself in large measure is, and will, pending changes not at present foreseeable, continue to be. It is not by ignoring this situation that the law will be advanced.

9. Given the Court's refusal to allow the appointment of a South African judge *ad hoc* in the present case, in spite of its clearly very contentious character (as to this, see section 4 of the Annex hereto), it is especially necessary that the difficulties I refer to should be stated, and fully gone into. This must be my excuse for the length of an Opinion which the nature of the case makes it impossible to reduce, except at the risk of important omissions.

10. The substance of my view is contained in the four sections A-D of Part II hereof (paragraphs 11-124). A postscriptum on certain related political aspects of the whole matter

is added (paragraph 125). As regards the various preliminary issues that have arisen, these — or such of them as I have felt it necessary to consider — are, together with one or two other matters that can more conveniently be treated of there, dealt with in the Annex that follows paragraph 125. On the substantive issues in the case my principal conclusions, stated without their supporting reasoning, are as follows :

(i) Although the various mandates comprising the League of Nations mandates system survived the dissolution of that entity in 1946, neither then nor subsequently did the United Nations, *which was not the League's successor in law*, become invested with the supervisory function previously exercised by the Council of the League, as the corollary or counterpart of the mandatories' obligation to render reports to it. It was only if a mandated territory was placed under the United Nations trusteeship system (but there was no obligation to do this) that the supervisory relationship arose. No mandates at all (and not merely South Africa's) were ever, *as* such, administered on behalf of the United Nations.[1]

(ii) The reporting obligation also survived the dissolution of the League, but became dormant until such time as arrangements for reactivating it, comparable to those which existed under the League, and acceptable to the Mandatory, could be made. It was not automatically transformed into, nor ever became, an obligation owed to the United Nations, such as to invest the latter with a supervisory function. The Mandatory's consent to what would, in effect, have been a *novation* of the obligation was never given.

(iii) Even if the United Nations did become invested with a supervisory function in respect of mandates not converted into trusteeships, this function, as it was originally conceived on a League basis, did not include any power of unilateral revocation. Consequently no such power could have passed to the United Nations.

(iv) Even if such a power was possessed by the Council of the League, the Assembly of the United Nations was not com-

---

1 With the exception of SW Africa, all the various mandated territories — apart of course from those that had become, or became, sovereign independent States — were placed under United Nations trusteeship. This did not by any means take place all at once, — but eventually SW. Africa was the only one to retain mandated status. However, as the Court found in its Advisory Opinion of 1950 concerning the *International Status of South West Africa (I.C.J. Reports 1950,* at p. 144), the mandatories were not under any legal obligation to place mandated territories under the trusteeship system.

petent to exercise it, because of the constitutional limitations to which its action as a United Nations organ was inherently subject having regard both to the basic structure and specific language of the Charter.

(v) Except as expressly provided in certain articles of the Charter not material in the present context, the Assembly's powers are limited to discussion and making recommendations. It cannot bind the Mandatory any more than the Council of the League could do.

(vi) Having regard to conclusions (i)-(iii) above, which relate to the United Nations as a whole, the Security Council did not, on a *mandates* basis, have any other or greater powers than the Assembly. Its action could not therefore, *on* that basis, replace or validate defective Assembly action. The Security Council equally had no power to revoke the Mandate.

(vii) The Security Council cannot, in the guise of peacekeeping, validly bring about a result the true character of which consists of the exercise of a purported supervisory function relative to mandates.

(viii) Even where the Security Council is acting genuinely for the preservation or restoration of peace and security, it has no competence as part of that process to effect definitive and permanent changes in territorial rights, whether of sovereignty or administration, — and a mandate involves, necessarily, a territorial right of administration, without which it could not be operated.

(ix) The "Legal consequences for States" of the foregoing conclusions are that the Mandate was not validly revoked by United Nations action in 1966 or thereafter, and still subsists; — that the Mandatory is still subject to all the obligations of the Mandate, whatever these may be and has no right to annex the mandated territory or otherwise unilaterally alter its status; — but that nor has the United Nations, — and that its member States are bound to recognize and respect this position unless and until it is changed by lawful means.

In Part II of this opinion, which comes next, the reasoning in support of these conclusions is distributed in the following way: as to conclusions (i) and (ii), in Section A, paragraphs 11-64; as to conclusion (iii), in Section B, paragraphs 65-89; as to conclusions (iv)-(viii), in Section C, paragraphs

90-116; and as to conclusion (ix), in Section D, paragraphs 117-124. The postscriptum (paragraph 125) follows. The Annex is separately paragraphed and footnoted.

11. There being no general rule of international law which would involve a process of automatic successorship on the part of such an entity as the United Nations to the functions and activities of a former entity such as the League of Nations, there are only three ways in which the United Nations could, upon the dissolution of the League, have become invested with the latter's powers in respect of mandates as such: namely, *(a)* if specific arrangement to that effect had been made, — *(b)* if such a succession must be implied in some way, — or *(c)* if the mandatory concerned — in this case South Africa — could be shown to have consented to what would in effect have been a *novation* of the reporting obligation, in the sense of agreeing to accept the supervision of, and to be accountable to, a new and different entity, the United Nations, or some particular organ of it.

12. It is my view that the United Nations did not in any of these three ways become clothed with the mantle of the League in respect of mandates; — but as regards the first of them, it is necessary to make it clear at the outset that the matter went far beyond the field of mandates. There was in fact a deliberate, *general,* politically and psychologically motivated, rejection of any legal or political continuity at all between the United Nations and the League (see paragraphs 35 and 36 below). Since mandates were regarded as one of the League's political activities, this raises a presumption that there was not any takeover by the United Nations of the League mandates system *as such,* — a view fully borne out by the creation of the parallel United Nations trusteeship system, and the fact that the mandatories were invited to convert their mandates into trusteeships, though without obligation to do so. These matters will however more conveniently be considered later, in their historical context; — and the same applies to the question of whether South Africa, as Mandatory, ever consented to the transfer to the United Nations of obligations which, at the date of the entry into force of the Charter, were owed to the League *which was then still in existence,* and remained so for some time after.

SIR GERALD FITZMAURICE (UK) DISSENTS

13. Meanwhile I turn to the second of the three possibilities mentioned in the preceding paragraph, — namely that there was an *implied* succession by the United Nations to League functions in respect of mandates, and correspondingly an *implied* transfer to the United Nations of the obligations owed by the Mandatory to the League. It is easy to assume that because the United Nations had certain resemblances to the League and might have been regarded as its "natural" successor, therefore it was the legal successor; — but this was not the case. It is no less easy to assume, as the Opinion of the Court clearly does — virtually without arguing the point — that if, and because, the various mandates survived the dissolution of the League, *therefore* the United Nations must necessarily and *ipso facto* have become entitled to exercise a supervisory role in respect of them, although they were a League, not a United Nations institution, and are mentioned in the Charter only as territories that can, but do not have to be, placed under United Nations trusteeship. The fallacy in this kind of reasoning — or rather, presupposition, is evident. Even the argument that only the United Nations *could* play such a part is, as will be seen, erroneous.

14. The Council of the League of Nations (of which three of the principal mandatories were permanent members) was never itself in terms invested *eo nomine* with what has become known as the supervisory function relative to the conduct of the various mandates.[2a] The very term "supervisory" is moreover misleading in the light of the League voting rule of unanimity including the vote of the member State affected, — that is to say, when mandates were in question, the mandatory. The so-called supervisory function was in reality predicated upon and derived from the obligation of the mandatories[2b] to furnish an annual report to the Council, through the then Permanent Mandate Commission, as a sort of inference, corollary or counterpart of that obligation. It was in that way and no other that what has been called the accountability of the mandatories arose. This point, which is of primary importance when it comes to determining what was the real nature of the supervisory function as exercisable by the League Council, and whether it included the power to revoke a mandatory's [2c] mandate, is developed in full in Section B below. Its relevance here is that it was this reporting obligation, and such "accoun-

tability" as an obligation of that order may imply[3], that gave rise to the *specific* function of supervision, not vice versa; — and what is incontestably clear is that the whole question of who, or what entity, was entitled to supervise, was bound up with and depended on the prior question of who, or what entity, mandatories were obliged to report to and, to that extent, become accountable to (but accountability did not in any event — see footnote[4] — imply *control*).

15. It follows that in order to determine what entity, if any, became invested with the supervisory function after the disappearance of the League and its Council, it is necessary to ascertain what entity, if any, the mandatories then became obliged to report to, if they continued to be subject *as* mandatories to the reporting obligation at all. More specifically, in the context of the present case, in order to answer the question whether the *United Nations,* in particular, became invested with any supervisory function, it will be necessary to determine whether, in respect of any mandated territory not placed under the United Nations trusteeship system, the mandatory concerned became obliged to report to some organ of the United Nations (and notably to its General Assembly, found by the Court in its 1950 Opinion to be the most appropriate such organ for the purpose). The underlying issue is whether the United Nations could claim not merely *a* right to be reported to, but an *exclusive* right, in the sense that the obligation arose in relation to it and it alone, and no other entity. In different terms: *first,* given, as is generally accepted[4], that the various mandates survived the dissolution of the League, then did the reporting obligation, the situation

2a,2b,2c The plural, or the indefinite article, and the small letter "M" is used in the present opinion whenever the context does not require the sense to be confined to the Mandate for SW. Africa or South Africa as Mandatory. Failure to do this must result in a distortion of perspective.
3 As will be seen later, reporting in the context of mandates had none of the implications that are involved when, for instance, it is said that "X" reports to "Y" (a superior), which implies that "X" takes his *orders* from "Y". This was not the position as between the League Council and the mandatories, any more than it is as between the competent organs of the United Nations and member States administering trust territories.
4 So far as this aspect of the subject is concerned, the South African contention that the Mandate is at an end is both conditioned and indirect. It is maintained on the one hand that the reporting obligation lapsed in its entirety on the dissolution of the League because it then became impossible to perform it according to its actual terms, — but also that it was not an essential part of the Mandate which could continue without it. At the same time it is maintained that if the obligation is nonseverable — if it *is* an essential part of the Mandate — then its lapse entails the lapse of the Mandate as a whole. These are alternative positions and there is no contradiction between them as the Opinion of the Court seeks to claim.

of accountability considered in the abstract so to speak, equally survive that dissolution as part of the concept of mandates; — and *secondly,* if so, did it survive in the form of, or become converted into, an obligation to report, to be accountable not just to *some* organ, but to that particular organ which was and is the Assembly of the United Nations?

(iii) *The reporting obligation, if it survived, was capable of implementation otherwise than by reporting to a United Nations organ*

16. It is of course evident that if a reporting obligation survived the dissolution of the League, the furnishing of reports to an organ of the United Nations, in particular the General Assembly, was not the only possible way in which that obligation could be discharged; nor was a United Nations organ, specifically as such, in any way indispensable as a recipient, and commentator on or critic of such reports. There were at the time, and there are now, several international bodies in existence, much more comparable in character to the League Council, or at least to the former Permanent Mandates Commission, than the United Nations Assembly, to which any mandatory preferring that course could have arranged to report, and with which it could have carried on the sort of dialogue that was carried on with the League organs; — *and here it is of primary importance to bear in mind that the absence of any compulsory powers vested in such a body would have had no bearing on the situation, since neither the League Council nor the Assembly of the United Nations had any such powers in this matter.* Alternatively, if no appropriate body could be found willing to act, it would have been open to any mandatory, perhaps acting in conjunction with others, to set one up, to which the necessary reporting undertakings would be given, — the ensuing reports, and comments thereon, being made public.

17. For present purposes it is unnecessary to express any final view as to whether the reporting obligation did or did not, in the abstract, or as a concept, survive the dissolution of the League, because in any event I do not consider that it survived in the form of an automatic self-operating obligation to report to and accept the supervision, specifically, of the United Nations, and in particular of its General Assembly. *The unconscious assumption* (or has it been deliberate?) which has

dogged the SW. Africa question for so many years, *that it was all the same thing for a mandatory whether it reported to the League Council or to the United Nations Assembly,* so why should it not do so, *is of course quite illusory, because the character of the supervisory organ affects the character and weight of the obligation.* Taking this view does not necessarily mean accepting the South African contention that the reporting obligation was so intimately bound up with the character of the entity to be reported to that, upon the extinction of that entity, it must lapse entirely. But I do accept the view that in no circumstances could an obligation to report to and accept supervision at the hands of one organ — the League Council — become converted automatically and *ipso facto,* and without the consent of the mandatory (indeed against its will), into an obligation relative to another organ, very differently composed, huge in numbers compared with the League Council, functioning differently, by different methods and procedures, on the basis of a different voting rule, and against the background of a totally different climate of opinion, philosophy and aim, unsympathetic by nature to the mandatory[5]. Indeed the very fact that the supervision of a *mandate* would have become exercisable by an organ which disapproved in principle of mandates that remained mandates, and held it from the start almost as an article of faith (this will be reverted to later, for it is a cardinal point) that all mandated territories should be placed under its own trusteeship system, — and whose primary aim moreover, in all its dealings whether with trust territories, mandated territories, or non-self-governing territories under Article 73 of the Charter, was to call into existence as speedily as possible a series of new sovereign independent States; — all this alone would have been sufficient to create, and perpetuate, a permanent state of tension between the United Nations Assembly as a supervisory organ and any mandatory held accountable to it. None of this existed under the régime of the League.

18. Exactly the same considerations apply to any Committee or sub-Committee of the Assembly which might be set up to deal with mandates, and which, however it might be dressed up to look like the former League Council or Permanent Mandates Commission (see the proposal made in Assembly resolution 449 (V) of 13 December 1950) would remain fully under

the Assembly's control, and reflect its tendencies and aims. Indeed this has been only too self-evidently the case as regards those Committees that have been (at later stages) set up with reference to the SW. Africa question.

19. For these reasons it seems to me to be juridically impossible to postulate such a metamorphosis as taking place automatically or unless by consent. *To do so would not merely be to change the identity of the organ entitled to supervise the implementation of the obligation but, by reason of this change, to change also the nature of the obligation itself.* Given the different character and methods of that organ, it would be to

5 The following table makes this clear:

I. International Organization:—	League of Nations.	United Nations.
II. Report receiving or supervisory body:—	League of Council.	General Assembly.
III. Numbers of same:—	Small (varied through 9-11-13) and included the then permanent members of which three were mandatories.	Potentially unlimited. 50/60 even in 1946— now 130-140 and still growing.
IV. Voting rule:—	Unanimity, including vote of Mandatory.	Two-thirds majority; sometimes possibly a bare majority.
V. Advisory sub-organ:—	Permanent Mandates Commission.	Trusteeship Council; Committee of the Assembly; or "subsidiary organ" set up under Art. 22 of the Charter.
VI. Composition of sub-organ:—	Experts acting in their personal capacity, not as representatives of governments.	Representatives of governments.
VII. Attitude and approach of supervisory body:—	Sympathetic to the mandatories — not over-political,	Unsympathetic to mandatories,— highly political.
VIII. Aim:—	Good administration of the mandated territory.	Earliest possible bringing about of the independence of the territory.

create a new and more onerous obligation (it is of course, *inter alia,* precisely because of the possibility of this, that novations require consent). I must therefore hold that no such transformation ever took place of itself so that, if consent was lacking, the United Nations never became invested with any supervisory function at all. This view will now be developed, first by way of answer to various counter-arguments that have been or may be advanced, — secondly on the basis of certain positive and concrete considerations which have never been given their true weight, but are to my mind decisive.

20. In the 1950 advisory proceedings there was a striking, though quite differently orientated parallelism between the South African arguments on this matter and the views expressed by the Court, due to a mutual but divergently directed confusion or telescoping of the two separate questions already noticed, of the survival of the reporting obligation as such, and the form of its survival, if survival there was. Contending that this obligation had never been contemplated except as an obligation relative to the Council of the League, and could not therefore upon the dissolution of the latter and the establishment of the United Nations, become automatically transformed into an obligation owed to that Organization, South Africa argued that *because* this was so, therefore *all* .obligations of accountability had disappeared. This deduction may have been natural, but clearly lacked logical rigour and necessity, — for the *obligation* as such could survive, even though becoming dormant for the time being.

21. The same process of ellipsis, though with quite another outcome, characterized the reasoning of the Court in 1950. Holding that the reporting obligation was an essential part of the mandates system, and must survive if the system itself survived, the Court went on to hold that *therefore* it survived as an obligation to report specifically to the Assembly of the United Nations. This last leg of the argument not only lacked all logical rigour and necessity but involved an obvious fallacy, — which was the reason for the dissenting views expressed by Judges Sir Arnold McNair (as he then was) and Read — dissenting views with which I agree. It obviously could not follow, as the Court in effect found, that *because* the United Nations happened to be there, so to speak, and, in the shape of the trusteeship system, had set up something rather similar to

the mandates system, *therefore* not merely trusteeships but mandates also were subject to United Nations supervision. This again was a *non sequitur.* It was tantamount to saying that although (as the Court found later in the same Opinion — *I.C.J. Reports 1950,* pp. 138-140) mandatories were not obliged to place their mandated territories under trusteeship, yet for all practical purposes they had to accept United Nations supervision just the same whether or not they had placed the territories under trusteeship. This does not make sense. The result was that in effect the Court cancelled out its own finding that trusteeship was not obligatory — and made it a case of "Heads I win: tails you lose"! It is not too much to say that the absence of any legal obligation to place mandated territories under trusteeship implied a *fortiori,* as a necessary deduction, the absence of any legal obligation to accept United Nations supervision in respect of mandates, or the one would be defeated by the other.

22. Clearly the existence of the United Nations, and its superficial resemblances to the League, had absolutely nothing to do in logic with the survival of the reporting obligation, except in so far as it provided a convenient (but not obligatory) method of discharging that obligation if it did survive. This was Judge Read's view in 1950. Having found that there had been no consent on the part of the Mandatory to the exercise of United Nations supervision, in the absence of which the only possible basis for such an obligation would be "succession by the United Nations," he continued *(I.C.J. Reports 1950,* p. 172):

"Such a succession could not be based upon the provisions of the Charter, because . . . no provisions of the Charter could legally affect an institution founded upon the Covenant or impair or extinguish (the) Legal rights and interests of those Members of the League which are not members of the United Nations. It could not be based on implications or inferences drawn from the nature of the League and the United Nations *or from any similarity in the functions of the organizations.* Such a succession could not be implied, either in fact or in law, in the absence of consent, express or implied by the League, the United Nations and the Mandatory Power. There was no such consent" — (my italics).

23. The Charter makes no specific mention of mandated territories at all, except in the two Articles (77, and 80, paragraph 2) where it refers to them, along with other types of territories, as candidates for being placed under trusteeship but without creating any obligation in that regard. It says nothing at all either about supervision or accountability. The contention that the Charter is to be read as if in fact it did so, is therefore founded entirely on a process of implication, — a process sought to be founded on two particular provisions, Articles 10, and 80, paragraph 1. These must now be considered.

24. For Article 10 to suffice in itself, it would be necessary to find in it not only a competence conferred on the Assembly to exercise a supervisory role in respect of mandates, but also an obligation for mandatories to accept that supervision and be accountable to the Assembly. Since the Article makes no mention of mandates as such, the argument would have to be that the faculty given to the Assembly by that provision "to discuss (and 'make recommendations . . . as to') any questions or any matters within the scope of the present Charter", not only invested the Assembly with a supervisory function in respect of mandates, but also obliged mandatories to *accept* the Assembly in that role and regard themselves as accountable to it. Quite apart from the fact that a faculty merely to "discuss . . . and . . . make (non-binding) recommendations" could not possibly extend to or include so drastic a power as a right unilaterally to revoke a mandate, it is evident that a *faculty* conferred on "A" cannot, in and of itself — even in relation to the same subject-matter — automatically and *ipso facto* create an *obligation* for "B". The *non sequitur* — the absence of any *nexus* is apparent, and the gap cannot be bridged in the way the Court seeks to do. Furthermore, since one of the basic questions at issue, is precisely, whether mandates *as such* — as opposed to trusteeships and mandated territories *placed under trusteeship* — *are* "within the scope of the Charter", the whole argument founded on Article 10 of the Charter is essentially circular and question-begging.

25. Article 10 was, and is, a provision which, without in terms mentioning mandates, or indeed anything specific at all, ranges over the vast field implied by the words "any questions or any matters within the scope of the present Charter". This could cover almost anything. Yet could it reasonably be con-

tended that in relation to anything the Assembly might choose to discuss under this provision, and which could fairly be regarded as included in it, authorities and bodies in all member States of the United Nations thereby, and without anything more, would become obliged at the request of the Assembly to submit reports to it, and accept its supervision concerning their activities? The question has only to be put, for its absurdity to be manifest. Nothing short of express words in Article 10 could produce such an effect. Upon what juridical basis therefore, can an obligation to report and accept supervision in respect of mandates be predicated upon this provision? It was precisely this absence of logical necessity, or even connexion, that motivated Lord McNair's dissent in 1950. After saying that he could not find any legal ground upon which the former League Council could be regarded as being replaced by the United Nations for the purpose of being reported to and exercising supervision, which "would amount to imposing a new obligation[6] upon the (mandatory) and would be a piece of judicial legislation", he continued (*I.C.J. Reports 1950,* p. 162):

"In saying this, I do not overlook the competence of the . . . Assembly . . . under Article 10 of the Charter, to discuss the Mandate . . . and to make recommendations concerning it, but that competence depends not on any theory of implied succession but upon the provisions of the Charter."

In other words, even if the provisions of the Charter might be sufficient to found the competence of the Assembly — (even so, only to discuss and recommend) — they must also be shown to establish the obligation of the mandatory, since no theory of implied succession could be prayed in aid; — and in so far as it is sought to rely on the terms of Article 10 for this purpose, it is clear that they will not bear the weight that would thereby be put upon them.

---

6 "New" because, since the League clearly had not *assigned* its supervisory rights to the United Nations (see further as to this, paragraph 42 below), only a *novation* could have produced the effect that the Court found in favour of in 1950. But a novation would have required the mandatory's consent, which Lord McNair did not think had been given. Speaking of the various contemporary statements made on behalf of South Africa, he said (*I.C.J. Reports 1950,* p. 161) that he did not find in them "adequate evidence" that the mandatory had "either assented to an implied succession by the United Nations . . ., or . . . entered into a new obligation towards (it) to revive the pre-war system of supervision".

26. This is another provision (its terms are set out below[7]) to which it has been sought to give an exaggerated and misplaced effect, and which equally cannot bear the weight thus put upon it. (It is true that the second paragraph manifests an expectation that mandated territories would be placed under the trusteeship system, — but expressions of expectation do not create obligations, as the Court found in 1950, specifically in relation to this provision — *I.C.J. Reports 1950*, p. 140). As for the first paragraph, the changes which it rules out are clearly those, and only those, that might result from Chapter XII (the trusteeship chapter) of the Charter ("nothing in this Chapter (i.e., XII) shall be construed . . . to alter . . . etc.), — and, as Lord McNair pertinently observed in 1950, "the cause of the lapse of the supervision of the League and of Article 6 of the Mandate is not anything contained in Chapter XII of the Charter, but is the dissolution of the League, so that it is difficult to see the relevance of this Article". It is of course possible to hold on other grounds that the principle of accountability, as expressed in the form of the *reporting* obligation, though becoming dormant, did not lapse with the dissolution of the League (paragraphs 17 and 20 above). What cannot legitimately be held is that if it did so lapse — or would otherwise have done so — it was preserved or revived by reason of Article 80, — for that provision's sole field of preservation was from extinction due to the effects of Chapter XII, not from extinction resulting from the operation of causes lying wholly outside that Chapter.

27. Still less can it be legitimate to hold that the reporting obligation was not only preserved as a concept, but became, by some sort of silent alchemy, actually *converted* by Article 80 into an obligation to report to an (unspecified) organ of the United Nations. The impossibility of attributing this last effect to Article 80 becomes manifest if it be recalled that at the date

7 Article 80 of the Charter reads as follows:

"1. Except as may be agreed upon in individual trusteeship agreements, made under Articles 77, 79 and 81, placing each territory under the trusteeship system, and until such agreements have been concluded, nothing *in this Chapter* shall be construed in or of itself to alter in any manner the rights whatsoever of any States or any peoples or the terms of existing international instruments to which Members of the United Nations may respectively be parties — (my italics).

2. Paragraph 1 of this Article shall not be interpreted as giving grounds for delay or postponement of the negotiation and conclusion of agreements for placing mandated and other territories under the trusteeship system as provided for in Article 77."

(24 October 1945) when the Charter, including Article 80, came into force, *the League of Nations was still in existence* (and continued so to be until 18 April 1946), so that the reporting obligation was still owed to the Council of the League. If therefore Article 80 could have operated at all to save this obligation from causes of lapse lying outside Chapter XII of the Charter, it is in *that* form that it must have preserved it — i.e., as an obligation in relation to the League Council; — and there is no known principle of legal construction that could, simply on the basis of a provision such as Article 80, cause an obligation preserved in that form, to become automatically and *ipso facto* converted six months later into an obligation *relative to a different entity of which no mention had been made.* If, to cite Article 80, Chapter XII was not to be "construed" as altering, "the terms of existing international instruments", then what was not to be altered were those provisions of the mandates and of Article 22 of the League Covenant (then still in force) for reporting to the League Council (then still in being). How then is it possible to read Article 80, not as preserving *that* obligation but (as if at the wave of the magician's wand) creating a new and different obligation to report to a new and very different kind of organ — the United Nations Assembly? — a change which could not have been a matter of indifference to the mandatories.

28. It comes to this therefore, that there is absolutely nothing in Article 80 to enable it to be read as if it said "The League is still in being, but if and when it becomes extinct, all mandatories who are Members of the United Nations will thereupon owe to the latter Organization their obligations in respect of mandated territories". *That* of course is precisely what (or something like it) the Charter ought to have stated, in order to bring about the results which — (once it had become clear that SW. Africa was not going to be placed under the United Nations trusteeship system) — it was then attempted to deduce from such provisions as Articles 10 and 80. But the Charter said no such thing, and these Articles, neither singly nor together, will bear the weight of such a deduction.

29. The truth about Article 80 can in fact be stated in one sentence: either the mandates, with their reporting obligations, would in any event have survived the dissolution of the League on a basis of general legal principle or, as some con-

tend, of treaty law, and there would have been no need of Article 80 for that particular purpose, — or else, if survival had to depend on the insertion of an express provision in the Charter, Article 80 was not effectual for the purpose — guarding as it did only against possible causes of lapse arising out of Chapter XII itself, which was not the cause of the dissolution of the League. In consequence, quite a different type of provision would have been required in order to produce the results now claimed for Article 80.

30. It is argued that the foregoing interpretation deprives Article 80 of all meaning, since (so it is contended) there is nothing in Chapter XII of the Charter that *could* alter or impair existing rights, etc. Even if this were the case, it would not be a valid juridical reason for reaching into this provision what *on any view* is not there, namely a self-operating United Nations successorship to League functions, — the automatic conversion of an obligation of accountability to the League Council (still extant when Article 80 came into force) into an obligation towards the Assembly of the United Nations. But in any event this argument is not correct. Article 80 remains fully meaningful, — and its intended meaning and effect, so far as mandates were concerned, was to safeguard against the possibility that the setting-up of the trusteeship system might be regarded as an excuse for not continuing to observe mandates obligations, *whatever these were,* and continued to be. *But it did not define what these were, or say whether they continued to be.* Furthermore it was only "in and of itself" (words all too frequently overlooked) that the creation of the trusteeship system was not to affect mandates. But if these lapsed from some other (valid) cause, Article 80 did not, and was never intended to operate to prevent it. In short, Article 80 did not *cause* them to survive, — but if they did (otherwise) survive, then the setting-up of the trusteeship system could not be invoked as rendering them obsolete.

31. The argument founded upon the reference to Article 80 contained in Article 76 *(d)* of the Charter is equally misplaced and turns in the same circle. Without doubt the effect of this reference was that *in so far as* any preferential economic or other rights were preserved by reason of Article 80, they formed exceptions to the régime of equal treatment provided for by Article 76 *(d).* But this left it completely open what

preferential rights were thus preserved. They were of course only those preserved from extinction because of the operation of Chapter XII of the Charter, not those that might be extinguished from other causes. The point is exactly the same as before.

32. If neither Article 10 nor 80, taken singly, created an obligation to report to the United Nations Assembly, it is evident that, taken together, they cannot do so either. If anything, the reverse is the effect, — two blanks only create a bigger blank.

33. The Organised World Community argument, not previously prominent, the essence of which is to postulate an *inherent* continuity between the League of Nations and the United Nations, as being only different expressions of the same overriding idea, emerged in the course of the *South West Africa* cases (Ethiopia and Liberia v. South Africa, 1960-1966). It is obviously directed to supplying a possibly plausible foundation for something that has no basis in concrete international law. It has no such basis because the so-called organized world community is not a separate juridical entity with a personality over and above, and distinct from, the particular international organizations in which the idea of it may from time to time find actual expression. In the days of the League there was not *(a)* the organized world community, *(b)* the League. There was simply the League, apart from which no *organized* world community would have existed. The notion therefore of such a community as a sort of permanent separate residual source or repository of powers and functions, which are re-absorbed on the extinction of one international organization, and then automatically and without special arrangement, given out to, or taken over by a new one, is quite illusory.

34. It is evident therefore that, in the instant case, this theory is put forward with a view to circumventing, *ex post facto,* what would otherwise be — what *is* — an insuperable juridical obstacle, — namely the lack of any true successorship in law between the League of Nations and the United Nations. In the absence of such successorship, the "organized world (or 'international') community" argument can be seen for what it is — an expedient; — for it is quite certain that none of the States that, as mandatories, assumed obligations to report to the League Council could for one moment have supposed that they were *thereby* assuming an open-ended obliga-

tion to report for all time to whatever organ should be deemed, at any given moment, to represent a notional and hypothetical organized world community, and regardless of how such a community might be constituted or might function.

35. In the foregoing sub-sections various theories of implied succession as between the United Nations and the League in the field of mandates have been considered and shown to be fallacious. The real truth is however, that they all fly in the face of some of the most important facts concerning the founding of the United Nations; — for the idea of taking over from the League, of re-starting where it left off, was considered and rejected — expectedly so. The United States had never been a member of the League for reasons that were still remembered. The Soviet Union had been expelled in 1939. The "Axis" Powers, on the other hand, under their then fascist regimes, *had* been members, and so on. The League had a bad name politically. It had failed in the period 1931-1939 to prevent at least three very serious outbreaks of hostilities, and it had of course been powerless to prevent World War II. It was regarded in many quarters as something which — so far from being an "organised world community" — was a paramountly European institution dominated by "colonialist" influences. The United Nations, so it was felt, must represent an entirely fresh initiative. Although it could hardly fail in certain ways to *resemble* the League, there must be no formal link, no juridical continuity. The League had failed and the United Nations must not start under the shadow of a failure.

36. *This* is why absolutely *no mention of the League is to be found in any part of the Charter.* (Even in connection with mandates, formerly generally known as "League of Nations mandates," the Charter makes no mention of the League. In Article 77, paragraph 1, and Article 80, paragraph 2 — the only provisions in which mandates as such are mentioned — they are referred to as "territories now held under mandate" and "mandated . . . territories.".) *This again* is why the Charter was brought into force without any prior action to wind up the League, and regardless of the fact that it was still, and continued to be, in existence. It is not too much to say therefore that, in colloquial terms, the founders of the United Nations bent over backwards to avoid the supposed taint of any League connexion.

37. The same attitude of regarding the League as a quasi-untouchable was kept up when, after the Charter had come into force and the United Nations was definitely established, action was taken to put an end to the League and take over its physical and financial assets — and to reach a final decision regarding its political and technical activities. This was done by the now well-known General Assembly Resolution XIV of 12 February 1946, the whole text of which will repay study and will, with one (non-pertinent) omission, be found set out verbatim on pages 625-626 of the 1962 volume of the Court's Reports. The parts relevant to mandates (though not mentioning them by name) were as follows:

"3. *The General Assembly* declares that the United Nations is willing in principle, and subject to the provisions of this resolution and of the Charter of the United Nations, to assume the exercise of certain functions and powers previously entrusted to the League of Nations and adopts the following decisions set forth in A, B and C below."

Decisions A ("Functions pertaining to a secretariat") and B ("Functions and powers of a technical and non-political character") are irrelevant in the present connexion; but decision C, under which the question of mandates was regarded as coming, read as follows:

"*Functions and Powers under Treaties, International Conventions, Agreements and other Instruments Having a Political Character.*

The General Assembly will itself examine, or will submit to the appropriate organ of the United Nations, any request from the parties that the United Nations should assume the exercise of functions or powers entrusted to the League of Nations bs treaties, international conventions, agreements and other instruments having a political character."

Commenting on this in 1950 *(I.C.J. Reports 1950,* p. 172), Judge Read, whose views I share said, speaking of the Mandate for SW. Africa, that it involved "functions and powers of a political character" and that in substance decision C provided that the General Assembly would examine a request "that the United Nations should assume League functions as regards report, accountability and supervision over the South-

West African Mandate." He then continued :

"No such request has been forthcoming, and the General Assembly has not had occasion to act under decision C. *The very existence of this express provision, however, makes it impossible to justify succession based upon implication*" — (my italics).

38. Nor was the Assembly's Resolution XIV of 12 February 1946 in any way the outcome of a hasty or insufficiently considered decision. It had been carefully worked out in the Preparatory Commission, and its committees and sub-committees, and it represented the culmination of a settled policy. The story is summarized on pages 536-538 of the 1962 joint dissenting Opinion already referred to (footnote 26 above) and a fuller version is given at pages 619-624 of the same volume of the Court's Reports. In the discussion in the Preparatory Commission of the drafts prepared by its Executive Committee, of what eventually became Resolution XIV, the use of the word "transfer" (of League functions and activities), which nowhere appears in that resolution, was specifically objected to, and dropped, on the ground that it would seem to apply a "legal continuity *that would not in fact exist*" — my italics — (see UN docts. PC/LN/2, pp. 2-3, and PC/LN/10, pp. 10-11).

39. As regards mandates, no fewer than three proposals were made in the Preparatory Commission for the setting up of what would have been an interim regime for *mandates* under the United Nations. In the first place the Executive Committee recommended the creation of a "Temporary Trusteeship Committee" to deal with various interim matters until the trusteeship system was fully working, and amongst them "any matters that might arise with regard to the transfer to the United Nations of any functions and responsibilities hitherto exercised under the Mandates System" — (references will be found in the footnotes to pp. 536 and 537 of the *I.C.J. Reports 1962*). Had this proposal been proceeded with, it would have resulted in the creation of some sort of interim regime in respect of mandates, pending their being placed, *or if they were not placed,* under trusteeship. But in the Preparatory Commission itself, the idea of a temporary trusteeship committee met with various objections, mainly from the Soviet Union, and was not proceeded with. Instead, the Commission made quite a different kind of recommendation to the General

Assembly, looking to the conversion of the mandates into trusteeships. This recommendation eventually emerged as Assembly Resolution XI of 9 February 1946, which will be considered in a moment.

40. Even more effective would have been the two United States proposals made in the Executive Committee on 14 October and 4 December 1945 respectively, which, had they been adopted, would have done precisely and expressly what is now claimed was (by implication) done, even though these proposals were not proceeded with. Subject to differences of wording they were to the same effect, and their character can be seen from the following passage recommending that one of the functions of a temporary trusteeship committee should be (UN doct. PC/EX/92/Add. 1):

> ". . . to undertake, following the dissolution of the League of Nations and of the Permanent Mandates Commission, the functions previously performed by the Mandates Commission in connection with receiving and examining reports submitted by Mandatory Powers with respect to such territories under mandate as have not been placed under the trusteeship system by means of trusteeship agreements, and until such time as the Trusteeship Council is established, whereupon the Council will perform a similar function".

But after tabling these proposals the United States delegation did not further proceed with them. Instead, the Preparatory Commission recommended, and the Assembly adopted, Resolution XI mentioned at the end of the preceding numbered paragraph above. The full text of the relevant parts of this Resoluton will be found on page 624 of *I.C.J. Reports 1962*. It was addressed to "States administering territories now held under mandate"; but all it did was to welcome the declarations made by "certain" of them as to placing mandated territories under trusteeship, and to "invite" all of them to negotiate trusteeship agreements for that purpose under Article 79 of the Charter; — not a word about the interim position, — not a word about the situation regarding any mandated territories in respect of which this invitation was not, and continued not to be, accepted. This piece of history confirms the existence

79

of a settled policy of avoidance of mandates as such.

41. Precisely the same attitude characterized the behaviour of those Members of the United Nations who were also Members of the League when, in their latter capacity, they attended the final Geneva meeting for the winding up of the League. Here again was an opportunity of doing something definite about mandates, — for (with the exception of Japan, necessarily absent) all the mandatories were present, and would be bound by any decisions taken, — since, according to the League voting rule, these had to be taken by unanimity. The terms of the resulting Resolution of 18 April 1946 will be considered in greater detail later, in connexion with the question whether they implied for the mandatories any *undertaking* of accountability *to the United Nations* in respect of their mandates as such. Suffice it for present purposes to say that after *recognizing* that, on the dissolution of the League, the latter's "functions with respect to Mandated Territories will come to an end", the Resolution merely *noted* that "Chapters XI, XII and XIII of the Charter of the United Nations embody principles corresponding to those declared in Article 22 of the Covenant of the League", — and then went on to take note of the "expressed intentions" of the mandatories to continue to administer their mandates "in accordance with the obligations contained" in them, "until other arrangements have been agreed between the United Nations and the respective (mandatories)"; — again an illusion to, and a looking towards, the trusteeship system which, under the Charter, required the negotiation of trusteeship *agreements*. The interim position, and the position concerning any mandates in respect of which no trusteeship agreement were negotiated, was thus left to the operation of an ambiguous general formula, the precise effect of which (to be considered later) has been in dispute ever since.

42. The view that it was once more the trusteeship system that those concerned had in mind is borne out by the fact that the Board of Liquidation set up by the League Assembly to dispose of the League's assets — in handing over the archives of the League's mandates section to the United Nations — said in a report, the relevant part of which was entitled *"Non-Transferable Activities, Funds and Services"* — (my italics), that these archives "should afford valuable guidance to those concerned with the administration of the *trusteeship* (not the

mandates) *system*" — (my italics). It then also declared that
"the mandates system inaugurated by the League has thus
been brought to a close" (L. of N. doc. C.5.M.5., p. 20). In
short, as Lord McNair said in 1950 (*I.C.J. Reports 1950*, P.
161), in a very pertinent verdict on the April 1946 resolution, it

> ". . . recognized that the functions of the League
> had come to an end; *but it did not purport to trans-
> fer them . . . to the United Nations*" (my italics).

After adding that he did not see how this resolution could
"be construed as having created a legal obligation . . . to make
annual reports to the United Nations and to transfer to that
Organization . . . the supervision of (the mandates)" he concluded that: "*At the most, it could impose an obligation to perform those obligations . . . which did not involve the activity of
the League*" — (my italics).

43. There were however two further circumstances which
suggest conclusively that no interim *mandates* rēgime was contemplated at Geneva —

(a) *The "Chinese" draft* — In the first place (and what must
resolve all doubts) is the fact that quite a different type of
resolution had previously been proposed but not proceeded
with. This was what has become known in the annals of the
SW. Africa complex of cases as the "Chinese" or "Liang"
draft, from its source of origination, and it was in complete
contrast to what was eventually adopted. It ran as follows:

> "The Assembly,
> Considering that the Trusteeship Council has not yet
> been constituted and that all mandated territories under
> the League have not been transferred into trusteeship
> territories;
> Considering that the League's function of supervising
> mandated territories should be *transferred* to the United
> Nations, *in order to avoid a period of inter-regnum in
> the supervision* of the mandatory rēgime in these terri-
> tories; — (my italics),
> *Recommends* that the mandatory powers as well as

81

those administering ex-enemy mandated territories shall
continue to submit annual reports to the United Nations
and to submit to inspection by the same until the Trusteeship Council shall have been constituted."

Although this proposal would have required amendment on
account of certain technical errors and defects, it needs but a
glance to see that, had the *substance* of it been adopted, it
would have done precisely what has since so continually and
tediously been claimed as having been done by the Resolution
actually adopted on 18 April 1946. It would have imposed
upon the mandatories an obligation at least to seek United
Nations supervision and submit to it, if forthcoming, during
what the proposal termed the "period of inter-regnum" in
respect of mandates. Whether the United Nations would have
accepted the suggested function — and naturally no resolution
of the League could have compelled it to do so — is beside the
point. The inescapable fact remains that, for whatever reason
(and that reason does not appear upon the record) the proposal
was not adopted; and matters cannot therefore, in law, be
exactly the same as if it had been. If any further proof were
needed it could be found in the fact that Dr. Liang himself, in
speaking on the Resolution of 18 April 1946, as actually
adopted, recalled his earlier (non-adopted) draft, and, after
stating that the trusteeship articles of the United Nations
Charter were "based largely upon the principles of the mandates system", added *"but the functions of the League in
that respect were not transferred automatically to the United
Nations"* — (my italics). Therefore, he said, the Assembly of
the League should "take steps to secure the continued application of (those) principles". But in fact the Assembly of the
League, like the Assembly of the United Nations, decided to
rely for that purpose on the (non-obligatory) conversion of
mandates into trusteeships, or else on Article 73 *(e)* of the
Charter to which I now come.

(b) *The reference to Chapter XI of the Charter in the Resolution of 18 April 1946* — This is the second significant circum-
stance showing how minds were working at Geneva in April
1946. The Resolution of 18 April (paragraph 3 — see *ante*
paragraph 41) referred not only to Chapters XII and XIII of
the Charter (trusteeships) but also to Chapter XI (non-
self-governing territories). The reasons for this were given in

the joint dissenting Opinion of 1962, at pages 541-545 of the 1962 volume of Reports, where attention was drawn to the virtual reproduction in the principal provision of Chapter XI (Article 73) of the language of Article 22, paragraph 1, of the League Covenant (both texts were set out for comparison in footnote 1 on p. 541 of that Opinion). The significance of the reference to Chapter XI in the Geneva Resolution — a reference that would otherwise have had no object — is as showing (i) that the delegates, including the various mandatories, regarded mandated territories as being in any event in the non-self-governing class, and (ii) that they regarded reporting under paragraph *(e)* of Article 73 as an alternative to the placing of mandated territories under trusteeship, *at least in the sense* of being something that would fill in the gap before the latter occurred, *or if it did not occur at all.* Furthermore, it had this advantage, that although it involved a less stringent form of reporting than specifically mandates or trusteeship reporting, and one moreover that did not involve actual accountability as such (see paragraph 59 below), it was *obligatory* for member States of the United Nations administering non-self-governing territories, — whereas the Charter created no obligation to place mandated or other territories under the trusteeship system. If therefore it be contended that there could not have been an intention to leave the "gap" totally unfilled, the answer is that this is how it was intended to be filled; — and there is evidence that several delegates and/or governments understood the matter in that sense (see *I.C.J. Reports 1962,* pp. 543-544). But equally clear it is that the gap was *not* intended to be filled on the basis that mandatories would, *as* mandatories, become accountable to the United Nations, — for if that had been the intention, the obvious course would have been followed of setting up an interim régime specifically for mandates as such, and inviting the United Nations to supervise it. There was therefore an implicit rejection of that course, — and if it is sought to explain matters (or explain them away) on the ground that the United Nations, being intent on the conversion of all mandates into trusteeships, would probably not have accepted the invitation, then surely this is an explanation that speaks for itself and can only confirm the view here put forward.

44. In relation to all these various attempts to bridge the gap

between mandates and trusteeships, or alternatively to place continuing mandates on a more regular footing, the claim made in the Opinion of the Court is that their non-adoption did not necessarily imply a rejection of the underlying idea contained in them. I myself had always thought that the absolutely classic case of implied rejection was when a proposal had been considered and not proceeded with — it being, as a matter of law, quite irrelevant why. [8]   When an idea has been put forward, in much the same terms, on several different successive occasions, but not taken up, only the strongest possible contra-indications (if any there could be) would suffice to rebut the presumption — if not of rejection — at least of deliberate non-acceptance. If something is suggested but not provided for, the situation cannot be the same as if it had been. If there is a series of proposals substantially in the same sense, none of which is adopted, the quite different resolutions that eventually were adopted cannot be interpreted as having the same effect as those that were not. Even a non-jurist can hardly fail to admit the logic of these propositions.

45. These persistent avoidances of any assumption of functions regarding mandates — even on an interim or temporary basis — are clear evidence of a settled policy of disinterest in anything to do with them that did not take the form of their conversion into trusteeships. This is borne out by an additional factor, namely that in spite of the considerations set out in paragraph 43 *(b)* above, the United Nations Assembly was, from the start, unwilling to allow that Article 73 of the Charter could be regarded as relating to mandated territories and, when it did receive reports about SW. Africa transmitted on that basis (see paragraphs 59 and 60 below), insisted on dealing with them through the Trusteeship Council. Individual episodes, occurring in isolation, might not have meant very much, but the cumulative effect of them, taken as a whole, is overwhelming, and can lead to only one conclusion; namely that the United Nations did not intend to take over any political

---

8 At international conferences proposals are often not proceeded with because their origina-tors realize that they would not be agreed to, — and this of course speaks for itself. Alternat-ively, they are often not proceeded with because, even though desirable in themselves, they would involve difficulties, or entail certain corresponding disadvantages; — but in that event a *choice* is made, and as a matter of law it cannot afterwards be claimed that "in reality" the proposal *was* accepted, or that at least it was not "truly" rejected. Such pleas are of a purely subjective character, — and psychology is not law.

function from the League except by special arrangements that were never made, — and that, as part of this policy, it did not want to become involved with mandates as such. This attitude was in fact understandable. In the first place, since the Charter made no express provision for the supervision of mandated territories by the United Nations, except if they were converted into trusteeships, which must be a voluntary act and could not be compelled, there was no legal basis upon which the Organization could claim to be *entitled* to supervise mandates not so converted. No separate machinery for doing so was instituted by the Charter, so that this would have had to be created *ad hoc* — with doubtful legality. To supervise *mandates* through the Trusteeship Council would have been tantamount to treating them as trust territories although they had not been placed under trusteeship, and did not have to be. In consequence, all efforts had to be concentrated on endeavouring to bring the various mandates into the trusteeship system.

46. Secondly, there cannot be any shadow of doubt that (apart from the general unwillingness to take over League functions) the reason for the reluctance to assume any role relative to mandates was the fear that to do so would or might tend to perpetuate the mandates system by acting as an inducement to mandatories to maintain the *status quo* and refrain from submitting to the trusteeship system (see *I.C.J. Reports 1962*, pp. 540-541). In this connexion a point to note — though only an incidental one — is that the latter system was in certain respects more onerous for the mandatories than the mandates system — in particular as regards the character and composition of the body that would be advising the supervisory authority. In the case of mandates, this was the Permanent Mandates Commission, which was made up of independent experts of great experience in such matters, acting in their personal capacity, not as representatives of their governments, and not acting under official instructions. In the case of the trusteeship system it was to be the Trusteeship Council, a political body consisting of representatives of governments acting under instructions. Be that as it may, it was evidently thought desirable to refrain from giving mandatories any excuse for not transferring their mandated territories to the trusteeship system, such as they might well have considered themselves to have had, if an alternative in the

shape of an *ad hoc* continuation of the mandates system had been afforded them. There was in addition the psychological factor of avoiding any suggestion, even indirect, that, possibly, not all mandated territories would be transferred to trusteeship, such as might have been conveyed by making provision for that eventuality.

47. Such then were the reasons for the United Nations attitude about mandates. But to establish the *reasons* for something is not to cancel out the *result,* as the Opinion of the Court often seems to be trying to maintain. Reliance on the proposition that, to find a satisfactory explanation of *why* a proposal was not adopted, is equivalent to demonstrating that it was not really *rejected* — and so it must be treated as if it had "really" been *adopted,* cannot enhance respect for law as a discipline.

48. What in actual fact did occur in the United Nations, in the period 1945/1946, was that the Assembly, in full awareness of the situation, made an *election* — or choice. The election, the choice, was this: it was, so far as the United Nations was concerned, to be "trusteeship" (though not obligatory trusteeship). The taking over of mandates on any other basis was, in effect, rejected. That being so, it was not thereafter *legally* possible to turn round and say, as regards any mandated territory not placed under trusteeship, that although the United Nations had not been given the right to supervise the administration of the territory as a trust territory, it nevertheless had the right to supervise it as a mandated territory. This would simply be an indirect way of in effect making trusteeship compulsory, which it was not and was never intended to be. It would be like allowing the man who draws the short straw to take the long one also! There is an unbridgeable inconsistency between the two positions. Despite various warnings, there was an expectation — or hope — that, in the end, trusteeship for all mandates would come about; but the risk that it might not do so had to be accepted. In the event this expectation or hope was realized except in the case of SW. Africa. The failure in this one case may have been very annoying or even exasperating, — but it could not afford juridical ground for deeming the United Nations *ex post facto* to be possessed of supervisory functions in respect of mandated territories which were not provided for in the Charter (outside the trusteeship

system), and which the Organization deliberately, and of set purpose, refused to assume. In short, so far as SW. Africa was concerned, the United Nations backed the wrong horse, — but backing the wrong horse has never hitherto been regarded as a reason for running the race over again!

49. The basic mistake in 1945/1946 was of course the failure either to make the conversion of mandates into trusteeships obligatory for Members of the United Nations, or else expressly to set up an interim rêgime for non-converted mandates. But by the time *political* awareness of this mistake was fully registered, it was already legally too late; — neither of these things having been done (because in effect the United Nations had preferred to trust to luck) it is hardly possible now to treat the situation virtually as if one of them had been. There is surely a limit to which the law can admit a process of "having it both ways". The cause of law is not served by failing to recognize that limit.

50. If the foregoing considerations are valid, it results that there is one and only one way in which the United Nations could have become invested with any supervisory function in respect of mandates, and that is by the consent of the mandatory concerned. Whether this was ever given by South Africa will now be considered.

51. *The issue of consent to accountability and United Nations supervision:* The question of consent can strictly speaking be disposed of in one sentence, — for, once it is clear that at the time, the United Nations was not accepting, was not wanting to assume any function in respect of mandates as such, was in fact aiming at the total disappearance of the mandates system, — it follows that there was nothing for the mandatories to consent to in respect of mandates, unless they were willing to start negotiations for the conclusion of trusteeship agreements, which they were not obliged to do. As Judge Read said (in *I.C.J. Reports 1950,* p. 171) speaking of events at an even later date (November 1946-May 1948), it was doubtful "whether the General Assembly was willing, *at any stage* (my italics), to agree to any arrangement that did not involve a trusteeship agreement . . ." In these circumstances there was no basis of consensus for any arrangement involving United Nations supervision of mandates as *mandates.* It would have been necessary for the mandatory's "consent" to have taken

the form of a positive petition or plea, which would unquestionably have received the answer that if the mandatory wanted, or was prepared to accept, United Nations supervision, all it had to do was to negotiate a trusteeship agreement.

52. Several references have been made to the principle that a novation was involved, which I believe has not, as such, been invoked in the previous proceedings before the Court except (implicitly) by Lord McNair and Judge Read in 1950. As has been seen in paragraphs 41 and 42 above, the League declared its functions with respect to mandates to be "at an end" and that the system "inaugurated by the League" had been "brought to a close". There was no assignment in favour of the United Nations of mandates as such, — nor could there have been without the consent of the mandatories, for what would have been involved was a new and different party and therefore, in effect, something in the nature of novation of the obligation. It is well established in law that a novation which involves the acceptance of a new and different party, needs consent in order to be good as such; — and, moreover, consent unequivocably and unambiguously expressed, or at least evidenced by unequivocal acts or conduct. It is in the light of this requirement that the question of consent must be viewed.

53. Given what has been said in the preceding paragraph concerning what would be needed in the present context in order to afford adequate evidence of consent, there is no need here to consider in detail the many so-called statements of intention made on behalf of South Africa and other mandatories in 1945 and 1946, indicative of their general attitude as to the future of their mandates, from which implications have been sought to be drawn in the sense of an acceptance or recognition of a United Nations function in respect of mandates as such — i.e., mandates not converted into trusteeships, — for hardly any of them is free from ambiguity. I therefore agree with Lord McNair's verdict in 1950 (*I.C.J. Reports 1950*, p. 161) that there were "also many statements to the effect that the Union Government will continue to administer the Territory 'in the spirit of the Mandate'. These statements are in the aggregate contradictory and inconsistent;" and, he continued, he did not "find in them adequate evidence that the Union Government has either assented to an implied succession by the United Nations . . . or has entered into a new obli-

gation . . ." I would however go further, and say that the various statements made, not only on behalf of South Africa but on behalf of the other mandatories (see next paragraph), taken broadly in the mass (many of them are given at various places from pp. 616-639 of the 1962 volume of the Court's Reports) show the following common characteristics: *(a)* they are statements of general attitude, insufficient, and not purporting, to convey any definite undertaking; *(b)* if there was any undertaking, it was to continue to *administer* the mandated territories concerned in accordance with the mandates, — and the administration of a mandate is of course a separate thing from reporting *about* that process; and *(c)* they none of them implied any recognition of the existence of a United Nations function relative to mandates, or any undertakings towards that Organization. I shall now consider the three episodes or complexes of episodes that have chiefly been relied on as indicative of South African recognition of accountability to the United Nations but which, in my view, do not justify that conclusion.

54. Features *(a)*, *(b)* and *(c)*, as set out in the preceding paragraph, strongly characterized the Geneva proceedings ending in the final League of Nations Resolution of 18 April 1946, on paragraphs 3 and 4 of which such heavy reliance was placed both in the 1950 and 1962 proceedings before the Court, and again now. Its effect has already been considered (paragraphs 41-43 above) in the related but separate context of the attitude of the States concerned on the question "mandates or trusteeships?" The question now is what if any undertakings for mandatories were implied by its paragraph 4 which is the operative one in the present connexion. This classic of ambiguity (text in footnote [9]) consists essentially of a *recital* describing a situation. Since it merely "takes note" of something — namely the "expressed intentions of the (mandatories)", it does not of

---

9 The full text of this resolution is given in footnote 1 on pp. 538-539 of the 1962 volume of the Court's Reports. It can be seen at a glance that only paragraphs 3 and 4 are relevant in the present context. The terms of paragraph 3 have in effect been cited in paragraph 41 above. Paragraph 4 was as follows :

"4. Takes note of the expressed intentions of the members of the League now administering territories under mandate to continue to administer them for the well-being and development of the peoples concerned in accordance with the obligations contained in the respective mandates until other arrangements have been agreed between the United Nations and the respective mandatory powers."

itself impose any obligations, so that the question is what these "expressed intentions" themselves were, and whether they amounted to binding undertakings, and if so to what effect. The statement made on behalf of South Africa is quoted in the next succeeding paragraph, and a summary of the key phrases used by the other mandatories will be found in footnote 2 on page 528 of the 1962 volume of the Court's Reports. Their vague and indeterminate character is immediately apparent. As summed up and described in paragraph 4 of the League resolution of 18 April 1946, the intentions expressed had nothing to do with the acceptance of United Nations supervision. They were, simply, "to administer (the territories) for the well-being and development of the peoples concerned." The further words "in accordance with the obligations contained in the respective mandates" at once involve the ambiguities to which attention has been drawn in paragraph 53 above. These words *need* mean, and were almost certainly intended by the mandatories to specify, no more than the obligations relative to administering "for the well-being and development . . .", etc., — for, as has already been noticed, reporting and supervision is *about* administration, not administration itself.

55. It is not upon flimsy and dubious foundations of this kind that binding undertakings (especially when dependent on unilateral declarations) can be predicated, more particularly where, as has been seen, a novation of an undertaking is involved, needing, in law, unambiguous consent. It is therefore instructive to see what, on this occasion, the "expressed intentions" of South Africa were, as stated by its delegate at Geneva on 9 April 1946 (*League of Nations Official Journal*, Special Supplement, No. 194, pp. 32-33). These were that, pending consideration of the South African desire, on the basis of the expressed wishes of the population, to incorporate SW. Africa in the territory of the Union (as it then was), the latter would in the meantime—

". . . continue to administer the territory scrupulously *in accordance with the obligations of the mandate, for the advancement for promotion of the interests of the inhabitants, as she has done during the past six years when meetings of the Mandates Commission could not be held.*

The disappearance of (the) organs of the League concerned with the supervision of mandates, primarily the Mandates Commission and the League Council, will necessarily preclude complete compliance with the letter of the mandate. The Union Government will nevertheless regard the dissolution of the League as in no way diminishing its obligations under the mandate, which it will continue to discharge with . . . full and proper appreciation of its responsibilities until such time as other arrangements are agreed upon concerning the future status of the territory" — (my italics).

For those who enjoy parlour games, an interesting hour could be spent in trying to decide exactly what this statement, equally a classic of ambiguity, amounted to as regards any South African acceptance of *United Nations* supervision, — for that, of course, is the point. The italicized passage clearly excludes the idea, — presaging as it does the continuation of a situation that had already lasted six years, in which no reports had been rendered, because there was no active *League* authority to which they could be rendered. The remainder of the statement, and in particular the phrase "as in no way diminishing its obligations under the mandate," involves precisely those ambiguities and uncertainties to which attention has already been drawn. To me it seems the very prototype of the non-committal, so far as concerns any recognition of accountability to the United Nations, and I am unable to find in it any indication whatever of such recognition. I realize that on this matter, as on most others my view and the reasoning of the Court are operating on different wavelengths. Seeing in the South African statement a recognition of the existence of a continuing obligation towards the peoples of the mandated territory — the reasoning of the Court then makes the great leap; — *because* there was that degree of recognition there was also, and *therefore* a recognition of accountability to the •United Nations. The lack of all rigour in this reasoning is evident. It involved exactly the same ellipses and telescopings of two distinct questions that characterized the reasoning of the Court in 1950, as already discussed in paragraphs 20-22 above. Nobody can have taken this declaration in that sense at the time, because everybody knew that United Nations supervision was to be exercised solely through the trusteeship system, and that there was no obligation to bring mandated territories within that system. This, to me, is one of the most decisive points in the whole case.

56. The approach made by South Africa to the United Nations in November 1946 for the incorporation in its own territory of SW. Africa on the basis of the expressed wishes of the inhabitants who had been consulted, constitutes the only episode which can plausibly be represented as a recognition — not indeed of accountability to the United Nations on a specifically mandates basis (nor, as will be seen, was it taken by the Assembly in that sense) — but of the existence, on a political basis, of a United Nations interest in matters having a "colonial" aspect. It was also a convenient way of obtaining a large measure of general international recognition for such an incorporation. This last aspect of the matter — that what was being sought through the United Nations was "international" recognition — had already been mentioned in another part of the statement cited in the preceding paragraph above, made on behalf of South Africa at Geneva earlier in the year, in which it was announced that at the next session of the United Nations Assembly there would be formulated "the case for according South West Africa a status under which it would be *internationally recognized* as an integral part of the Union (of South Africa)" — my italics.

57. This was not the first mention of the matter. The possibility of incorporation had been foreshadowed in the most explicit terms as far back as 11 May 1945 in the long and detailed statement then made by the representative of South Africa in Committee II/4 of the San Francisco Conference, which there is every reason to believe ended with a remark to the effect that the matter was being mentioned—

". . . so that South Africa *may not afterwards be held to held acquiesced in the continuance of the Mandate* or the inclusion of the territory in any form of trusteeship under the new International Organisation" — (my italics).

From this, it was already clear that any definite approach to the United Nations on incorporation, if and when made, would be a political one, on a voluntary basis, not in recognition of accountability.

58. When however the matter was raised in the Fourth Committee of the United Nations Assembly in November 1946 by

Field-Marshal Smuts in person, it became clear that the probable reaction of the Committee would be a demand that the territory should be placed under trusteeship. Accordingly Field-Marshal Smuts later made a further statement in the course of which he said that :

"It would not be possible for the Union Government *as a former mandatory* to submit a trusteeship agreement in conflict with the clearly expressed wishes of the inhabitants. The Assembly should recognize that the implementation of the wishes of the population was the course prescribed by the Charter and dictated by the interests of the inhabitants themselves. If, however, the Assembly did not agree that the clear wishes of the inhabitants should be implemented, the Union Government could take no other course than to abide by the declaration it had made to the last Assembly of the League of Nations to the effect that it would continue to administer the territory as heretofore as an integral part of the Union, and to do so *in the spirit of the principles* laid down in the mandate" — (my italics).

Two things may be noted about this statement:first the speaker referred to South Africa as a "former" mandatory. Whether or not it was correct to speak of South Africa as not still being a mandatory is not the point. The point is that such a remark is quite inconsistent with any recognition of accountability in respect of the mandate. *Secondly,* when at the end of this passage, the speaker stated his Government's intention to continue to administer the territory "in the spirit" of the "principles" laid down in the Mandate — (and it would be difficult to find a phrase less recognizatory of obligation) — he did not mention, and was clearly not intending to include reporting of the kind indicated in the Mandate. Instead, he went on to state an intention to report on the non-self-governing territory basis of Article 73 *(e)* of the Charter (the effect of which will be considered in the next succeeding subsection); and what he said was that his Government would "in accordance with" (not, be it noted, Article 6 of the Mandate, but) "Article 73, paragraph *(e),* of the Charter" transmit reports to the Secretary-General "for information purposes", — this last phrase being the language of Article 73 *(e)* itself. He then concluded by saying that there was—

93

> ". . . nothing in the relevant clauses of the Charter, nor
> was it in the minds of those who drafted these clauses,
> to support the contention that the Union Government
> could be compelled to enter into a trusteeship agreement
> even against its own view or those of the people con-
> cerned."

And what was the reaction of the Assembly in its ensuing
resolution 65 (I)? — was it to demand the submission of
reports and the acceptance of supervision under Article 6 of
the Mandate? Not at all, — it was to recommend that SW.
Africa be placed under *the trusteeship system.* Clearly, no
more than the Mandatory was the Assembly contemplating the
exercise of any functions in respect of the territory on a mandates basis.

59. In the case of SW. Africa the Mandatory had no intention either of negotiating a trusteeship agreement or of submitting to United Nations supervision of the territory on a mandates basis; — and here again, it is not the ethics of this attitude that constitutes the relevant point, but the evidence it
affords of lack of *consent* to any accountability to the United
Nations. Nothing could make this — or the absence of all
common ground — clearer than the next episode, starting with
the statement made on behalf of South Africa in the Fourth
Committee of the Assembly, on 27 September 1947, relative to
the South African proposal, originally made in November 1946
(see previous paragraph), to transmit information of the same
type as was required by Article 73 *(e)* of the Charter in respect
of so-called "non-self-governing territories." Such information, given about colonies, protectorates, etc., *does not imply
accountability,* and is not in the formal and technical sense
"reporting." The Report of the Fourth Committee on this
occasion (dated 27 October 1947) describes the statement of
the South African representative as follows:

> "It was the assumption of his Government, he said,
> that the report (i.e., the information to be transmitted)
> would not be considered by the Trusteeship Council and
> would not be dealt with as if a trusteeship agreement had
> in fact been concluded. He further explained that as the
> League of Nations had ceased to exist, the right to sub-
> mit petitions could no longer be exercised, since that
> right presupposes a jurisdiction which would only exist

where there is a right of control and supervision, *and in the view of the Union of South Africa no such jurisdiction was vested in the United Nations with regard to South West Africa"* — (my italics).

What was said of petitions was a *fortiori* applicable in respect of, reports of the kind contemplated by Article 6 of the Mandate. The italicized words constituted a *general* denial of United Nations jurisdiction.

60. There were further offers to furnish information on the same basis in the period 1947/1948, and one or two reports were actually transmitted. But all along the line statements were made on behalf of South Africa indicating clearly that this was done voluntarily and without admission of obligation. Thus at a Plenary Meeting of the Assembly on 1 November 1947 the representative of South Africa said that:

".. . the Union of South Africa has expressed its readiness to submit annual reports for the information of the United Nations. That undertaking stands. Although these reports, if accepted, will be rendered *on the basis that the United Nations has no supervisory jurisdiction in respect of this territory* they will serve to keep the United Nations informed in much the same way as they will be kept informed in relation to Non-Self-Governing Territories under Article 73 *(e)* of the Charter" — (my italics).

And in a letter of 31 May 1948 to the Secretary-General an explicit re-statement was given of the whole South African position as follows (UN doct., T/175, 3 June 1948, pp. 51-52):

".. . the transmission to the United Nations for information on South West Africa, in the form of an annual report or any other form, *is on a voluntary basis and is for purposes of information only. They* (the Government) *have on several occasions made it clear that they recognise no obligation to transmit this information to the United Nations,* but in view of *the wide-spread interest* in the administration of the Territory, and *in accordance with normal democratic practice,* they are willing and anxious *to make available to the world* such

95

facts and figures as are readily at their disposal . . . The Union Government desire to recall that in offering to submit a report on South West Africa for the information of the United Nations, they did so on the basis of the provisions of Article 73 *(e)* of the Charter. This Article calls for 'statistical and other information of a technical nature' and makes no reference to information on questions of policy. In these circumstances the Union Government do not consider that information on matters of policy, particularly future policy, should be included in a report (or in any supplement to the report) which is intended to be a factual and statistical account of the administration of the Territory over the period of a calendar year. Nevertheless, the Union Government are anxious to be as helpful and as co-operative as possible and have, therefore, on this occasion replied in full to the questions dealing with various aspects of policy. The Union Government do not, however, regard this as creating a precedent. Furthermore, the rendering of replies on policy should not be construed as a commitment as to future policy *or as implying any measure of accountability to the United Nations on the part of the Union Government.* In this connexion the Union Government have noted that their declared intention to administer the Territory in the spirit of the mandate *has been construed in some quarters as implying a measure of international accountability.* This construction the Union Government cannot accept *and they would again recall that the League of Nations at its final session in April 1946, explicitly refrained from transferring its functions in respect of mandates to the United Nations* — (my italics).

And then again in the Fourth Committee of the Assembly in November 1948 (Official Record of the 76th Meeting, p. 288), it was stated that:

". . . the Union could not admit the right of the Trusteeship Council to use the report for purposes for which it had not been intended: *still less could the Trusteeship Council assume for itself the power claimed in its resolution, i.e.,* 'to determine whether the Union of South

Africa is adequately discharging its responsibilities *under the terms of the mandate* . . .' Furthermore, that power was claimed in respect of a territory which was not a trust territory and in respect of which no trustee-ship agreement existed. The South African delegation considered that in so doing the Council had exceeded its powers" — (my italics).

Since however the Assembly persisted in dealing with the reports through the Trusteeship Council, they were subsequently discontinued. It is of course evident that the "parties", so to speak, were completely at loggerheads. But no less clear is it *(a)* that the Assembly would agree to nothing, except on a trusteeship basis, and *(b)* that South Africa would agree to nothing that involved recognition of an obligation of accountability to the United Nations. In consequence there was no agreement, no consent.

61. Whatever may be thought of the South African attitude from a wider standpoint than that of law, there can surely be no doubt as to what, *in* law, the character of that attitude was. In the face of the statements above set-out, it is impossible to contend that there was any recognition, or acceptance, of accountability to the United Nations as a *duty* arising for the Mandatory upon the dissolution of the League. There was in fact an express rejection of it. Consequently, in a situation in which, for the reasons given in paragraphs 51 and 52 above, nothing short of positive expressions of recognition or acceptance would have sufficed, there were in fact repeated positive denials and rejections. This being so, all attempts to *imply* it must fail in principle on *a priori* grounds; for implications are valid only in situations of relative indeterminacy where, if there are no very positive indications "for", there are also no very positive ones "against". Where however, as here, there are positive indications "against", mere *implications* "for" cannot prevail. Recognition of accountability could be attribut-able to South Africa only on the basis of conduct not other-wise explicable. In fact, it was both otherwise explicable, and repeatedly explained.

62. An important point of international legal order is here involved. If, whenever in situations of this kind a State volun-tarily, and for reasons of policy, brings some matter before an

international body, it is thereby to be held to have tacitly admitted an *obligation* to do so (as it has quite erroneously been sought to maintain in connexion with the United Kingdom's reference of the Palestine question to the United Nations in 1948), then there must be an end of all freedom of political action, within the law, and of all confidence between international organizations and their member States.

63. Exactly the same is applicable to attempts to read binding undertakings into the language of what are really only statements of policy, as the declarations made at one time or another by the various mandatories essentially were. Clearly in the formative period of the United Nations and the dissolution of the League, the question of mandates was a matter of general interest. They were bound to be discussed, — the mandatories were bound to make known in a general way what their views and attitudes were. Clearly some conclusion had to be reached about their future. *But equally clearly, if not more so, is the fact that the conclusion reached as to their future was that they ought to be placed under the trusteeship system, and that the United Nations should not have anything to do with them as mandates. In other words United Nations supervision was to be exercised through the trusteeship not the mandates system.* At the same time no legal obligation was created under the Charter for mandatories to convert their mandates into trusteeships. Therefore it is not now legally possible (SW. Africa not having been placed under trusteeship and there having been no legal obligation so to place it) to contend that the United Nations is entitled *none the less* to exercise supervision on a mandates basis. Such a contention constitutes a prime example of a process to which I will not give a name, but which should not form part of any self-respecting legal technique.

64. Since for all these reasons the United Nations as an Organization (including therefore both the General Assembly and the Security Council) never became invested with the powers and functions of the Council of the former League in respect of mandates, in any of the possible ways indicated in paragraph 11 above, I must hold that it was incompetent to revoke South Africa's mandate, irrespective of whether the League Council itself would have had that power. It is nevertheless material to enquire whether the latter did have it, — for

if not, then *cadit quaestio* even if the United Nations had inherited. To this part of the subject I now accordingly turn.

65. On the assumption — or postulate as it really has to be — that, contrary to the conclusion reached in the preceding section the United Nations did inherit — or did otherwise become invested with — a supervisory function in respect of those mandates which remained mandates and were not converted into United Nations trusteeships; — it then becomes necessary to enquire what was the nature and scope (or content) of that function, as it was exercised, or exercisable, by the Council of the League of Nations. Such an enquiry is rendered necessary because of an elementary yet fundamental principle of law. In so far as (if at all) the United Nations could legitimately exercise any supervisory powers, these were perforce *derived* powers — powers inherited or taken over from the League Council. They could not therefore exceed those of the Council, for *derived* powers cannot be other or greater than those they derive from. There could not have been transferred or passed on from the League what the League itself did not have, — for *nemo dare potest quod ipse non habet*, or (the corollary) *nemo accipere potest id quod ipse donator nunquam habuit.* This incontestable legal principle was recognised and applied by the Court in 1950, and was the basis of its finding (*I.C.J. Reports 1950,* at p. 138) that:

> "The degree of supervision to be exercised by the General Assembly should not therefore exceed that which applied under the Mandates System, and should conform as far as possible to the procedure followed in this respect by the Council of the League of Nations."

This finding was specifically affirmed in the later *Voting Procedure* and *Oral Petitions* cases (1955 and 1956), both of which indeed turned on whether the way in which the Assembly was proposing or wanting to interpret and conduct its supervisory role in certain respects, would be consistent with the principle thus enunciated. Furthermore, in the second of these cases the Court gave renewed expression to the principle. Referring to its original (1950) Opinion, it said (*I.C.J. Reports 1956,* at p. 27):

"In that Opinion the Court . . . made it clear that the obligations of the Mandatory were those which obtained under the Mandates System. Those obligations could not be extended beyond those to which the Mandatory had been subject by virtue of the provisions of Article 22 of the Covenant and of the Mandate for South West Africa under the Mandates System. The Court stated therefore that the degree of supervision to be exercised by the General Assembly should not exceed that which applied under the Mandates System (and that) the degree of supervision should conform as far as possible to the procedure followed by the Council of the League . . ."

66. The correctness of this view has never been challenged, and seems on principle unchallengeable. It follows inevitably therefore that if the League possessed no power of unilateral revocation of [10] a mandate the United Nations could not have become subrogated to any such power. It equally follows on the procedural side — (and here there is an important connexion) — that if, under the mandates system as conducted by the League, the position was that the supervisory body, the League Council, could not bind a mandatory without its consent, then neither could the organs of the United Nations do so, whether it was the General Assembly or the Security Council that was purporting so to act. In short, let the Assembly — or for that matter the Security Council — be deemed to have all the powers it might be thought that either organ has, or should have, — these still could not, in law, be exercised in the field of *mandates* to any other or greater effect than the League Council could have done. (Both organs are of course also subject to *Charter* limitations on their powers which will be considered below.)

67. The case for deeming League of Nations mandates to have been subject to a power of unilateral revocation by the Council of the League does not rest on any provision of the mandates themselves, or of the League Covenant. (These indeed, as will be seen presently, imply the exact opposite.)

10 The "indefinite" article — "a" not "the" mandate is here employed of set purpose, — for whatever the position was as regards the League's powers of revoking a mandate, it was the same for all mandates, not merely that for SW. Africa. The view that the latter could unilaterally be revoked entails that the various Australian, Belgian, French, Japanese, New Zealand and United Kingdom mandates equally could be.

The claim is one which, as noted earlier, is and can only be advanced on the assumption of fundamental breaches of the mandate concerned, such as, if the case were one of a private law contract for instance, could justify the other party in treating it as terminated?[11] The claim therefore rests entirely on the contention that, in the case of institutions such as the League mandates were, there must exist an inherent power of revocability in the event of fundamental breach, even if no such power is expressed; — that indeed there is no need to express it. This is in fact the Court's thesis.

68. In support of this view, comparisons are drawn with the position in regard to private law contracts and ordinary international treaties and agreements, as to which it may be said that fundamental breaches by one party will release the other from its own obligations, and thus, in effect, put an end to the treaty or contract. The analogy is however misleading on this particular question, where the contractual situation is different from the institutional, — so that what may be true in the one case cannot simply be translated and applied to the other without inadmissible distortions (see footnote 12).

69. There is no doubt a genuine difficulty here, inasmuch as a régime like that of the mandates system seems to have a foot both in the institutional and the contractual field. But it is necessary to adhere to at least a minimum of consistency. If, on the basis of contractual principles, fundamental breaches justify unilateral revocation, then equally is it the case that contractual principles require that a new party to a contract cannot be imposed on an existing one without the latter's consent (novation). Since in the present case one of the alleged fundamental breaches is precisely the evident non-acceptance of this new party, and of any duty of accountability to it (such an acceptance being *ex hypothesi*, on contractual principles, *not* obligatory), a total inconsistency is revealed as lying at the root of the whole Opinion of the Court in one of its most essential aspects.

---

11 Note the intentional use of the phrase "in treating it as terminated" and not "in putting an end to it." There is an important conceptual difference. Strictly speaking, all that one party alleging fundamental breaches by the other can do, is to declare that it no longer considers itself bound to continue performing *its own* part of the contract, which it will regard as terminated. But whether the contract *has*, in the objective sense, come to an end, is another matter and does not necessarily follow (certainly not from the unilateral declaration of that party) — or there would be an all too easy way out of inconvenient contracts.

70. If, in order to escape this dilemma — and it is not the only one — a shift is made into the international institutional field, what is at once apparent is that the entities involved are not private persons or corporate entities, but sovereign States. Where a sovereign State is concerned, and where also it is not merely a question of pronouncing on the legal position, but of ousting that State from an administrative role which it is physically in the exercise of, it is not possible to rely on any theory of implied or inherent powers. It would be necessary that these should have been given concrete expression in whatever are the governing instruments. If it is really desired or intended, in the case of a sovereign State accepting a mission in the nature of a mandate, to make the assignment revocable upon the unilateral pronouncement of another entity, irrespective of the will of the State concerned [12] it would be essential to make express provision for the exercise of such a power.

71. Nor would that be all, — for provision would also need to be made as to how it was to be exercised, — since clearly, *upon* its exercise a host of legal and practical questions would at once arise, requiring speedy solution, and possibly demonstrating the existence of potential problems more serious than those supposed to be solved by the revocation. To leave such matters in the air — to depend on the chance operation of unexpressed principles or rules — is an irresponsible course, and not the way things are done. If the possibility of changes of mandatory had really been contemplated, the normal method would have been to provide for a review after an initial period of years, or at stated intervals, — and even this would not imply any general or unconstrained power of revocation, but rather an ordered process of periodical re-examination in which the mandatory itself would certainly participate.

72. In consequence, within a jurisprudential system involving sovereign independent States and the major international organizations whose membership they make up, there must be a natural presumption *against* the existence of any such drastic thing as a power of unilaterally displacing a State from a position or status which it holds. No implication based on sup-

12 If it be objected that no State would willingly or knowingly accept such conditions, I can only agree, — but this in fact reinforces and points up the whole of my argument. The obvious absurdity of the whole idea at once emerges.

posed inherency of right — but only concrete expression in some form — could suffice to overcome this presumption, — for what is in question here is not a simple finding that international obligations are considered to have been infringed, but something going much further and involving action — or purported action — of an executive character on the objective plane. *It is as if the King of Ruritania were declared not only to be in breach of Ruritania's international obligations but also, on that account, be no longer King of Ruritania.* The analogy is not claimed to be exact, but it will serve to make the point, — namely that infringements of a mandate might cause the mandatory concerned to be in breach of its international obligations but could not cause it thereby to cease to be the mandatory or become liable to be deposed as such, at the fiat of some other authority, *unless* the governing instruments so provided or clearly implied. In the present case they not only do not do so but, as will be seen, indicate the contrary.

73. *Essentially non-peremptory character of the mandates system.* This point will be more fully dealt with in connexion with the basic voting rule of the League which, with certain exceptions not applicable in the case of mandates, was that of unanimity including the vote of the interested party, and therefore of the mandatory concerned. It is mentioned here by way of introduction as being an essential piece of background knowledge, — for since it was the case that mandatories could not in the last resort become bound by the decisions of the League Council unless they agreed with them, or at least tacitly acquiesced in, or did not oppose them, the system was necessarily non-peremptory in character; — and in relation to such a system there is obviously an element of total unreality in speaking of a power of unilateral revocation, — for any decision to revoke would itself, in order to be valid, have required the concurrence of the mandatory. It could not therefore have been unilateral. Any other view involves an inherent logical contradiction.

74. As was mentioned early in this Opinion (paragraph 14 above), no supervisory role in respect of mandates was, *in terms,* conferred upon the League Council, or any other organ of the League, either by the relevant mandate itself or by Article 22 of the League Covenant, which established the mandates system as a régime, and indicated its character in

103

considerable detail — but not in this particular respect. The supervisory role or function was left to emerge entirely — or virtually so — as a kind of deduction from, or corollary of the obligation of the mandatory concerned to furnish annual reports to the Council. It is therefore to the character of *that* obligation to which regard must be had in order to establish what kind and scope of supervision could legitimately be inferred as flowing from it.

> Where a right or power has not been the subject of a specific grant, but exists only as the corollary or counterpart of a corresponding obligation, this right or power is necessarily defined by the nature of the obligation in question, and limited in its scope to what is required to give due effect to such correlation.

75. All the various mandates (with one exception not here pertinent, and subject to minor differences of language) dealt with the reporting obligation in the same way. Citing that for SW. Africa, it was provided (Article 6) that the Mandatory was to render to the Council of the League "an annual report to the satisfaction of the Council [13] containing full information with regard to the territory and indicating the measures taken to carry out the obligations assumed . . . ". This was a reflection and expansion of paragraph 7 of Article 22 of the Covenant, which provided for an annual report to the Council "in reference to the territory committed to (the Mandatory's) charge." The only other relevant clause was paragraph 9 of Article 22, which provided for the setting up of what became the Permanent Mandates Commission, "to receive and examine the annual reports of the Mandatories and to advise the Council on all matters relating to the observance of the mandates." Later, by special arrangement, written petitions from the inhabitants of the mandated territories, forwarded through the mandatories, could also be received and examined.

---

13 The phrase "to the satisfaction of the Council" cannot have related to the measures reported on, for the mandatory only had to render one annual report, and could not know, at the reporting stage, what view the Council would take as to those measures. Nor did the mandatory subsequently revise its *report*, though it might revise its measures. The object of the report was, precisely, to inform the Council about these; and, considered as a piece of reporting, the report was necessarily satisfactory if it contained full and accurate information as to what was being done, so that the Council, having thus been put in possession of all the facts, would, on the basis of the report, be able to indicate to the mandatory whether it approved of the measures concerned or what other or additional measures it advocated.

76. It is clear therefore that the sole real *specific* function of the Council was (via the Permanent Mandates Commission) to "receive and examine" these reports and petitions. The Council could require that the reports should be to its satisfaction, namely "contain full information" about the mandated territory, and "indicate the measures taken" by the mandatory, etc. It would also be a natural corollary that the Council could comment on these reports, indicate to the mandatory what measures it thought wrong or inadequate, suggest other measures, etc., — but in no case with any binding effect unless the mandatory agreed. The Council could exhort, seek to persuade and even importune; but it could not require or compel, — and it is not possible, from an obligation which, on its language, is not more than an obligation to render reports of a specified kind, to derive a further and quite different obligation to act in accordance with the wishes of the authority reported to. This would need to be separately provided for, and it is quite certain that none of the various mandatories ever understood the reporting obligation in any such sense as that, and equally certain that they never would have undertaken it if they had.

77. In other words, the supervisory function, as it was contemplated for League purposes, was really a very limited one — a view the principle of which was endorsed by Sir Hersch Lauterpacht in the *Voting Procedure* case when, speaking of United Nations trusteeships (but of course the same thing applies *a fortiori* to the case of mandates) he said this (*I.C.J. Reports 1955*, p. 116):

". . . *there is no legal obligation, on the part of the Administering Authority, to give effect to a recommendation of the General Assembly to adopt or depart from a particular course of legislation or any particular administrative measure.* The legal obligation resting upon the Administering Authority is to administer the Territory in accordance with the principles of the Charter and the provisions of the Trusteeship Agreement, *but not necessarily in accordance with any specific recommendation of the General Assembly or of the Trusteeship Council*" — (my italics).

78. Such then was the real and quite limited nature of the supervisory function to which the General Assembly became subrogated, if it became subrogated to any function at all in respect of mandates. It was, as the term implies, strictly a right of "supervision"; it was not a right of *control* — it did not comprise any executive power; — and therefore clearly could not have comprised a power of so essentially executive a character as that of revocation. Between a function of supervision (but not of control) and a power to *revoke* a mandate and, so to speak, evict the mandatory — and to do this unilaterally without the latter's consent — there exists a gulf so wide as to be unbridgeable. It would involve a power different not only (and greatly) in degree, but in kind. This is a consideration which, in the absence of express provision for revocation, makes it impossible to imply such a power, — and indeed excludes the whole notion of it, as being something that could not have fallen within the League Council's very limited supervisory role, and accordingly cannot fall within that of the United Nations Assembly — assuming the latter to have any supervisory role.

79. The views just expressed are more than confirmed by the League Council's voting rule, as embodied in paragraph 5 of Article 4 of the Covenant in combination with Paragraph 1 of Article 5. The effect, in the case of all matters involving mandates, was to enable the mandatories, if not already members of the Council (as several invariably were), to attend if they wished, and to exercise a vote which might operate as a veto. No exception was provided for the possibility of a revocation, and no such exception can be implied from the fact that mandatories did not always attend the Council when invited to do so, or might abstain on the vote, or that certain devices might be employed on occasion to avoid direct confrontations between them and the other members of the Council. The fact that there may be no recorded case of the actual use of this veto does not alter the legal position, — it merely shows how well the system worked *in the hands of reasonable people.* None of this however can alter the fact that mandatories always had the right to attend and exercise their votes. The existence of this voting situation was confirmed by the Court not only in its Judgment of 1966 *but also in that of 1962 (I.C.J. Reports 1966,* pp. 44-45; and *I.C.J. Reports 1962,* pp.

336-337). It is obvious that a situation in which the League Council could not impose its views on the mandatories without their consent, is with difficulty reconcilable with one in which it could unilaterally revoke their mandates without their consent; — and therefore, *a fortiori,* with the idea that the United Nations possessed such a power.

Where a provision (such as the League Council's voting rule) is so worded that it can only have one effect, any intended exceptions, in order to be operative, must be stated in terms.

80. This principle of interpretation is, as it happens, well illustrated, and the view expressed in the preceding paragraph is given the character of a virtual certainty, by the fact that (though not in the sphere of mandates) the League Covenant did specifically provide for certain exceptions to the basic League unanimity rule, — namely, in particular under paragraphs 4, 6, 7 and 10 of Article 15 and paragraph 4 of Article 16, dealing with matters of peace-keeping. This serves to show that those who framed the Covenant fully realized that there were some situations in which to admit the vote of the interested party would be self-defeating — and these they provided for. They do not seem to have thought so in the case of mandates, nor was such a suggestion ever made in the course of the League's dealings with mandates. It can only be concluded that terminations or changes of administration were never contemplated, except on a basis of agreement.

81. Nor was it in, any way a question of a mere oversight. Earlier proposals for a mandates system, in particular as put forward by President Wilson on behalf of the United States, did contain provision for the replacement of mandatories, or for the substitution of another mandatory, — and these things (contrary to what is implied in the Opinion of the Court) could of course only be done by revoking (or they would amount to a revocation of) the original mandate. Even the possibility of breaches was not overlooked, for the Wilson proposals also provided, as is correctly stated in the Opinion of the Court, for a "right to appeal to the League for the redress or correction of any breach of the mandate". There can however be no point in following the Opinion of the Court into a debate as to the precise period and the precise context in which the idea of revocability was discussed, — because what is beyond doubt

107

is that, whether on the basis of President Wilson's proposal, or of some other proposal, it *was* discussed. The proof of this is something of which the Court's Opinion makes no mention, namely that objections were entertained to the notion of revocability by all the eventual holders of "C" mandates, and by the representatives of governments destined to hold most of the "A" and "B" mandates — in particular by M. Simon on behalf of France and Mr. Balfour (as he then was) on behalf of Great Britain, both of whom pointed out the difficulties, economic and other, that would arise if mandatories did not have complete security of tenure. The idea was accordingly not proceeded with, and the final text of the mandates, and of Article 22 of the Covenant, contained no mention of it. This makes it quite impossible in law to infer that there nevertheless remained some sort of unexpressed intention that a right of revocation should exist, for this would lead to the curious legal proposition that it makes no difference whether a thing is expressed or not. Yet the classic instance of the creation of an irrebuttable presumption in favour of a given intention is, precisely, where a different course has been proposed but not followed. The motives involved are juridically quite irrelevant, but were in this case clear.[14]

Applicable Principle of Interpretation

Where a particular proposal has been considered but rejected, for whatever reason, it is not possible to interpret the instrument or juridical situation to which the proposal related as if the latter had in fact been adopted.

82. The episode described in the preceding paragraph directly illustrates and confirms the view expressed in paragraphs 70-72 above. When Statesmen such as President Wilson thought of making mandates revocable (which could only be in a context of possible breaches) they were not content to rely

---

14 For sheer audacity, it would be hard to equal the attempts made in the course of the present proceedings to represent M. Simon's statement to the effect that every mandate would be revocable and there could be no guarantee of its continuance (which of course *would* have been the case on the basis of the *earlier* idea which M. Simon was *contesting*), as affording evidence of an intention that mandates should be revocable; and that this was only not proceeded with because of a desire to be "tactful" towards the mandatories, — although it is perfectly clear on the face of the record that M. Simon (and Mr. Balfour) were *objecting* to the idea of revocability, — not on grounds of its want of tact, but for economic and other reasons of a highly concrete character, — i.e., France and Great Britain, no less than the "C" mandatories, were not prepared to accept mandates on such a basis.

on any inherent principle of revocability but made a definite proposal which, had it been adopted, would have figured as an article in the eventual governing instrument, or instruments. Since however the idea met with specific objections, it was not proceeded with and does not so figure. Therefore to treat the situation as being exactly the same as if it nevertheless did, is inadmissible and contrary to the stability and objectivity of the international legal order. Again, the process of having it both ways is evident.

83. Article 22 of the League Covenant drew a clear distinction between the "C" mandated territories and the other ("A" and "B") territories, inasmuch as in its paragraph 6 it described the former as being territories that could "be best administered under the laws of the Mandatory as integral portions of its territory", — and a clause to that effect figured in the "C" mandates accordingly. This distinction was not, however, fully maintained; for a similar clause eventually appeared in the "B" mandates as well, — though without warrant for this in the Covenant. But this does not invalidate the point to be made because, as has been seen in the previous sub-section (paragraph 81), the notion of revocability was as inacceptable to the "B" as to the "C" mandatories. The point involved is that the "integral portion" clause came very close in its wording to the language of incorporation — indeed it only just missed it. It did not amount to that of course, for annexation or cession in sovereignty of the mandated territory was something which it was one of the aims of the mandates system to avoid. But this clause did create a situation that was utterly irreconcilable with unilateral *revocability*, — with the idea that at some future date the existing administrative and legal integrations, and applicable laws of the mandatory concerned, could be displaced by the handing over of the territory to another mandatory, to be then administered as an integral portion of *its* territoy and subjected to another set of laws; — and of course this process could in theory be repeated indefinitely, if the revocability in principle of mandates once came to be admitted.

84. In consequence, although the mandates did not contain any provision affirmatively ruling out revocability, the "integral portion" clause in the "B" and "C" mandates had in practice much the same effect. Significantly, no such clause

figured in any of the "A" mandates which were, from the start (paragraph 4 of Article 22 of the Covenant), regarded as relating to territories whose "existence as independent nations can be provisionally recognized". Naturally the insertion of the "integral portion" clause in the "B" and "C" mandates did not in any way preclude the eventual attainment of self-government or independence by the territories concerned, as indeed happened with most of them some forty years later, — *with the consent of the mandatory concerned;* but that is another matter. What it did preclude was any interim change of régime *without* the consent of the mandatory.

85. As is well known, the mandates system represented a compromise between, on the one hand, President Wilson's desire to place all ex-enemy territory outside Europe or Asia Minor (and even some *in* Europe) under direct League of Nations administration, — and, on the other hand, the desire of some of the Allied nations (more particularly as regards the eventual "C" mandates) to obtain a cession to themselves of these territories, which their forces had overrun and occupied during the war. The factor of "geographical contiguity to the territory of the Mandatory", specifically mentioned in paragraph 6 of Article 22 of the Covenant, was of course especially (indeed uniquely) applicable to the case of SW. Africa, and had unquestionably been introduced with that case in mind. The compromise just referred to was accepted only with difficulty by some of the mandatories and, in the case of the "C" mandates only after assurances that the mandates would give them ownership in all but name. Whether this attitude was unethical according to present-day standards (it certainly was not so then) is juridically beside the point. It clearly indicates what the *intentions* of the parties were, and upon what basis the "C" mandates were accepted. This does not of course mean that the mandatories obtained sovereignty. But it does mean that they could never, in the case of these territories contiguous to or very near their own, have been willing to accept a system according to which, at the will of the Council of the League, they might at some future date find themselves displaced in favour of another entity — possibly a hostile or unfriendly one — (as is indeed precisely the intention now). No sovereign State at that time — or indeed at any other time — would have accepted the administration of a territory on

such terms. To the mandatories, their right of veto in the Council was an essential condition of their acceptance of this compromise, — and that they viewed it as extending to any question involving a possible change in the identity of the mandatory is beyond all possible doubt. Here once more is a consideration that completely negatives the idea of unilateral revocability.

86. Taking these various factors together, as they have been stated in the preceding paragraphs, the conclusion must be that no presumptions or unexpressed implications of revocability are applicable in the present case, and that in any event they would be overwhelmingly negatived by the strongest possible contra-indications.

87. *Test of this conclusion* — a good test of this conclusion is to enquire what happened as regards those former mandated territories that were eventually placed under the United Nations trusteeship system. Here was an opportunity for the Assembly to introduce an express power of unilateral revocation into the various trusteeship agreements entered into under Article 79 of the Charter. This however was not done, for one very simple reason, namely that not a single administering authority, in respect of any single trusteeship, would have been prepared to agree to the inclusion of such a power — any more than, as a mandatory, it had been prepared to agree to it in the time of the League. The point involved is of exactly the same order (though in a different but related context) as that to which attention was drawn in paragraphs 93-95 of the 1966 Judgment of the Court, where it was stated (*I.C.J. Reports 1966*, p. 49) that there was *one* test that could be applied in order to ascertain what had really been intended, namely,

". . . by enquiring what the States who were members of the League when the mandates system was instituted did when, as Members of the United Nations, they joined in setting up the trusteeship system that was to replace the mandates system. In effect . . . they did exactly the same as had been done before . . .".

And so it was over revocation. No more than before was any provision for it made. Is it really to ascribe this to a belief that it was not necessary because all international mandates and trusts were inherently subject to unilateral revocation, irrespective of the consent of the administering authority? — or

111

would it be more reasonable to suppose that it was because no such thing was intended? If no such thing was intended in the case of the *trust* territories (all of them formerly mandated territories), this was because no such thing had been intended, or had ever been instituted, in the case of the mandated territories themselves, *as mandates*. The former mandatories were simply perpetuating in this respect the same system as before *(and the Assembly tacitly agreed to this under the various trusteeship agreements)*. This previous system of course applied, and continues to apply, to the mandated territory of SW. Africa.

88. Since the conclusion reached is that League of Nations mandates would not have been subject to unilateral revocation by the Council of the League or — what comes to the same thing — that the concurrence of the mandatory concerned would have been required for any change of mandatory, or for the termination of the mandate on a basis of self-government or independence; — and since the United Nations cannot have any greater powers in the matter than had the League, it follows that the Assembly can have had no competence to revoke South Africa's mandate, even if it had become subrogated to the League Council's supervisory role — for that role did not comprise any power of unilateral revocation.

89. There are however other reasons, resulting from the United Nations Charter itself, why the organs of the United Nations had no competence to revoke the Mandate, whether or not they would otherwise have had it; and these will now be considered in the next main section.

90. In the two preceding main sections it has been held, *first* that the United Nations as an Organization never became invested with any supervisory function in respect of mandates not voluntarily converted into trusteeships, and never became subrogated to the sphere of competence of the former League of Nations in respect of mandates; and *secondly* that since in any event that competence did not include any power of unilateral revocation of a mandate, or of terminating it without the consent of the mandatory concerned, the United Nations would equally have had no competence to exercise such a power even if it had, in principle, become subrogated to the role of the League in respect of mandates. But in addition to the limitations thus arising, both from general rules of law and

from the provisions of the relevant governing instruments, there is also the question of the limitations imposed upon the competence and sphere of authority of the organs of the United Nations by the constitution of the latter, as embodied in its Charter. Since these organs (in the present context the General Assembly and the Security Council) are the creations of the Charter, they are necessarily subject to such limitations, and can prima facie, take valid action only upon that basis.

91. So far as the Assembly is concerned, there arises at the outset an important preliminary question, namely whether it was competent to act as (in effect) a court of law to pronounce, as judge in its own cause, on charges in respect of which it was itself the complainant. In my opinion it was not; and this suffices in itself to render Resolution 2145, by which the Assembly purported to revoke the Mandate for SW. Africa, invalid and inoperative. However, in order not to break the thread of the present argument, I deal with the matter in the first section of the Annex to this Opinion.

92. In contrast with the former League of Nations, in which both main bodies, except in certain specified cases, acted by unanimity, the basic structure adopted in the drafting of the United Nations Charter consisted in the establishment of a careful balance between a small organ — the Security Council, acting within a comparatively limited field, but able, in that field, to take binding decisions for certain purposes; — and a larger organ, the General Assembly, with a wide field of competence, but in general, only empowered to discuss and recommend; — this distinction being fundamental. The powers of the Security Council will be considered at a later stage. As to the Assembly, the list appended below in footnote [15] indicates

15 The list shows that the Assembly is either limited to making recommendations, or that where it can do more, it is as a result of a specific power conferred by the express terms of some provision of the Charter. In other words the Assembly has no inherent or residual power to do more than recommend.

The recommendatory functions are described as follows:—

(The General Assembly)

Article 10: "may discuss . . . and . . . make recommendations";
Article 11, paragraph 1: "may consider . . . and . . . make recommendations";
Article 11, paragraph 2: "may discuss . . . and . . . make recommendations";
Article 11, paragraph 3: "may call . . . attention . . . to";
Article 12, paragraph 1: "*shall not make any recommendation . . . unless (so requested)*";
Article 13: "shall initiate studies and make recommendations";
Article 14: "may recommend measures";

the general character of what it was empowered to do. From what this list reveals (seen against the whole conceptual background of the Charter), there arises an irrebuttable presumption that except in the few cases (see section *(d)* of the list) in which executive or operative powers are specifically conferred on the Assembly, it does not, so far as the Charter is concerned, have them. In consequence, anything else it does outside those specific powers, whatever it may be and however the relevant resolution is worded, *can* only operate as a recommendation. It should hardly be necessary to point out the fallacy of an argument which would attribute to the Assembly a residual power to take executive action at large, because it has a *specific* power so to do under certain particular articles (4, 5, 6 and 17). On the contrary, the correct inference is the reverse one — that where no such power has been specifically given, it does not exist.

93. It follows ineluctably from the above, that the Assembly has no *implied* powers except such as are mentioned in *(e)* of footnote. [15] *All* its powers, whether they be executive or only recommendatory, are precisely formulated in the Charter and there is no residuum. Naturally any organ must be deemed to have the powers necessary to enable it to perform the specific functions it is invested with. This is what the Court had in mind when, in the *Injuries to United Nations Servants* (Count Bernadotte) case (*I.C.J. Reports 1949*, p. 182), it said that the

Article 15: "shall receive and consider (reports)";
Article 16: "*shall perform such functions . . . as are assigned to it (by Chapters XII and XIII of the Charter)*";
Article 105, paragraph 3: "may make recommendations".

(b) *The peace-keeping functions conferred upon the Assembly by Article 35, are, by its third paragraph, specifically stated to be "subject to the provisions of Articles 11 and 12" (as to which, see above).*
(c) *As regards Chapters XII and XIII of the Charter (trusteeships, the only provisions which refer to the Assembly are:*

Article 85, which (without any indication of what the functions in question are) provides that the non-strategic area functions of the United Nations "with regard to *trusteeship agreements*" (italics added) "including the approval of the terms of" such agreements, "shall be exercised by the . . . Assembly".

Article 87, under which the Assembly may "consider reports" ("submitted by the administering authority"); "accept petitions and examine them" ("in consultation with (that) authority"); "provide for periodic visits" to trust territories ("at time agreed upon with the (same) authority"); and "take these and other actions *in conformity with the terms of the trusteeship agreements*" (italics added).

United Nations:

". . . must be deemed to have those powers which, though not expressly provided in the Charter, are conferred upon it by necessary implication as being essential to the performance of its duties".

This is acceptable if it is read as being related and confined to existing and specified duties; but it would be quite another matter, by a process of implication, to seek to bring about an *extension* of functions, such as would result for the Assembly if it were deemed (outside of Articles 4, 5, 6 and 17) to have a non-specified power, not only to discuss and recommend, but to take executive action, and to bind.

94. In the same way, whereas the practice of an organization, or of a particular organ of it, can modify the manner of exercise of one of its functions (as for instance in the case of the veto in the Security Council which is not deemed to be involved by a mere abstention), such practice cannot, in principle, modify or add to the function itself. Without in any absolute sense denying that, through a sufficiently steady and long-continued course of conduct, a new tacit *agreement* may arise having a modificatory effect, the presumption is against it, — especially in the case of an organization whose constituent instrument provides for its own amendment, and prescribes with some particularity what the means of effecting this are to be. There is a close analogy here with the principle enunciated by the Court in the *North Sea Continental Shelf* case (*I.C.J. Reports 1969*, p. 25) that when a convention has in

---

None of this invests the Assembly with any binding or executive powers except in so far as might specifically be conferred upon it by the express terms of the trusteeship agreements. These did not in fact any of them do so (see footnote 64 below).

(d) In the result, the only provisions of the Charter which confer executive or quasi-executive powers on the Assembly are:

Articles 4, 5 and 6, which enable the Assembly to admit a new Member, or suspend or expel an existing one, — in each case only upon the recommendation of the Security Council; and *Article 17,* under paragraph 1 of which the Assembly is to "consider and approve" the budget of the Organization, with the corollary (paragraph 2) that the expenses of the Organization are to be borne by the Members "as apportioned by the Assembly". Under paragraph 3, the Assembly is to "consider and approve" financial arrangements with the specialized agencies, but is only to "examine" their budgets "with a view to making recommendations" to them.

(e) The Assembly naturally has those purely domestic, internal, and procedural executive powers without which such a body could not function, e.g., to elect its own officers; fix the dates and times of its meetings; determine its agenda; appoint standing committees and *ad hoc* ones; establish staff regulations; decide to hold a diplomatic conference under United Nations auspices, etc., etc.

terms provided for a particular method whereby some process is to be carried out (in that case it was the method of becoming bound by the convention), it was "not lightly to be presumed that", although this method had not been followed, the same result had "nevertheless somehow (been achieved) in another way" — a principle which, had it been applied by the Court in the present case, would have led to a totally different outcome, as can be seen from Sections A and B above.

95. Translating this into the particular field of mandates, it is clear that, just as the Assembly would have no power to make a grant of sovereign independence to a non-self-governing territory under Articles 73 and 74 of the Charter, nor to terminate a trusteeship without the consent of the administering authority (see relevant clauses of the various trusteeship agreements made under Article 79 of the Charter), — so equally, given the actual language of the Charter, does the Assembly have no power to evict a mandatory. Any resolution of the Assembly purporting to do that could therefore only have the status of, and operate as, a non-binding recommendation. The power given to the Assembly by Articles 5 and 6 of the Charter to suspend or expel a member State (upon the recommendation of the Security Council) would of course enable it to suspend or expel a mandatory *from its membership of the United Nations;* but this cannot be extended on a sort of analogical basis to the quite different act of purporting to revoke the mandatory's mandate.

96. From all of this, only one conclusion is possible, namely that so far as the terms of the Charter itself are concerned, *the Assembly has no power to terminate any kind of administration over any kind of territory.*

97. It may however be contended that the matter does not end there, for it may be possible for powers other or greater than its normal ones to be conferred upon an international organ *aliunde* or *ab extra,* for some particular purpose — e.g., under a treaty, — and if so, why should it not exercise them? This contention must now be considered.

98. The question here is whether it is legally possible for a body such as the Assembly, in the purported exercise of what may conveniently be called "extra-mural" powers, to act in a manner in which, in the *intra*-mural exercise of its normal functions, it would be precluded by its constitution from

doing. To put the matter in its most graphic form, suppose for instance a group of member States of the United Nations — in a particular region perhaps — entered into a treaty under which they conferred on the Assembly, in relation to themselves and for that region, exactly those peace-keeping powers which, under the Charter, the Security Council is empowered to take as regards the member States of the United Nations collectively. Could it then validly be argued that although it would be *ultra vires* for the Assembly so to act under the *Charter,* if Charter action were involved, nevertheless it could in this particular case do so because it had acquired, *aliunde,* the necessary power vis-a-vis the particular States members of the regional group concerned, by reason of the treaty concluded between them investing the Assembly with such power? It is in fact approximately upon the basis of a theory such as this one, that those who (to their credit) feel some difficulty in attributing executive powers to the Assembly, outside those specified in Articles 4, 5, 6 and 17 of the Charter, rely in contending that, although under the Charter the Assembly could not do more than discuss and recommend in the field of mandates, yet it would go further than this if it had derived from the League of Nations the power to do so.

99. It should be realized that the question asked in the preceding paragraph is not merely an academic one; it is closely related to situations that have actually arisen in the history of the United Nations. There have been times when the majority of the member States have been dissatisfied with the functioning of the Security Council, whose action had become paralyzed owing to the attitude of one or more of the Permanent Members. In these circumstances recourse was had to the Assembly, which adopted resolutions containing recommendations that were not, indeed, binding but which could be, and were by most of the States concerned, regarded as authorizing them to adopt courses they might not otherwise have felt justified in following. If such situations were to arise again and continue persistently, it could be but a step from that to attempts to invest the Assembly with a measure of executive power by the process already described, or something analogous to it.

100. It so happens that the principle of the question under discussion arose in the *Voting Procedure* case, and was dealt

with both by the Court and by three individual judges in a sense adverse to the contention now being considered. It was Sir Hersch Lauterpacht who gave the most direct general negative; and though he was speaking with reference to the question of the voting rule, the principle involved was exactly the same *(I.C.J. Reports 1955,* at p. 109): ". . . the . . . Assembly cannot act in that way. It cannot override a seemingly mandatory provision of the Charter *by the device of accepting a task conferred by a treaty. It might otherwise be possible to alter, through extraneous treaties, the character of the Organization in an important aspect of its activity"* — (my italics).

The passage italicised is precisely applicable to the situation that would arise if the Assembly were deemed able to accept, *ab extra,* functions of an executive character going beyond its basic Charter role of consideration, discussion and recommendation. Even if it may not be outside the scope of the Charter for the Assembly to deal in *some* form with mandated territories not placed under trusteeship — e.g., as being, at the least, non-self-governing territories within the meaning of Article 73 — it can only deal with them by way of discussion and recommendation, not executive action.

101. In the *Voting Procedure* case, the Court itself was of the same way of thinking as Sir Hersch. Having regard to the view expressed in its earlier (1950) Opinion to the effect that the degree of supervision in the Assembly should not exceed that of the League Council, and should as far as possible follow the latter's procedure (see paragraph 65 above), it became evident that if the Assembly applied its usual majority, or two-thirds majority, voting rule in the course of its supervision of the mandate, it would *not* be conforming to the procedure of the League Council, which was based on a unanimity rule, including even the vote of the mandatory. Moreover, it was clear that the latter rule (being more favourable to the mandatory by making decisions adverse to its views harder to arrive at) involved in consequence a lesser degree of supervision than the Assembly's voting rule would do. This being so, the question arose whether the Assembly, in order to remain within the limits of the powers derived by it from or through the instrument of mandate, as those powers had been exercised by the League Council, could proceed according to a voting rule which was not that provided for by the *Charter* —

in short could depart from the Charter in this respect. The Court answered this question by a decided negative in the following terms (*I.C.J. Reports 1955*, at p. 75):

"The constitution of an organ usually prescribes the method of voting by which the organ arrives at its decisions. The voting system is related to the composition and functions of the organ. It forms one of the characteristics of the constitution of the organ. Taking decisions by a two-thirds majority vote or by a simple majority vote is one of the distinguishing features of the General Assembly, while the unanimity rule was one of the distinguishing features of the Council of the League of Nations. These two systems are characteristic of different organs, and one system cannot be substituted for another without constitutional amendment. To transplant upon the General Assembly the unanimity rule of the Council of the League . . . would amount to a disregard of one of the characteristics of the . . . Assembly."

This view was independently concurred in by Judges Basdevant, Klaestad and Lauterpacht. Judge Basdevant said (at p. 82):

"The majority rule laid down by Article 18 of the Charter and the unanimity rule prescribed by the Covenant of the League of Nations are something other than rules of procedure: they determine an essential characteristic of the organs in question and of their parent international institutions." (For Judge Klaestad's view see paragraph 104 below.)

102. The criteria thus enunciated by the Court and by Judge Basdevant were, be it noted, formulated precisely in the context of the mandates system. It is therefore legitimate to apply them to the present case; and if this is done in terms of the last two sentences of the foregoing quotation from the 1955 Opinion of the Court, the result is that there "cannot . . . without constitutional amendment" "be substituted" for a system which only allows the Assembly to discuss and recommend, "another" system which would allow it, in addition, to take executive and peremptory action, — and that, to deem the Assembly to be invested with such a power "would amount to a disregard of one of its characteristics" within the system of the Charter.

119

103. It must be concluded that even if the League Council's supervisory powers had in principle passed to the Assembly, and had included the right to revoke an existing mandate, such a right could not, constitutionally, be exercised by the Assembly, since this would be inconsistent with the basic philosophy of its role within the general structure of the United Nations.

104. *Dilemma of Judges Klaestad and Lauterpacht in the Voting Procedure case* — The problem in the *Voting Procedure* case was that, as had already been mentioned, the fact that decisions could be more easily arrived at under the Assembly's voting rule than under the League's rule of unanimity including the vote of the mandatory, involved for the latter a "greater degree of supervision" than the League's. Yet, as the Court found (see *ante,* paragraph 101), the Assembly could not, conformably with the Charter, depart from its own voting rule. The Court solved this problem by holding that although, in the exercise of its supervisory function, the Assembly must not depart from the substance of the mandate, the procedure by which it carried out that function must be the procedure provided for by the Charter; and that the Court's previous (1950) pronouncement, indicating that the degree of supervision must not be greater than the League's, was intended to apply only to matters of substance, not procedure. Given that the Assembly's voting rule *did* however, in principle, involve a greater degree of supervision than the League rule, by making it possible for decisions to be arrived at without the concurrence of the mandatory, this pronouncement of the Court in the *Voting Procedure* case involved a distinct element of inconsistency. That solution accordingly did not satisfy Judges Klaestad and Lauterpacht who arrived at a different and more logical one, avoiding contradictions and, at the same time, operating to confirm in a very striking manner the views expressed above as to the limits imposed by the Charter on the powers of the Assembly. They pointed out that the decisions reached by that organ in the course of supervising the mandate, not being in the nature of domestic, internal or procedural decisions (see head *(e)* in note 62 above) *could only operate as recommendations,* and could not therefore in any case be binding on the mandatory unless it had at least voted in favour of them. Hence the Assembly's two-thirds

rule, though theoretically more burdensome for the mandatory than the League's rule of unanimity including the mandatory's vote, would not in practice be so, since in neither case could the mandatory be bound without its own concurrence. In this way the balance between the weight of the League Council's supervision and that of the Assembly would be maintained or restored.

105. This conclusion could not be other than correct, — for if the Assembly's decisions bound the mandatory without the latter's consent, whereas the League's did not, there would be imposed a degree of supervision not only far heavier, but *differing totally in kind* from that of the League. To put the matter in another way, if the substitution of the Assembly for the League Council could not be allowed to operate so as to increase the Mandatory's obligations, it correspondingly could not be allowed to operate to increase the supervisory organ's powers, still less to give it a power that the former supervisory organ never had, or could never have exercised except in a certain way and by a certain kind of vote. It follows that such a power could not be exercised by the Assembly either, especially since the latter equally cannot bind the mandatory and cannot go beyond recommendations without exceeding its constitutional Charter powers. In consequence, Resolution 2145, even if it were otherwise valid, could not have any higher status or effect than, or operate except as, a *recommendation* that South Africa's administration should terminate, and not as an actual termination of it. I have to point out in conclusion that the whole of this most important aspect of the matter, resulting from the Court's own jurisprudence as it was enunciated in the 1955 *Voting Procedure* case, is now completely ignored, and not even mentioned, in the present Opinion of the Court; — for the sufficient reason no doubt that there is no satisfactory answer that can be given to it.

106. *The answer given by the Court in 1950 to the question lettered* (c) *put to it in the then advisory proceedings* — This question asked where the competence to modify the international status of SW. Africa lay, upon the assumption that it did not lie with South Africa acting unilaterally. The Court replied (*I.C.J. Reports 1950,* at p. 144):

    "... that the Union of South Africa acting alone has not the competence to modify the international status of the territory of South West Africa, and that the competence to determine and modify the international status of the Territory *rests with the Union of South Africa acting with the consent of the United Nations"* — (my italics).

It is clear that even if the Mandate itself persisted under another authority the *change* of authority (particularly if the new one was the United Nations as such) would unquestionably involve a modification of the international status of the territory, not only by substituting a new administration for the existing one, but by substituting one which could not itself be subjected to any supervision at all, except its own, and which would have to render reports to itself (and so — *quis custodiet ipsos custodes?)* [16] It therefore follows from what the Court said about modifying the status of the territory, that the competence to effect any substitution of this kind (or any other change of mandatory) would rest "with the Union of South Africa acting with the consent of the United Nations," — which view invests *South Africa* with the initiative, and negatives the existence of any independent right of termination resident in the United Nations acting alone. Even allowing for the fact that the issue at that time was whether the *mandatory* had any unilateral power of modification it is impossible to reconcile the phraseology employed with the idea that the Court in 1950 could have thought the United Nations, or any organ of it, acting *alone,* had such a power. As my colleague Judge Gros points out, both aspects of the matter had been raised in the course of the proceedings.

107. The foregoing considerations lead to the conclusion that even if the Assembly inherited a supervisory role from the League Council, it could exercise it only within the limits of its competence under the Charter namely by way of discussion and recommendation. Such a situation has no room for, and is entirely incompatible with, any power to revoke a mandate. In consequence, Assembly Resolution 2145 could have effect only as a recommendation.

---

16 Even if the Assembly had "inherited" the supervisory function from the League, this function manifestly cannot include administration, — for the essence of supervision is its exercise by a *separate* body, not being the *administering* authority. The idea of mandates administered direct by the League itself without a mandatory as intermediary, which formed part of President Wilson's original proposals at Versailles, was not adopted, and formed no part of the *League* mandates system which it is claimed that the United Nations inherited.

108. It is strictly superfluous to consider what (if any) were the Security Council's powers in relation to mandates, because it is quite clear that the Council never took any independent action to terminate South Africa's mandate. All its resolutions were consequential, proceeding on the basis of a supposed termination already effected or declared by the Assembly. Without the Assembly's act, the acts of the Security Council, which were largely in the nature of a sort of attempted enforcement of what the Assembly had declared, would have lacked all *raison d'etre*; — while on the other hand, if the Assembly's resolution 2145 lacked *in se* validity and legal effect, no amount of "confirmation" by the Security Council could validate it or lend it such effect, or independently bring about the revocation of a mandate.

109. It is necessary to distinguish clearly between what the Security Council can do on a *mandates* basis and what it might be able to do on the only other possible basis on which it could act, namely a peace-keeping basis. On a mandates basis the Security Council has not greater powers than the Assembly, — for (see the 1950 Opinion of the Court at p. 137) it was the United Nations as a whole which inherited — or did not inherit — the role of the League of Nations in respect of mandates, together with (if it did) such powers as were comprised in that role. Consequently, as regards any power of revocation, the Security Council stands on exactly the same footing as the Assembly in respect of such questions as whether the United Nations has any supervisory function at all and, if so, whether it includes any power of revocation; — subject however to this one qualification, namely that in 1950 the Court very definitely *(loc. cit.)* indicated the Assembly as the *appropriate* organ to exercise the supervisory function it found the United Nations to be invested with. It must therefore be questioned whether the Security Council has any specific role whatever in respect of mandates as such, similar to that which it has in respect of strategic trusteeships. If this is so, it would be solely for peace-keeping purposes that the Security Council would be competent to take action in respect of a mandate.

110. As regards the alternative basis of Security Council intervention, clearly that organ cannot be precluded from exercising its *normal* peacekeeping functions merely because the threat to the peace, if there is one, has arisen in a mandates

context, — *provided* the intervention has a genuinely peace-keeping aim and is not a disguised exercise in mandates supervision. What the Security Council cannot properly do is, in the guise of peace-keeping, to exercise functions in respect of mandates, where those functions do not properly belong to it either as a self-contained organ or as part of the United Nations as a whole. It cannot, in the guise of peace-keeping revoke a mandate any more than it can, in the guise of peace-keeping order transfers or cessions of territory.

111. However, in my opinion, the various Security Council resolutions involved did not, on their language, purport to be in the exercise of the peace-keeping function. There is in fact something like a careful avoidance of phraseology that would be too unambiguous in this respect. That being so, their effect was as indicated in paragraphs 108-109 above. They were not binding on the Mandatory or on other member States of the United Nations. Like those of the Assembly they could only have a recommendatory effect in the present context.

112. *Proper scope of the Security Council's peace-keeping powers under the Charter:* This matter, so far as the actual terms of the Charter are concerned, is governed by paragraphs 1 and 2 of Article 24 which read as follows:

"1. In order to ensure prompt and effective action by the United Nations, its Members confer on the Security Council primary responsibility for the maintenance of international peace and security and agree that in carrying out its duties under this responsibility the Security Council acts on their behalf.

2. In discharging these duties the Security Council shall act in accordance with the purposes and principles of the United Nations. *The specific powers granted to the Security Council for the discharge of these duties are laid down in Chapters VI, VII, VIII and XII"* — (my italics.).

I am unable to agree with the extremely wide interpretation which the Opinion of the Court places on this provision. No doubt it does not limit the *occasions* on which the Security Council can act in the preservation of peace and security, provided the threat said to be involved is not a mere figment or pretext. What it does do is to limit the type of action the Council can take in the discharge of its peace-keeping responsibilities, — for the second paragraph of Article 24 states in terms that the *specific* powers granted to the Security Council for these purposes are laid down in the indicated Chapters (VI, VII, VIII and XII). According to normal canons of interpretation this means that so far as *peace-keeping* is concerned, they are not to be found anywhere else, and are exercisable only as those Chapters allow. It is therefore to them that recourse must be had in order to ascertain what the *specific* peace-keeping powers of the Security Council are, *including the power to bind.* If this is done, it will be found that only when the Council is acting under Chapter VII, or possibly in certain cases under Chapter VIII, will its resolutions be binding on member States. In other cases their effect would be recommendatory or hortatory only. (Peace-keeping action under Chapter XII — strategic trusteeships — does not really seem to me to be a separate case, since it is difficult to see how it could fail to take the form of action under Chapters VI or VII as the case might be.

113. These limitations apply equally to the effect of Article 25 of the Charter, by reason of the proviso "in accordance with the present Charter". If, under the relevant chapter or article of the Charter, the decision is *not* binding, Article 25 cannot make it so. If the effect of that Article were automatically to make *all* decisions of the Security Council binding, then the words "in accordance with the present Charter" would be quite superfluous. They would add nothing to the preceding and only other phrase in the Article, namely "The Members of the United Nations agree to accept and carry out the decisions of the Security Council," which they are clearly intended to qualify. They effectively do so only if the decisions referred to are those which *are* duly binding "in accordance with the present Charter". Otherwise the language used in such parts of the Charter as Chapter VI for instance, indicative of recommendatory functions only, would be in direct contradiction with Article 25 — or Article 25 with them.

114. Since, in consequence, the question whether any given resolution of the Security Council is binding or merely recommendatory in effect, must be a matter for objective determination in each individual case, it follows that the Council cannot, merely by *invoking* Article 25 (as it does for instance in its Resolution 269 of 12 August 1969) impart obligatory character

125

to a resolution which would not otherwise possess it according to the terms of the chapter or article of the Charter on the basis of which the Council is, or must be deemed to be, acting.

115. There is more. *Even when acting under Chapter VII of the Charter itself,* the Security Council has no power to abrogate or alter territorial rights, whether of sovereignty or administration. Even a war-time occupation of a country or territory cannot operate to do that. It must await the peace settlement. This is a principle of international law that is as well-established as any there can be, — and the Security Council is as much subject to it (for the United Nations is itself a subject of international law) as any of its individual member States are. The Security Council might, after making the necessary determinations under Article 39 of the Charter, order the occupation of a country or piece of territory *in order to restore peace and security,* but it could not thereby, or as part of that operation, abrogate or alter territorial rights; — and the right to administer a mandated territory is a territorial right without which the territory could not be governed or the mandate be operated. It was to keep the peace, not to change the world order, that the Security Council was set up.

116. These limitations on the powers of the Security Council are necessary because of the all too great ease with which any acutely controversial international situation can be represented as involving a latent threat to peace and security, even where it is really too remote genuinely to constitute one. Without these limitations, the functions of the Security Council could be used for purposes never originally intended, — and the present case is a very good illustration of this: for not only was the Security Council not acting under Chapter VII of the Charter (which it obviously could not do — though it remains to be seen by what means and upon what grounds the necessary threat to, or breach of the peace, or act of aggression will be determined to exist); — not only was there no threat to peace and security other than such as might be artificially created as a pretext for the realization of ulterior purposes, — but the whole operation, which will not necessarily end there, had as its object the abrogation of the Mandatory's rights of territorial administration, in order to secure (not eventually but very soon) the transformation of the mandated territory into, and its emergence as, the sovereign independent State of

"Namibia". This what is declared in terms, not only in Resolution 2145 itself, but also in the subsequent Assembly Resolution 2248 (S-V) of 1967, specifying June 1968 as the intended date of transfer, — and this is par excellence the type of purpose, in promoting which, the Security Council (and *a fortiori* the Assembly) exceeds its competence, and so acts *ultra vires*.

117. On the basis of the foregoing conclusions, the answer to the question put to the Court in the present proceedings, as to what are the legal consequences for States of the continued presence of South Africa in the mandated territory of SW. Africa, despite Security Council resolution 276 of 1970 is strictly, that there are no specific legal consequences for States, for there has been no change in the legal position. Since neither the Security Council nor the Assembly has any competence to revoke South Africa's Mandate, the various resolutions of these organs purporting to do so, or to declare it to be at an end, or to confirm its termination, are one and all devoid of legal effect. The result is that the Mandate still subsists, and that South Africa is still the Mandatory. However, from this last conclusion there do follow certain legal consequences both for South Africa and for other States.

118. *For South Africa* there is an obligation
(1) to recognize that the Mandate survived the dissolution of the League, — that it has an international character, — and that in consequence SW. Africa cannot unilaterally be incorporated in the territory of the Republic;
(2) to perform and execute in full all the obligations of the Mandate, whatever these may be.

119. With regard to this last requirement, I have given my reasons for thinking that, the United Nations not being the successor in law to the League of Nations, the Mandatory is not, and never became subject to any duty to report to it, or accept its supervision, particularly as regards the Assembly. But as was pointed out earlier in this Opinion (paragraphs 17 and 20), it does not follow that the reporting obligation has lapsed entirely; and it is the fact that it could be carried out by the alternative means indicated in paragraph 16. This being so, the question arises whether the Mandatory has a legal duty to take some such steps as were there indicated. The matter is not free from doubt. The Court in 1950 considered the report-

ing obligation to be an essential part of the Mandate. Judge Read on the other hand thought that although its absence might "weaken" the Mandate, the latter would not otherwise be affected. Again if the Mandate is viewed as a treaty or contract, the normal effect of the extinction of one of the parties would be to bring the treaty or contract to an end entirely.

120. However, the better view seems to be that the reporting obligation survived, though becoming dormant upon the dissolution of the League, and certainly not transformed into an obligation relative to the United Nations. Nevertheless, if not an absolutely essential element, it is a sufficiently important part of the Mandate to place the Mandatory under an obligation to revive and carry it out, if it is at all possible to do so, by some other means. But the Mandatory would have the right to insist (a) on the new supervisory body being acceptable to it in character and composition — (such acceptance not to be unreasonably withheld), — (b) on the nature and implications (as to degree of supervision) of the reporting obligation being as they are indicated to be in paragraphs 76-78 above, — and (c) that, just as with the League Council, the Mandatory would be under no legal obligation to carry out the recommendations of the supervisory body, no more than States administering trust territories are obliged to accept the views of the United Nations Assembly as supervisory organ — (see supra, paragraphs 77 and 104).

121. A further, or rather alternative, course that could be considered incumbent on South Africa, though as a consequence of the Charter not the Mandate, would be to resume the rendering of reports under Article 73 (e) of the Charter (see as to this the joint dissenting Opinion of 1962, I.C.J. Reports 1962, pp. 541-548 and paragraph 43 (b) above), seeing that on any view SW. Africa is a non-self-governing territory. This resumption must however be on the understanding that the reports are not dealt with by the Trusteeship Council unless South Africa so agrees.

122. For other States the "legal consequences" of the fact that South Africa's Mandate has not been validly revoked, and still subsists in law are:

(1) to recognize that the United Nations is not, any more than the Mandatory, competent unilaterally to change the status of the mandated territory;

(2) to respect and abide by the Mandatory's continued right to administer the territory, unless and until any change is brought about by lawful means.

123. On the foregoing basis it becomes unnecessary for me to consider what the legal consequences for States would be if the view taken in the Opinion of the Court were correct; although, since the measures indicated by the Court seem to be based mostly on resolutions of the Security Council that — for the reasons given in paragraphs 112-114 above — I would regard as having only a recommendatory effect, I would be obliged to question the claim of these measures to be in the proper nature of "legal consequences", even if I otherwise agreed with that Opinion. (I also share the views of my colleagues Judges Gros, Petren, Onyeama and Dillard as to the standing of certain of these measures.)

124. There is however another aspect of the matter to which I attach importance and which I think needs stressing. It was for this reason, that, on 9 March 1971, during the oral proceedings (see Record, C.R. 71/19, p. 23), I put a question to Counsel for the United States of America, then addressing the Court. I do not think I can do better than cite this question and the written answer to it, as received in the Registry of the Court some ten days later (18 March 1971):

Question: In the opinion of the United States Government is there any rule of customary international law which, in general, obliges States to apply sanctions against a State which has acted, or is acting illegally — such as cutting off diplomatic, consular and commercial relations with the tortfeasor State? If not, in what manner would States become compelled so to act — not merely by way of moral duty or in the exercise of a faculty, but as a matter of positive legal obligations?

Reply: It is the opinion of the United States that there is no rule of customary international law imposing on a State a duty to apply sanctions against the State which has acted, or is acting, illegally. However, under the Charter of the United Nations, the Security Council has the power to decide that member States should apply sanctions against the State which acts in certain illegal ways. Thus, should the Security Council determine that an illegal act by a State constitutes "a threat to the peace, breach of the peace, or act of aggression", it would have a duty under Article 39 to "make recommendations, or decide what measures shall be taken in accordance with Articles 41 and 42, to maintain or restore international peace and security". When ever the Security Council makes such a determination and decides that diplomatic, consular and commercial relations shall be cut off in accordance with Article 41 of the Charter, all Members of the United Nations have the duty to apply such measures.

If the latter part of this reply is intended to indicate that it is broadly speaking only in consequence of decisions taken under Chapter VII of the Charter, after a prior determination of the existence of a "threat to the peace, breach of the peace or act of aggression", that a legal duty for member States would arise to take specific measures, I can only agree.

POSTSCRIPTUM

125. In the latter part of his separate declaration, the President of the Court has made certain observations which, though closely related to the legal issues involved in this case, have a different character. Taking my cue from him, I should like to do the same. In the period 1945/1946, South Africa could have confronted the United Nations with a *fait accompli* by incorporating SW. Africa in its own territory, as a component province on a par with Cape province, Natal, the Transvaal and the Orange Free State. Had this been done, there would have been no way in which it could have been prevented, or subsequently undone, short of war. Wisely however, though at the same time exercising considerable restraint from its own point of view, South Africa refrained from doing this. If however "incorporation" is something which the United Nations believes it could never accept, there should equally be a reciprocal and corresponding realization of the fact that the conversion of SW. Africa into the sovereign independent State of Namibia (unless it were on a very different basis from anything now apparently contemplated) could only be brought about by means the consequences of which would be incalculable, and which do not need to be specified.

Clearly therefore, in a situation in which no useful purpose can be served by launching the irresistible force against the immovable object, statesmanship should seek a *modus vivendi* — while there is yet time.

ANNEX

1. When, by its Resolution 2145 of 1966, the Assembly purported to declare the termination of South Africa's mandate, on the basis of alleged fundamental breaches of it, and to declare this not merely as a matter of opinion but as an *executive* act having the intended operational effect of bringing the Mandate to an end — or registering its termination — and of rendering any further administration of the mandated territory by South Africa illegal, — it was making pronouncements of an essentially juridical character which the Assembly, not being a judicial organ, and not having previously referred the matter to any such organ, was not competent to make.

2. There is nothing unusual in the view here expressed. On the contrary it represents the normal state of affairs, which is that the organ competent to perform an act, in the executive sense, is not the organ competent to decide whether the conditions justifying its performance are present. In all other fields a separation of functions is the rule. Thus the legislature is alone competent to enact a law, — the executive or administration alone competent to apply or enforce it, — the judiciary alone competent to interpret it and decide whether its application or enforcement is justified in the particular case. In the institutional field, the justification for the act of some organ or body may turn upon considerations of a political or technical character, or of professional conduct or discipline, and if so, the political, technical or professional organ or body concerned will, in principle, be competent to make the necessary determinations. But where the matter turns, and turns exclusively, on considerations of a legal character, a political organ, even if it is competent to take any resulting action, is not itself competent to make the necessary legal determinations on which the justification for such action must rest. This can only be done by a legal organ competent to make such determinations.

3. It must be added that besides being *ultra vires* under this head, the Assembly's action was arbitrary and high-handed, inasmuch as it acted as judge in its own cause relative to charges in respect of which it was itself the complainant, and without affording to the "defendant" any of the facilities or safeguards that are a normal part of the judicial process.

4. It has been contended that the competence of the Assembly to make determinations of a legal character is shown by the fact that Article 6 of the Charter confers upon it the right (upon the recommendation of the Security Council) to expel a member State "which has persistently violated the principles contained in . . . the Charter". This however merely means that the framers of the Charter did confer this particular specific power on the Assembly, in express terms, without indicating whether or not it was one that should only be exercised after a prior determination of the alleged violations by a competent juridical organ. To argue from the power thus specifically conferred by Article 6, that the Assembly must therefore be deemed to possess a *general* power under the Charter to make legal determinations, is clearly fallacious.

5. The contention that Resolution 2145 did not actually terminate South Africa's mandate, but merely registered its termination by South Africa itself, through its breaches of it, i.e., that the Resolution was merely declaratory not executive, is clearly nothing but an expedient directed to avoiding the difficulty; — for even as only declaratory, the resolution amounted to a finding that there had been breaches of the Mandate, — otherwise there would have been no basis even for a declaratory resolution. It is moreover a strange and novel juridical doctrine that, by infringing an obligation, the latter can be brought to an end, — but doubtless a welcome one to those who are looking for an easy way out of an inconvenient undertaking.

6. No less of an expedient is the plea that South Africa had itself "disavowed the Mandate" ever since 1946. South Africa's attitude has always been that, as a matter of *law,* either the Mandate was so bound up with the League of Nations that it could not survive the latter's dissolution, or else, that if it did, it did not survive in the form claimed in the United Nations. Whether this view was correct or not it was in no sense equivalent to a "disavowal" of the Mandate. To deny the existence of an obligation is *ex hypothesi* not the same as to repudiate it. Nor can any such deduction legitimately be drawn from the failure to render reports to, and accept the supervision of the Assembly, based as this was on the contention (considered correct by an important body of professional opinion) that no legal obligation to that effect existed. If this were not so, no party to a dispute could argue its case without being told that, by doing so, it had "disavowed" its obligations.

7. It has also been argued that the Assembly had "vainly" tried to obtain the necessary findings from the Court via the contentious proceedings brought by Ethiopia and Liberia in the period 1960-1966. But this would be tantamount *(a)* to saying that because the Assembly did not get the judgment it wanted in 1966, it was therefore justified in taking the law into its own hands, which, however, would in no way serve to validate Resolution 2145; — *(b)* to admitting that the 1966 Judgment was right in seeing the then Applicants in the light of agents of the United Nations and not, as they represented themselves to be, litigants in contentious proceedings sustaining an interest of their own; — and *(c)* recognizing that, as was strongly hinted in paragraphs 46-48 (especially the latter) of the 1966 Judgment, the correct course would have been for the Assembly as an organ to have asked the Court for an advisory opinion on the question of breaches of the Mandate, in relation to which the objection as to legal interest would not have been relevant. It was still open to the Court to do this, for instance in 1967. It cannot therefore do other than give a wrong impression if it is said that the Assembly in 1966 had no other course open to it but to adopt Resolution 2145 without having previously sought legal advice on this basis.

8. These various purported justifications for the Assembly making legal determinations, though not itself a competent legal organ, and without any reference to such an organ, or even to an *ad hoc* body of jurists (such as was the settled practice of the League Council in all important cases), are clearly illusory. In the result, the conclusion must be that the Assembly's act was *ultra vires* and hence that Resolution 2145 was invalid, even if it had not been otherwise ineffective in law to terminate South Africa's mandate.

9. Although the Court has to some extent gone into the question of the validity and effect of Assembly Resolution

2145, it has not adequately examined the question of its right to do so having regard to the way in which the Request of an Advisory Opinion in the present case was worded. The matter is however so important for the whole status and judicial function of the Court that it becomes necessary to consider it.

10. The Court could not properly have based itself on the literal wording of the Request, in order to regard its task in the present proceedings as being confined solely to indicating what, on the assumptions contained in the Request, and without any prior examination of their validity, are the legal consequences for States of South Africa's continued presence in SW. Africa, — those assumptions being that the Mandate for that territory had been lawfully terminated and hence that this presence was illegal. The Court cannot do so for the simple but sufficient reason that the question whether the Mandate is or is not legally at an end goes to the root of the whole situation that has led to the Request being made. If the Mandate is still, as a matter of law, in existence, then the question put to the Court simply does not arise and no answer could be given. Alternatively the question would be a purely hypothetical one, an answer to which would, in those circumstances, serve no purpose, so that the situation would, on a different level, resemble that which, in the *Northern Cameroons* case (*I.C.J. Reports 1963,* p. 15), caused the Court to hold (at p. 38) that it could not "adjudicate upon the merits of the claim" because *inter alia,* the circumstances were such as would "render any adjudication devoid of purpose". It has constantly been emphasized in past advisory cases — (and this was also confirmed in the contentious case just mentioned, in which occasion arose to consider the advisory practice) — that in advisory, no less than in contentious proceedings, the Court must still act as a court of law (and not, for instance, as a mere body of legal advisers), — that "the Court's authority to give advisory opinions must be exercised as a judicial function" (*ibid.,* at p. 30), — and that, to use the wording of one of the most quoted dicta of the Permanent Court in the *Eastern Carelia* case, *P.C.I.J., Series B, No. 5* (1923) at page 29, the Court "being a Court of Justice, (it) cannot, even in giving advisory opinions, depart from the essential rules guiding (its) activity as a Court".

11. So much is this the case that the original tendency in the past was to question whether the mere giving of *advice,* even in solemn form such as by means of an advisory opinion of the Court, was compatible with the judicial function at all. The Court has not of course taken this view but, to cite a very high authority and former judge of the Permanent Court:

". . . the Court . . . has conceived of its advisory jurisdiction as a judicial function, and in its exercise of this jurisdiction it has kept within the limits which characterize judicial action. It has acted *not as an 'academy of jurists' but as a responsible 'magistrature' "* — (my italics).

The words italicized in the passage just quoted contain the key to the question. If an organ such as the General Assembly or Security Council of the United Nations likes to refer some question to a body of legal experts, whether a standing one or set up *ad hoc* for the purpose, which that body is instructed to answer on the basis of certain specified assumptions that are to be taken as read, it will be acting perfectly properly if it proceeds accordingly, because it is not a court of law and is not discharging or attempting to discharge any *judicial* function; it is indeed bound by its instructions, which the organ concerned is entitled to give it. But the Court, which is itself one of the six original main organs of the United Nations, and not inferior in status to the others, is not bound to take instruction from any of them, in particular as to how it is to view and interpret its tasks as a court of law, which it is and must always remain, whatever the nature and context of the task concerned; — and whereas a body of experts may well, as a sort of technical exercise, give answers on the basis of certain underlying assumptions irrespective of their validity or otherwise, a court cannot act in this way; it is bound to look carefully at what it is being asked to do, and to consider whether the doing of it would be compatible with its status and function as a court.

12. This faculty constitutes in truth the foundation of the admitted right of the Court, deriving from the language of Article 65, paragraph 1, of its Statute, and consecrated in its jurisprudence, to refuse entirely to comply with a request for

135

an advisory opinion if it thinks that, for sufficient reasons, it would be improper or inadvisable for it to do so; — and if the Court can thus refuse entirely, *a fortiori* can it, and must it, insist on undertaking a preliminary examination of the assumptions on which any request is based, particularly where, as in the present case, those assumptions are of such a character that, unless they are well-founded, the question asked has no meaning or could admit of only one reply. Otherwise put, for a court to give answers that *can only* have significance and relevance if a certain legal situation is presumed to exist, but without enquiring whether it does (in law) exist, amounts to no more than indulging in an interesting parlour game, which is not what courts of law are for. In the present case, if the Court had lent itself to such a course, it would not have been engaging in a judicial activity, — it would have to abnegate its true function as a court-of-law and would indeed have acted as if, in the words used by Judge Hudson, it were "an academy of jurists".

13. There can be no doubt that the question put to the Court was a legal one, such as it had the power to answer if it considered it proper to do so, — more especially if (as it must be) the question is regarded as relating not only to the legal *consequences* of the General Assembly Resolution 2145 but also to the validity of that Resolution itself, and its effect upon the Mandate for South West Africa.

14. On the other hand, had the Court considered that the form of the question addressed to it precluded it from following any but the first course (i.e., dealing with the "consequences" alone), and excluded, or was intended to exclude, any consideration by it of the validity and effect of the act from which those consequences are supposed to flow — i.e., Assembly Resolution 2145 — then this would have been a ground for declining to comply with the Request since, for the reasons given in the preceding section of this Annex, it is unacceptable for any organ making such a request to seek to limit the factors which the Court, as a court of law, considers it necessary to take into account in complying with it, or to prescribe the basis upon which the question contained in it must be answered. A further element is that the Court, not being formally obliged to comply with the Request at all (even though it might otherwise be right for it to do so), is necessarily the master, and the only master, of the basis upon which it will do so, if in fact it decides to comply.

15. Subject to what has just been said, I agree with the conclusion of the Court that it should comply with the Request, though not with some of the reasoning on which that conclusion is based. I take this view even though I have no doubt that the present proceedings represent an attempt to use the Court for a purely political end, namely as a step towards the setting up of the territory of South West Africa as a new sovereign independent State, to be called "Namibia", irrespective of what the consequences of this might be at the present juncture. This aim is made perfectly clear by operative paragraphs 1, 2 and 6 of Resolution 2145 itself, which is reproduced here *in extenso*:

> "*The General Assembly,*
>
> *Reaffirming* the inalienable right of the people of South West Africa to freedom and independence in accordance with the Charter of the United Nations, General Assembly resolution 1514 (XV) of 14 December 1960 and earlier Assembly resolutions concerning the Mandated Territory of South West Africa,
>
> *Recalling* the advisory opinion of the International Court of Justice of 11 July 1950, accepted by the General Assembly in its resolution 449 A (V) of 13 December 1950, and the advisory opinions of 7 June 1955 and 1 June 1956 as well as the judgement of 21 December 1962, which have established the fact that South Africa continues to have obligations under the Mandate which was entrusted to it on 17 December 1920 and that the United Nations as the successor to the League of Nations has supervisory powers in respect of South West Africa,
>
> *Gravely concerned* at the situation in the Mandated Territory, which has seriously deteriorated following the judgement of the International Court of Justice of 18 July 1966,
>
> *Having studied* the reports of the various committees which had been established to exercise the supervisory functions of the United Nations over the administration of the Mandated Territory of South West Africa,

137

Convinced that the administration of the Mandated Territory by South Africa has been conducted in a manner contrary to the Mandate, the Charter of the United Nations and the Universal Declaration of Human Rights,

Reaffirming its resolution 2074 (XX) of 17 December 1965, in particular paragraph 4 thereof which condemned the policies of apartheid and racial discrimination practised by the Government of South Africa in South West Africa as constituting a crime against humanity,

Emphasizing that the problem of South West Africa is an issue falling within the terms of General Assembly resolution 1514 (XV),

Considering that all the efforts of the United Nations to induce the Government of South Africa to fulfil its obligations in respect of the administration of the Mandated Territory and to ensure the well-being and security of the indigenous inhabitants have been of no avail,

Mindful of the obligations of the United Nations towards the people of South West Africa,

Noting with deep concern the explosive situation which exists in the southern region of Africa,

Affirming its right to take appropriate action in the matter, including the right to revert to itself the administration of the Mandated Territory,

1. *Reaffirms* that the provisions of General Assembly resolution 1514 (XV) are fully applicable to the people of the Mandated Territory of South West Africa and that, therefore, the people of South West Africa have the inalienable right to self-determination, freedom and independence in accordance with the Charter of the United Nations;

2. *Reaffirms further* that South West Africa is a territory having international status and that it shall maintain this status until it achieves independence;

3. *Declares* that South Africa has failed to fulfil obligations in respect of the administration of the Mandated Territory and to ensure the moral and material well-being and security of the indigenous inhabitants of South West Africa and has, in fact, disavowed the Mandate;

4. *Decides* that the Mandate conferred upon His Britannic Majesty to be exercised on his behalf by the Government of the Union of South Africa is therefore terminated, that South Africa has no other right to administer the Territory and that henceforth South West Africa comes under the direct responsibility of the United Nations;

5. *Resolves* that in these circumstances the United Nations must discharge those responsibilities with respect to South West Africa;

6. *Establishes* an *Ad Hoc* Committee for South West Africa — composed of fourteen Member States to be designated by the President of the General Assembly — to recommend practical means by which South West Africa should be administered, so as to enable the people of the Territory to exercise the right of self-determination and to achieve independence, and to report to the General Assembly at a special session as soon as possible and in any event not later than April 1967;

7. *Calls upon* the Government of South Africa forthwith to refrain and desist from any action, constitutional, administrative, political or otherwise, which will in any manner whatsoever alter or tend to alter the present international status of South West Africa;

8. *Calls the attention* of the Security Council to the present resolution;

9. *Requests* all States to extend their whole-hearted co-operation and to render assistance in the implementation of the present resolution;

10. *Requests* the Secretary-General to provide all the assistance necessary to implement the present resolution and to enable the *Ad Hoc* Committee for South West Africa to perform its duties.

> *1454th plenary meeting,*
> *27 October 1966."*

If there could be any doubt it would be resolved by the two following more recent and conclusive pieces of evidence:

(a) General Assembly Resolution 2248 (S-V) of 19 May 1967, after re-affirming Resolution 2145 and appointing a

"Council for South West Africa" which later became known as the "Council for Namibia", ended as follows:

> "*Decides* that South West Africa shall become independent on a date to be fixed in accordance with the wishes of the people and that the Council shall do all in its power to enable independence to be attained by June 1968."

(b) On 29 January 1971, when the whole matter was already *sub judice* before the Court and the oral proceedings had actually started, the United Nations "Council for Namibia" issued a statement commenting on the South African proposal for holding a plebiscite in SW. Africa under the joint supervision of the Court and the Government of the Republic, and finishing as follows:

> "Furthermore, the issue at stake is the independence of Namibia, and not whether the Government of South Africa or the United Nations should administer the Territory. The United Nations decisions in this matter are aimed at achieving the independence of Namibia, and not its administration by the United Nations, except for a brief transitional period."

16. Despite the revealing character of these statements, and despite its obvious political background and motivation, the question put to the Court is, in itself, essentially a legal one. Moreover, in fact, most advisory proceedings have a political background. It could hardly be otherwise, as the Court pointed out in the *Certain Expenses* case with reference to interpretations of the Charter (*I.C.J. Reports 1962,* p. 155, *in fine*). But as the Court equally pointed out in that case (echoing a similar dictum made on a previous occasion), such a background does not of itself impart a political character to the *question* the Court is asked to answer, and this is the important consideration. It would seem therefore that the political background of a question would only justify a refusal to answer where this background loomed so large as to impart a political character to the question also. In spite of doubts as to whether something of the kind has not occurred in the present case [17] the legal character of the questions themselves remains.

17. The Court's rejection of the South African request to be allowed to appoint a judge *ad hoc* in the present case was embodied in the Order of the Court of 29 January 1971 to which my colleagues Judges Gros, Petren and I appended a joint dissenting declaration reserving our right to give reasons for this at a later stage. In my opinion this rejection was wrong in law, and also unjustified as a matter of equity and fair dealing, — for it was obvious, and could not indeed be denied by the Court, that South Africa had a direct, distinctive and concrete special interest to protect in this case, quite different in kind from the general and common interest that other States had as Members of the United Nations. In short, South Africa had, and was alone in having, precisely the same type of interest in the whole matter that a litigant defendant has, — and should therefore have been granted the same right that any litigant before the Court possesses, namely that, if there is not already a judge of its own nationality amongst the regular judges of the Court, it can, under Article 31 of the Statute of the Court, appoint a judge *ad hoc* to sit for the purposes of the case.

18. The Court's refusal to allow this was thrown into particular relief by the almost simultaneous rejection in the three Orders of the Court dated 26 January 1971, of the South African challenge concerning the propriety of three regular judges of the Court sitting in the case, — a matter on which, as to the third of these Orders, I wish to associate myself with the views expressed in the early part of his dissenting opinion in the present case by my colleague Judge Gros. In the light of the explanations as to this, given in the Opinion of the Court, it has now to be concluded that, outside the literal terms of Article 17, paragraph 2, of the Statute, no previous connexion with the subject-matter of a case, however close, can prevent

---

17 The present case might well be regarded as being at the least a borderline one, for the political nature of the background is unusually prominent. Yet the two main questions involved, namely whether the Mandate has been validly terminated or not and, if it has, what are the legal consequences for States, are in themselves questions of law. The doubt arises from the way in which the request is framed, suggesting that the Court is to answer the second question only, and postulating the first as already settled. It is above all this which imparts a political twist to the whole Request.

a judge from sitting, unless he himself elects as a matter of conscience not to do so.

19. On the question of a judge *ad hoc,* the immediately relevant provision is Article 83 of the Court's Rules, which reads as follows:

> "If the advisory opinion is requested upon a legal question actually pending between two or more States, Article 31 of the Statute shall apply, as also the provisions of these Rules concerning the application of that Article."

If this provision was the only relevant one, it would be a reasonable inference from it that a judge *ad hoc* could not be allowed unless the case had the character specified. In the present one it was obvious that a legal question was involved, — or the Court would have lacked all power to comply with the Request for an advisory opinion (see Article 96, paragraph 1, of the United Nations Charter and Article 65, paragraph 1, of the Court's Statute). But could it be said to be a question "actually pending between two or more States"? I shall give my reasons later on for thinking that it was of this kind. But for the purposes of my principal ground for holding that the South African request should have been allowed, it is not strictly necessary for me to determine whether the legal questions concerned were "pending"; and if pending, "actually pending"; and if actually pending, then actually pending "between two or more States", and if so which ones, etc., etc.; — for in my view the matter is not exclusively governed by the provisions of Article 83 of the Rules, which I consider do not exhaust the Court's power to allow the appointment of a judge *ad hoc.*

20. The contrary view is based on a misreading of the true intention and effect of Rule 83 when considered in relation to Article 68 of the Statute which reads as follows:

> "In the exercise of its advisory functions, the Court shall . . . be guided by the provisions of the present statute which apply in contentious cases to the extent to which it recognizes them to be applicable."

This provision of course covers Article 31 of the Statute, and hence confers on the Court a general power to apply that

Article by allowing the appointment of a judge *ad hoc* if requested. Furthermore, the provisions of the Rules are subordinated to those of the Statute. The Court has no power to make Rules that conflict with its Statute: hence any rule that did so conflict would be *pro tanto* invalid, and the Statute would prevail.

21. However, I can see no conflict between Rule 83 and Article 68 of the Statute. They deal with different aspects of the matter. The *latter* (Article 68), despite its quasi-mandatory form, confers what is in effect a power or discretion on the Court to assimilate requests for advisory opinions to contentious cases, either in whole or in part. Rule 83 on the other hand contains what amounts to a direction by the Court to itself as to how it is to exercise this discretion in certain specified circumstances. If those circumstances are found to obtain, then the Rule obliges the Court to allow the appointment of a judge *ad hoc*. But this in no way means, nor was ever intended to mean, that by making Rule 83 the Court parted with the residual discretion it has under Article 68 of the Statute, and that in *no other* circumstances than those specified in Rule 83 could the Court allow such an appointment. The object of the Rule was *not* to specify the only class of case in which the Court could so act, but to indicate the *one* class in which it *must* do so, and to ensure that, at least in the type of case contemplated in the Rule, the Court's discretion should be exercised in a positive way, in the sense of applying Article 31 of the Statute. This was entirely without prejudice to the possibility that there might be other cases than those indicated in the Rule, as to which the Court might feel that, though not *obliged* to apply Article 31, it ought nevertheless for one reason or another to do so. This view is borne out by the language of Article 82, paragraph 1, of the Rules, which relates to the application in advisory proceedings of *any* of the contentious procedure provisions, not merely those of Article 31. After recapitulating the general language of Article 68, it goes on to say that "for this purpose" (i.e., in order to determine the sphere of application — if any — of the contentious procedure), the Court is "above all" to consider "whether the request . . . relates to a legal question actually pending between two or more States". This wording clearly makes the test of legal pendency a primary, but equally clearly not a conclusive factor.

22. It has been contended that although the foregoing description of the relationship between the various provisions concerned might otherwise be correct, it must nevertheless break down on the actual wording of Article 31 itself, particularly its second and third paragraphs which, it has been claimed, not only clearly contemplate the case of "parties" to an actual litigation but are virtually incapable of functioning in any other circumstances, so that at the very least the requirements of Rule 83 constitute a minimum and *sine qua non,* in the absence of which no application of Article 31 is possible. I have difficulty in following the logic of this view which, if it were correct, would go far in practice to clawing back almost everything supposed to have been conferred by Rule 83, and rendering that provision a piece of useless verbiage, — for even where the case is indubitably one of a legal question actually pending between two or more States, it would be rare in advisory proceedings to find a situation such that Article 31 could be applied to it integrally as that provision stands, and without gloss or adaptation. It is in fact manifest that the provisions of the Statute and Rules concerning contentious cases were quite naturally and inevitably drafted with litigations and parties to litigations in mind. Hence these provisions are bound to be — as they are — full of passages and expressions that are not literally applicable to cases where there is no actual litigation and no parties technically in the posture of litigants, — in short to the vast majority of the cases in which there are advisory proceedings. Consequently the power given to the Court by Article 68 of the Statute to be guided by the contentious procedure would be largely nullified in practice unless it were deemed to include a power to adapt and tailor this procedure to the advisory situation. The very words "shall be guided by" indicate that such a process is contemplated.

23. In the present case in particular, no difficulty could have arisen, for the sufficient reason that, apart from South Africa, no other State presenting written or oral statements asked to be allowed to appoint a judge *ad hoc,* although they in fact had the opportunity of doing so, — and moreover representatives of four such States actually attended the separate and prelimi-

nary oral hearing held *(in camera* [18] *)* on this matter, but none of them intervened either to oppose the application or to make a similar one. Had any two or more such applications been received, in addition to South Africa's, the Court would have had to consider, under Article 3, paragraph 2, of its Rules, whether the States concerned, or any group of them, not already comprising between them a judge of the nationality of one of them amongst the regular judges of the Court, were "in the same interest", in which event only one *ad hoc* judge *per* such group could have been allowed.

24. Reference is made in the Opinion of the Court to the Permanent Court's Order of 31 October 1935 in the *Danzig Legislative Decrees* case (Annex 1 to *Series A/B, No. 65,* at pp. 69-71). That case however has no relevance to the present one; for in 1935 no provision corresponding to what is now Article 68 of the Statute figured in the Statute as it then stood. The latter, in fact, contained no provisions at all about the advisory jurisdiction, which rested entirely on Article 14 of the Covenant of the League and the Court's own Rules. It was therefore inevitable that the Court should feel it had no discretion as to the appointment of a judge *ad hoc* unless the matter fell strictly within the terms of those Rules. Hence the *Legislative Decrees* case constitutes no precedent, either for the view that the Court lacks a discretion *now,* or for a refusal to exercise that discretion (which the Parmanent Court, not then having one, could not in any event have exercised). The situation being in consequence quite different, it becomes evident that if, under Article 68, of the Statute — which takes precedence of the Rules, there is (as is unquestionably the case) a discretion to "be guided by the provisions of the . . . Statute which apply in contentious cases" (including therefore Article 31) there must be a discretion to allow the appointment of a judge *ad hoc* — one of the most important parts of the contentious process. No (manifestly non-existent) doctrine of the Court's inability to regulate its own composition could operate to prevent this.

---

18 See Article 46 of the Statute. The hearing takes place before the full Court and in the main Court-room as if for a public sitting, but press and public are excluded. The decision to sit in private despite South Africa's strong representations to the contrary, was in my view mistaken and unwise (as was indeed subsequently impliedly admitted by the decision to publish the verbatim record of the sitting).

25. In the light of these various considerations, it is clear that the Court in no way lacked the power to grant the South African request, but was simply unwilling to do so. In this I think the Court was not justified, particularly in view of the fact that the request was unopposed which, to my mind, indicated a tacit recognition by the other intervening States of the contentious features of the case. The present proceedings, though advisory in form, had all the characteristics of a contentious case as to the substance of the issues involved [19] , no less than had the actual litigation between South Africa and certain other States which terminated five years ago, and of which these advisory proceedings have been but a continuation in a different form. Even if, therefore, the Court did not consider the matter to come under Article 83 of its Rules, in such a way as to *oblige* it to allow a judge *ad hoc* to be appointed, it should have exercised its residual discretionary powers to the same effect.

26. The above expression of view has proceeded upon the assumption that, in order to determine whether the Court *could* grant the South African request, and should do so, it was unnecessary to decide whether the case fell within the strict terms of Rule 83. In fact, however, I consider that it does, and that any other conclusion is unrealistic and can only be reached by a closing of the eyes to the true position. It really involves something that gets very near to equating the words "a legal question actually pending between two or more States" in Rule 83, with circumstances in which two or more States are in a condition of actual or immediately impending litigation. But, as I have already pointed out, such an interpretation would virtually nullify the intended effect of Rule 83 by restricting its scope to situations that seldom take that precise form in advisory proceedings.

27. The nub of the whole difficulty lies in the word "pending"; but if this is taken on its normal dictionary acceptation of "remaining undecided" or "not yet decided", and "not terminated" or "remaining unsettled", — or in short "still outstanding", — then it is evident that there is a whole series of legal

---

19 In consequence of which the Court found itself obliged in practice, and in a manner tually unprecedented in previous advisory proceedings, to conduct the oral hearing as if a litigation were in progress.

questions in issue (or in dispute) between South Africa on the one hand and a number of other States, and that these questions are, in this sense, outstanding and unresolved, inasmuch as the view held on one side as to their correct solution differs *in toto* from that taken on the other. Would it be possible for instance to find a more concrete and fundamental issue of this kind than one which turns on whether the Mandate for SW. Africa has been legally terminated or is still in existence; whether South Africa is *functus officio* in SW. Africa or is still entitled to administer that territory, and whether South Africa's continued presence there is an illegal usurpation or is in the legitimate exercise of a constitutional authority? It would surely be difficult to think of a more sharply controversial situation than one in which, depending on the answers to be given to these questions, South Africa is on the one side being called upon to quit the territory, while she herself asserts her right to remain there, — in which it is maintained on the one side that the whole matter has been settled by the General Assembly resolution 2145 of 1966, and on the other that this resolution was *ultra vires* and devoid of legal effect, — and therefore settled nothing. The case in fact falls exactly within the definition of a dispute which, following my former colleague Judge Morelli, I gave in my separate opinion in the *Northern Cameroons* case (*I.C.J. Reports 1963*, at p. 109), when I said that the essential requirement was that: ". . . the one party (or parties) should be making, or should have made, a complaint, claim or protest about an act, omission or course of conduct, present or past of the other party, which the latter refutes, rejects or denies the validity of, either expressly, or else implicitly by persisting in the acts, omissions or conduct complained of, or by failing to take the action, or make the reparation, demanded".

If this does not describe the situation as it has long existed, and now exists, between the United Nations or many of its member States, and South Africa, I do not know what does.

28. Nevertheless it may be suggested that these issues, concrete and unresolved as they are, and hence, in the natural and ordinary sense, "pending" and "actually pending", are not, within the primarily intended meaning of the words, pending "between two or more States", because they lie too much at large between South Africa and either the United Nations as an entity, or a group of its Members rather than as individual States. In other circumstances there might be a good deal to be said in favour of this view. But the Assembly resolution purporting to terminate the Mandate has led to a situation in which, as it was one of its objects, this resolution is being made the basis of *individual* action taken outside the United Nations by a number of States in their relations with South Africa over SW. Africa, as described in some detail by Counsel for South Africa at the preliminary oral hearing held on 27 January 1971.

29. One example must (but will) suffice — namely the situation which has arisen over the application to South West Africa of the 1965 Montreux International Telecommunication Convention. When becoming a party to this Convention, South Africa gave notice in proper form applying it to SW. Africa also. Thereupon a number of States addressed official communications to the Secretariat of the International Telecommunication Union, which were all to the same effect, namely that *precisely by reason of Assembly resolution 2145* purporting to terminate the Mandate, South Africa no longer had the right to administer or speak for SW. Africa, and that, in consequence, the application of the Convention to that territory was invalid and of no effect. The Administrative Council of the Union then, in May 1967, circularized the member States with a request for their views on the matter, which was put to them in the form whether South Africa's right to represent SW. Africa "should be withdrawn". To this South Africa, on 23 May 1967, sent a full and reasoned reply affirming its continuing right to represent SW. Africa. Nevertheless at the next session of the Union a majority voted in favour of the "withdrawal". There now in consequence exists a clear-cut and concrete dispute, not only between South Africa and a majority of the members of the Union as such, but also individually between South Africa and those specific members who initiated and raised the issue in the first place. The subject-matter of this dispute is whether or not the 1965 Convention is or is not applicable to SW. Africa; — and this dispute, or legal question (to use the language of Rule 83), not only is actually pending between South Africa and those States, and continues so to be, *but also constituted one of the alleged possible "legal consequences" of the purported termination of the Mandate*

which the Court might have to consider in the present proceedings.

30. For these reasons, were it necessary to hold (as in my view it is not) that the Court had no residual power outside Rule 83 to allow the appointment of a South African judge *ad hoc,* I should take the view that the conditions specified in the Rule were fully satisfied and that it was applicable so as to oblige the Court to grant the request, as justice and equity in any event called for, in the exercise of its undoubted discretionary power. In fact, if ever there was a case for allowing the appointment of a judge *ad hoc* in advisory proceedings, that case was this one.

31. On the basis of the foregoing views two somewhat serious consequences would ensue. The first is that, in refusing to allow the appointment of a judge *ad hoc,* the Court in effect decided that the proceedings did not involve any dispute, and thus prejudged the substance of a number of issues raised by South Africa which turned on the existence or otherwise of a dispute, — although no argument had yet been heard on these issues, nor was it until after the Order embodying the Court's decision on the matter had been issued. This created a situation in which, in most national legal systems, the case would, on appeal, have been sent back for a re-trial. Similarly the Court virtually precluded itself from going into any question of fact: for disputed issues of fact are difficult to deal with except on the basis of a contentious procedure involving recognition of the existence of a dispute. This again was in advance of having heard the South African argument on the question of the admission of further factual evidence, — although the Court was, from the start, under written notice of the South African view that such further evidence was relevant and important. These views are not affected by the fact that, as the Opinion of the Court correctly observes, a decision on the questiom of a judge *ad hoc,* being a matter of the composition of the Court, had to be taken in advance of everything else, — although this situation may well point to a somewhat serious flaw in the present Rules. It cannot however affect the fact that, having rejected the request for the appointment of a judge *ad hoc* — and *on the very ground* that there was no dispute or legal question pending (for if the Court had thought there was, Rule 83 would have obliged it to grant the request) — the Court was thenceforward precluded in practice, in connexion with anything arising later in the case, from coming to a different conclusion as to the existence of a dispute or legal question pending. Had the Court, without prejudging these matters, simply exercised its discretion in the sense of allowing the appointment (as in my view it should in any case have done), no difficulty would have arisen. But it should at least, and *at that stage*, have heard full argument on the question, in the course of ordinary public hearings.

32. Secondly, the failure to allow the appointment of a judge *ad hoc*, coupled with the views expressed by my colleague Judge Gros, which I share, concerning the third of the three Orders of the Court referred to in paragraph 18 of this Annex, arouses in me a number of misgivings, as to which it will suffice here to say that I associate myself entirely with what is stated at the end of paragraph 17 of Judge Gros' Opinion.

6

JUDGE ANDRÉ GROS (FRANCE)

DISSENTS

HERE FOLLOWS the full list of the Dissenting Opinion of André Gros, the distinguished international jurist from France, at the World Court in 1971.

TO MY REGRET, I am unable to concur in the Advisory Opinion, whether in regard to the substance or in regard to certain problems of a preliminary character, and I propose to explain my disagreement below.

1. By way of preliminary decision, the Court made four Orders on questions concerning its composition, and as I voted against two of them I should give my reasons for doing so. The first concerned is Order No. 3 of 26 January 1971, which, having regard to Article 48 of the Statute, rejected by 10 votes to 4 an objection raised against a Member of the Court, but gave no reasons. The second Order on which I have to comment is that of 29 January 1971, which, having regard to Articles 31 and 68 of the Statute and Article 83 of the Rules of Court, rejected by 10 votes to 5 a request by the Government of South Africa for the appointment of a judge *ad hoc*: it likewise gave no reasons, and it was accompanied by two joint declarations, one made by three and the other by two Members of the Court.

2. The Court has said: "The Court itself, and not the parties, must be the guardian of the Court's judicial integrity" (*I.C.J. Reports 1963*, p. 29). Even if one of the Governments represented in the proceedings had not raised the problem decided by Order No. 3 of 26 January 1971, the Court would

151

have been obliged to examine it in the application of its Statute. The observance of the provisions of its own Statute is a strict obligation, as the Court's 1963 decision emphasizes.

3. At the meeting of the Security Council on 4 March 1968, the representative of Pakistan, speaking on behalf of the co-sponsors of draft resolution S/8429 on Namibia, which was to become Security Council resolution 246 (1968), stated:

"The seven co-sponsors acknowledge with gratitude the constructive co-operation extended to them by Mr. . . . and Mr. . . . . and the great contribution which they made to the formulation of the draft resolution" (S/PV. 1395, p. 32).

The first person mentioned has since become a Member of the Court; now, resolution 246 (1968) of 14 March 1968, in its preamble, takes into account the General Assembly resolution, 2145 (XXI), "by which the General Assembly of the United Nations terminated the Mandate of South Africa over South West Africa and assumed direct responsibility for the territory until its independence" (14 March 1968, S/PV. 1397, pp. 6-10). The records likewise contain summaries of several speeches, some of them lengthy, which that same person made on the substantive problem now decided by the Court (see S/PV. 1387, pp. 61-66; S/PV. 1395, pp. 41 and 43-45; S/PV. 1397, pp. 16-20).

4. Such are the facts. Hitherto it has been the practice of the Court to determine in each case of this kind whether Article 17 of the Statute was applicable and to ascertain whether there had been any active participation on the part of a Member, before his election, in a question laid before the Court (cf. Stauffenberg, *Statut et Règlement de la Cour permanente de Justice internationale*, 1934, P. 76, citing a decision of the Permanent Court, taken at its twentieth session in which the material point was that a Member had not played an "active part" in the treatment of the question by the Council of the League). It was in application of that principle that one Member of the Court decided not to sit in the case concerning the *Anglo-Iranian Oil Company* because he had represented his country in the Security Council when it had been considering a matter arising out of the claim of the United Kingdom against Iran, and that the Court expressed its agreement with that decision (*I.C.J. Yearbook 1963-1964*, p. 100).

No reader of the records I have cited in paragraph 3 can be left in any doubt as to the character and substance of the positions adopted by the then representative, now a judge, on the question of the revocation of the Mandate by the effect of resolution 2145 (XXI). Yet that resolution is the fundamental problem of the present proceedings, inasmuch as they are concerned with the determination of its legal consequences. It must therefore be noted that Order No. 3 of 26 January 1971 marked a change in practice, and that the Court has discarded the criterion of active participation.

It was indeed, in the present case, no participation in the drafting of a general convention that had to be considered, but the expression of opinion on the international status of the Mandate after and in function of the declaration of revocation by resolution 2145 (XXI), which is the underlying legal point of the proceedings. Thus we see that the representative in the Security Council pronounced upon the substance of the case after the critical date of October 1966. There is therefore no comparison with certain precedents cited in the Advisory Opinion (para. 9), which are instances of judges having contributed to the drafting of international treaties applicable in cases which arose much later in which they had taken no part.

The Court's decision contradicts the principle, to which Article 17 of the Statute lends formal expression, that a Member must not participate in the decision of any case in which he has previously taken part in some other capacity. This Article, moreover, is an application of a generally accepted principle of judicial organization deriving from an obvious concern for justice. The new interpretation which has been placed upon it cannot, therefore, be justified.

5. I have now to explain why I consider that Article 68 of the Statute and Articles 82 and 83 of the Rules ought to have been given a different application from the one chosen by the Court in adopting the Order of 29 January 1971.

The Order of 29 January 1971 rejecting the request for a judge *ad hoc* was made after a closed hearing, held on 27 January, at which the observations of the South African Government were heard. Judge Sir Gerald Fitzmaurice, Judge Petren and I reserved the right to make known the reasons for our dissent, which, inasmuch as they concerned the substance from certain aspects, could not be disclosed at the moment when the Order which discounted them was issued. The Court gave definitive shape to its interpretation of the relevant articles of the Statute and Rules by refusing the appointment of a judge *ad hoc* — a question which it thus made irreversible — without, however, disclosing any reasons for the Order embodying the decision. In that this was an interpretation of rules which are binding on the Court, it is necessary to examine the reasons for it.

The refusal of a judge *ad hoc* is justified only if the legal conditions for the exercise of the faculty to request such an appointment have not been satisfied. The Court has not, in effect, any freedom of choice in the matter, for Article 83 of the Rules expressly provides that if "a legal question actually pending between two or more States" is involved in proceedings on a request for advisory opinion, the Court is to apply Article 31 of the Statute, which concerns the appointment of a judge *ad hoc* on the application of a State not represented on the Bench. Furthermore, the Court ought to have pronounced upon this legal problem *"avant tout"* ("above all") (Rules, Art. 82), but this it failed to do, not treating the question as a preliminary one to be thrashed out in full cognizance of all the factors concerned, including those related to questions of substance. Needless to say, the idea of a preliminary question is nothing new in advisory procedure, and it would have been natural, in view of the particular circumstances of the case, to adopt on this point an approach analogous to that of contentious procedure, as is recommended by Article 68 of the Statute. This is a point with which the Court had to deal, for example, in connection with its Advisory Opinion on *Judgments of the Administrative Tribunal of the ILO upon Complaints Made against Unesco (I.C.J. Reports 1956)*: Poland's objection to the Court's jurisdiction in *International Status of South West Africa (Pleadings*, p. 153, in para. 2) was of a preliminary nature, as was also that raised in *Interpretation of Peace Treaties with Bulgaria, Hungary and Romania* by the Government of Czechoslovakia, which specifically relied on Article 68 of the Statute and Article 82 of the Rules in requesting the Court to apply preliminary objection procedure *(Pleadings*, p. 204). (Note also the Permanent Court's Order of 20 July 1931 on the appointment of judges *ad hoc* in *Customs Regime between Germany and Austria*, ruling by way of preliminary decision on the applicability of Article 71 of its Rules (Art. 82 in those of the present Court) and Article 31 of the Statute: *P.C.I.J., Series A/B, No. 41*, p. 89; see also the Advisory Opinion on the *Consistency of Certain Danzig Legislative Decrees with the Constitution of the Free City, 1935, P.C.I.J. Series A/B, No. 65*, p. 69, and the explanation of it given by my colleague Judge Sir Gerald Fitzmaurice in his dissenting opinion, Annex, para. 24). A thorough preliminary examination would not have resulted in any delay, as the deliberation would only have required a few meetings and the interval separating the Order from the oral argument on that point, which was two days, would scarcely have been lengthened. To deal with the problem by a rejection not giving reasons, and without adequate examination, is to confuse the preliminary with the prima facie. A preliminary question is the subject of exhaustive treatment and final decision; a prima facie examination can never, by definition, be thoroughgoing, and can never lead but to a provisional decision. Articles 82 and 83 entail irrevocable decisions, as has been seen in the present proceedings.

6. The fact that the Court did not *avant tout* consider whether the request related to a pending legal question constitutes a refusal to apply a categorical provision of the Rules touching a problem with regard to the Court's composition. It is no reply to argue (para. 36 of the Opinion) that, in any case, the decision to refuse a judge *ad hoc* left the question of the Court's competence on the points of substance open; what Article 82 prohibits, in requiring an examination *avant tout* of the point of law, is to fix the composition of the Court otherwise than as provided by Article 83, and it is only subsequent to that point's being decided for sound reasons after a thorough legal examination that any refusal of a judge *ad hoc* may ensue — and not the reverse.

7. The manner in which the problem was decided therefore constitutes, in my judgment, a violation of the general system laid down in the Statute and Rules, whatever view one may hold of the idea of a legal question actually pending. Moreover, I consider that the present proceedings are in fact related to a legal question actually pending (see paras. 37-45 below), and this ought to have occasioned a deliberation as to the

appointment of a judge *ad hoc* or, possibly, judges *ad hoc* in the plural.

The Advisory Opinion affirms the existence of a legal obligation on the part of States which have never ceased to affirm that that obligation did not exist. The existence or non-existence of legal obligations *for States* is the question put to the Court; it was even the subject of lively controversy during the discussions in the General Assembly and the Security Council, according to the documentation in the present proceedings (cf. paras. 20 et seq. below). Judging by the declarations made on behalf of States, there was a conflict of views and much hesitation as to the law applicable.

8. The Court finds in its Opinion that the question is not a dispute between States, nor even one between the Organization and a State. That is a purely formal view of the facts of the case which does not, to my mind, correspond to realities. While it is true that an advisory opinion is given to the organ entitled to request it, and not to States *(Interpretation of Peace Treaties, First Phase, I.C.J. Reports 1950,* p. 71), the present request has been so framed as to seek an opinion on "the legal consequences for States", a formulation which the Court in its reply has not sought to modify despite its ambiguity in relation to the rule stressed by the Court in *Interpretation of Peace Treaties.* The course taken by the oral proceedings before the Court, as also the text of the Court's present Opinion, have placed South Africa in the position of respondent in a manner difficult to distinguish from contentious proceedings. (See paras. 133, 118 and 129, which are framed like judicial pronouncements in the form of decisions.)

9. The Court observed in its Judgment of 21 December 1962:

"A mere assertion is not sufficient to prove the existence of a dispute any more than a mere denial of the existence of the dispute proves its non-existence" *(I.C.J. Reports 1962,* p. 328).

One need only substitute "legal question actually pending" for "dispute" to establish that the Court had an obligation to treat the matter in depth and take it beyond the mere assertion that, while questions did lie in dispute between States, this represented, as in the case of the 1950, 1955 and 1956 Opinions, a divergence of views on points of law, as in nearly all advisory proceedings (para. 34).

10. Rather than generalizations, it is necessary to apply to the present proceedings the test adopted by the Court in 1950, when it stated that the application of the provisions of the Statute which apply in contentious cases "depends on the particular circumstances of each case and that the Court possesses a large amount of discretion in the matter" *(I.C.J. Reports 1950,* p. 72).

What then are the particular circumstances of the case which might have led the Court to exercise that "large amount of discretion"? The request for an advisory opinion relates to a substantive problem over which South Africa and other States are opposed; the existence of slight divergences of view on some points among those other States is immaterial, the basic legal question for all of them without exception being that of the revocation of the Mandate with which, as a binding decision, certain States confront South Africa, but which gives rise to doubts and hesitations on the part of others; the purpose of the Advisory Opinion is to apprise the international community of the present legal position of the Territory of Namibia (South West Africa), and thus to determine the purport of a certain international status. It is another way of putting afresh the question laid before the Court in 1950: "What is the international status of the territory?" That, with the addition of "since General Assembly resolution 2145 (XXI)", could in fact have been the request.

However, any reply purporting to apprise *States* of the extent of their obligations subsequent to resolution 2145 (XXI) must connote not only the disposal of the conflict of views between the holder of the revoked Mandate and the States which instigated and eventually pronounced the revocation, but also the imposition on all States of a certain line of conduct.

11. It is not enough to describe the problem as a "situation" for the difficulties to cease. As the Court said in respect of disputes, "a mere assertion is not sufficient". From the viewpoint of law the description "situation" used by the Security Council has no effect so far as the Court is concerned. Without denying that the Namibia affair is and remains for the

Security Council a situation, the Court, in order to determine its own competence, had to enquire whether, quite apart from what the Security Council may have thought, the request of 29 July 1970 did or did not relate to a legal question actually pending between States, within the meaning of the Rules of Court (as the Court did in its Opinion on the *Interpretation of Peace Treaties with Bulgaria, Hungary and Romania, First Phase, I.C.J. Reports 1950*, pp. 72-74). Any other view would confer on the political organs of the United Nations the right to interpret, subject to no appeal, the Rules of Court.

12. The Court was faced with a legal question with pronounced political features, which is often the case, but which is not enough to overrule the argument that the issue is, at bottom, a legal one. The subject of the dispute is the conflict of views between, on the one hand, those States which, through the procedures available to the United Nations, have sought and procured the revocation of South Africa's Mandate for the Territory of South West Africa and, on the other hand, South Africa, which attacks that revocation and such effects as it might have. The way in which the request was framed adds to this basic question that of the effects for all States, that is to say even for States which have not taken any active part in the development of the action proceeded with in the United Nations; but this relates to consequences, as the request itself says, and not to the essential legal question. All this emerges strikingly from the written and oral proceedings, in which the Government of South Africa behaved like a respondent, replying to veritable claims and submissions presented by other Governments (with the exception of the French Government, whose written statement is more in the nature of an intervention by an *amicus curiae*).

13. There is, said the Court in 1962, a "conflict of legal views and interests — between the respondent on the one hand, and the other Members of the United Nations . . . on the other hand" (*South West Africa, Preliminary Objections, Judgment, I.C.J. Reports 1962*, p. 345); and this observation was not modified in the Judgment of 1966, which dismissed the Applications not on the ground that there was no dispute, but solely in regard to the question whether the Applicants had a legal interest in the carrying-out of the "conduct" clauses of the Mandate. It is therefore impossible to deduce therefrom

any refusal on the part of the Court to pronounce in any circumstances on whether there had been breaches of the Mandate (on the contrary, one might note the allusion in paras. 11 and 12 of the 1966 Judgment to Article 5 of the Mandate for South West Africa and to the right of every League member to take action to secure its observance, which connotes recognition of a legal interest in the proving of certain breaches of the Mandate). The Advisory Opinion, as is apparent from its contents, meets the concern, expressed during the discussions in the Security Council preceding its request, for proof that the Mandate was lawfully revoked; and this, by the Opinion's own admission, comprises a legal question rooted in the very origins of the Mandate, one which at all events, as we shall see below (para. 25), made its appearance before the Court as long ago as 1950.

The Court might perhaps have been encouraged to admit the existence of a genuine dispute between States if it had taken note of the fact that the General Assembly itself, in its resolution 1565 (XV) of 18 December 1960, made a pronouncement on "the dispute which has arisen between *Ethiopia, Liberia and other member States, on the one hand, and the Union of South Africa on the other*" (my emphasis). Need one do more than recall this fact and raise the question as to whether, in the words of the Court's Advisory Opinion of 30 March 1950 on the *Interpretation of Peace Treaties*, "the legal position of the parties . . . cannot be in any way compromised by the answers that the Court may give to the question put to it" *(I.C.J. Reports 1950,* p. 72)? Judge Koretsky had a similar point in mind when, in what was in many respects a comparable case, he observed that the Court, in its Advisory Opinion, would be giving "some kind of judgment as if it had before it a concrete case" *(Certain Expenses of the United Nations (Article 17, paragraph 2, of the Charter),* dissenting opinion, *I.C.J. Reports 1962,* p. 254).

14. The fact that a political organ of the United Nations places a situation on its agenda cannot have the legal effect of the disappearance of a dispute between two or more States interested in the maintenance or modification of the situation. These are two different and parallel planes: one is the manifestation of the United Nations political interest in facilitating settlement of a situation of general concern for the community

F

of States, the other is the determination of the existence as between certain States of opposed legal interests which give them a special position in the appraisal of the situation of general concern. Naturally, the fact that there is a divergence of views on the law does not rob the Security Council or the General Assembly of the rights they derive from the Charter to consider the situation as it presents itself. But in the same way it is impossible to admit that the mere calling-in of a general situation by the political organs of the United Nations could bring about the disappearance of the element of a dispute between States if there exists such an element underlying the general situation, when such a case is in fact provided for in the Rules of Court. This is why, in each case, the question arises of whether one is or is not confronted with what is really a dispute. Articles 82 and 83 of the Rules of Court would otherwise have no meaning, whereas their purpose is to reassure States that, if an advisory opinion be requested in relation to a legal question over which they are divided, they will enjoy the right to present their views in the same way and with the same safeguards as in contentious procedure, more particularly where the composition of the Court is concerned.

15. To conclude in regard to this point, to say, as the Opinion does, that there is no dispute, and that the question of the application of Articles 82 and 83 of the Rules does not arise, is to suppose that the Court was, on the very first day of the proceedings, able to resolve the substantive question, namely the existence of a power in the United Nations, as an international organization, to revoke the Mandate. But on the day the Order of 29 January 1971 was made, before any discussion or deliberation of the substantive issues, the least that can be said is that this was still a point which remained to be proved. This is a question which was so important for all the subsequent examination of the case that the Court ought to have resolved it *"avant tout"*, but this it failed to do. The argument that it was the Order of 29 January 1971 which established that there was no legal question pending between South Africa and other States, but merely an opinion to be given to a political organ on the consequences and repercussions of its decisions, is equivalent to an assertion that, before any oral proceedings on the substance of the case, the Court could have judicially decided the substantive problem to which the request for an

advisory opinion related. To refuse the judge *ad hoc* applied for by South Africa before settling this basic question was to prejudge it irremediably. The questions whether a dispute existed, what it consisted of and who the parties might be were all disposed of *in limine litis* by the mere effect of the dismissal of the application for a judge *ad hoc*, for it was thereafter impossible to go back and modify that refusal, even if the examination of the substantive issues had eventually led the Court to conclude that there was in fact a legal question pending between States. The fact that the Court has confirmed the decision to refuse a judge *ad hoc* in its consideration of the substance does not exonerate it from the charge of having failed to consider the point of law *"avant tout"*.

16. I would add that, even if the Court, after thorough preliminary examination of the point of law, had decided that Article 83 did not oblige it to accept the application for the appointment of a judge *ad hoc*, Article 68 of the Statute left it the power to do so, and on this point I would refer to the declaration of my colleagues Judges Onyeama and Dillard appended to the Order of 29 January 1971. When it is a matter of deciding whether a legal title has lawfully been withdrawn from a State and determining the legal consequences of that revocation, it is in the compelling interest of the Court that it should apply that clause of its Statute which provides for the closer approximation of advisory to contentious procedure. I am unable to accept the contention in paragraph 39 of the Opinion, to the effect that the circumstances contemplated in Article 83 of the Rules are the only ones in which the Court may agree to the appointment of a judge *ad hoc* in advisory proceedings (cf. the reasoning of Judge Sir Gerald Fitzmaurice in paragraph 25 of the Annex to his dissenting opinion, and that of Judge Onyeama in his separate opinion).

17. The two decisions of the Court concerning its composition affect the constantly followed rule that the Court, when it gives an advisory opinion, is exercising a judicial function (*Constitution of the Maritime Safety Committee of the Inter-Governmental Maritime Consultative Organization, Advisory Opinion, I.C.J. Reports 1960*, p. 153: "The Court as a judicial body is . . . bound in the exercise of its advisory function to remain faithful to the requirements of its judicial character"; a formula reiterated in *Northern Cameroons, I.C.J. Reports*

1963, p. 30). For it is certain that while advisory judgments and advisory opinions are for the Court two different forms of decision, they are always the expression of its confirmed view as a tribunal on rules of international law. There are no two ways of declaring the law. For the reasons I have set down in the foregoing paragraphs, Order No. 3 of 26 January 1971 and the Order of 29 January 1971 do not appear to me to satisfy the requirements of that good administration of justice which it is the purpose of the Statute and Rules to secure.

18. Another deviation from the line of the Court's case-law is to be observed in the way in which the Court has hesitated to examine the lawfulness of the legal step which gave rise to the question upon which the Court is asked to pronounce, i.e., General Assembly resolution 2145 (XXI). In paragraphs 88 and 89 of the Opinion the Court declares that the question of the validity or the conformity with the Charter of resolution 2145 (XXI), or of the Security Council resolutions, did not form the subject of the request for advisory opinion. It used not to be the Court's habit to take for granted the premises of a legal situation the consequences of which it has been asked to state; in the case concerning *Certain Expenses of the United Nations* it declared that:

"The rejection of the French amendment does not constitute a directive to the Court to exclude from its consideration the question whether certain expenditure were 'decided on in conformity with the Charter', if the Court found such consideration appropriate. It is not assumed that the General Assembly would seek to hamper or fetter the Court in the discharge of its judicial functions; the Court must have full liberty to consider all relevant data available to it in forming an opinion on a question posed to it for an advisory opinion." *(I.C.J. Reports 1962,* p. 157.)

The situation in the two cases is parallel; in *Certain Expenses of the United Nations,* as in the present case, there was some question as to the desirability of stating that the Court should examine the whole of the legal situation and in particular the validity of the acts of the General Assembly. But unlike what has occurred in the present case, and although the General Assembly eschewed placing the Court's terms of reference on the broadest basis when it rejected the amendment of France submitted for that purpose, the Court nevertheless, on that occasion, found that it had competence and was bound to conduct that thorough examination in order to acquit itself fully of its judicative task. How indeed can a court deduce any obligation from a given situation without first having tested the lawfulness of the origins of that situation? Between the Court's decision in 1962 and the present Opinion a change of attitude is manifest.

19. In the present case, in which the Court has based its Opinion on an interpretation of Articles 24 and 25 of the Charter as to the powers of the Security Council, and on an interpretation of the legal nature of the powers of the General Assembly, it would have seemed particularly appropriate to have exercised unambiguously the Court's power to interpret the Charter, which the General Assembly itself, in resolution 171 (II) of 14 November 1947, formally recognized that it possesses. That resolution recommends the reference to the Court of points of law "relating to the interpretation of the Charter".

20. I must therefore briefly indicate the reasons why I disagree with the Court with regard to the legal nature of resolution 2145 (XXI) and its effects.

It is the content of resolution 2145 (XXI) which determines the scope of that decision; it contains various declarations:

(a) as to the right of the peoples of South West Africa to freedom and independence, based on the Charter, General Assembly resolution 1514 (XV), and its previous resolutions concerning the Territory (first and seventh paragraphs of the preamble, para. 1 of resolution 2145 (XXI);

(b) recalling the obligations under the Mandate and the supervisory powers of the United Nations as the successor to the League of Nations (second paragraph of preamble, para. 2 of the resolution);

(c) as to the administration of the Territory in a manner regarded as contrary to the Mandate, the Charter, and the Universal Declaration of Human Rights (fifth paragraph of preamble, para. 3 of resolution);

(d) as to condemnation of *apartheid* and racial discrimination as constituting a crime against humanity (sixth paragraph of preamble);

(e) as to the right to take over the administration of the mandated territory (eleventh paragraph of pramble; paras. 4, 5, 6 and 7 of resolution).

21. It is also important to recall that underneath the quasi-unanimity which is often urged in favour of resolution 2145 (XXI) having certain legal effects there lie serious differences of view.

(a) The Soviet Union and nine other States (Albania, Byelo-russia, Cuba, Czechoslovakia, Hungary, Poland, Romania, Ukraine, Yugoslavia) expressed reservations (see Secretary-General's second written statement, paras. 30 to 39) with regard to the setting-up of a United Nations organism for the administration of the Territory of Namibia, which is one of the essential objects of resolution 2145 (XXI) (cf. last paragraph of preamble and paras. 4 and 5 of the resolution).

(b) Australia and Japan drew attention to the complexity of the legal problems involved and reminded the General Assembly that it "must keep strictly within the frame-work of the Charter and of international law" (*ibid.,* Australia: para. 49; Japan: para 57).

(c) Canada said that "the General Assembly was not called upon to make a juridical judgment as to whether in one respect or another the government in charge of the Man-date had been delinquent in carrying out the Mandate entrusted to it . . ." (*ibid.,* para. 50), whereas, as we have seen in paragraph 20 above, the fifth and sixth para-graphs of the preamble and paragraph 3 of the resolution make formal declarations on that subject.

(d) The representative of Belgium explained "that his deleg-ation's support of the text (resolution 2145 (XXI)) for which he had voted did not, in any way, imply that the delegation approved it without doubts or reservations. His delegation would have preferred the point of law of the General Assembly's competence to be clarified as fully as possible" (*ibid.,* para. 40).

In the same way, Brazil declared that the decision for the Mandate to be revoked and the United Nations to take over direct responsibility for the Territory "would be based on doubtful juridical grounds" and "expressed a series of reservations". For example: "it was not . . . legitimate for the General Assembly to decide to revoke the Mandate" (*ibid.*, para. 60).

(e) Italy and the Netherlands formally reserved their position with regard to paragraph 4, concerning an essential point of resolution 2145 (XXI): the assumption by the United Nations of direct responsibility for Namibia (*ibid.*, paras. 45 et seq.). New Zealand reserved its position with regard to the methods of implementation.

(f) Israel considered "that the political aspect of the question of South West Africa outweighed the possible legal problems, and that even the most scrupulous concern for legal niceties might at this juncture cede its place to the political wisdom of the majority of the General Assembly" (*ibid.*, para. 51).

(g) It will be recalled that two States voted against resolution 2145 (XXI) and that three abstained, while all indicating definite reservations.

22. Thus there were 24 States which, in one way or another, expressed opposition, reservations or doubt. The fact that 19 of these States voted for resolution 2145 (XXI) does not in any way diminish the effect of the observations and reservations they made upon the text, for in voting for it the States in question did not withdraw them; thus their votes signified acceptance of a political solution of which some features remained, for each of them, the subject of the opinions expressed. Resolution 2145 (XXI), therefore, was not voted with quasi-unanimity of intention; it was voted by a large majority, clearly under the strong impression that law was not being made.

It was argued before the Court on behalf of the Secretary-General that the concept of reservations was not applicable to the voting of decisions in organs of the United Nations (hearing of 8 March 1971). As the Opinion makes no pronouncement on that point, suffice it to recall that the practice is a constant one, necessitated through the need to provide States wishing to dissociate themselves from a course of action with a means of making their attitude manifest (on the usefulness and meaning of such reservations, see the opinion of Judge

Koretsky in *Certain Expenses of the United Nations, I.C.J. Reports 1962*, p. 279). The consequence of the rejection of this practice and its effects would be to treat the political organs of the United Nations as organs of decision similar to those of a State or of a super-State, which, as the Court once declared in an oft-quoted phrase, is what the United Nations is not. For if a minority of States which are not in agreement with a proposed decision are to be bound, however they vote, and whatever their reservations may be, the General Assembly would be a federal parliament. As for the Security Council, to affirm the non-existence of the rights of making reservations and of abstention would, for the permanent members, be a simple encouragement to use the veto. The everyday operation of the United Nations would be deprived of all the flexibility made possible by statements of reservation and by abstention; as Judge Koretsky put it:

> "Abstention from the vote on the resolutions on these or those measures proposed by the Organization should rather be considered as an expression of unwillingness to participate in these measures (and eventually in their financing as well) and as unwillingness to hamper the implementation of those measures by those who voted 'in favour' of them." (*I.C.J. Reports 1962*, p. 279.)

23. Resolution 2145 (XXI) is a recommendation of the General Assembly concerning a mandated territory. With certain exceptions, recommendations have no binding force on member States of the Organization. It is therefore either in the law of mandates or in the Charter that justification for an exception must be discovered.

24. First, let us re-examine the question of revocation under the mandates system as it was originally established. The international status of the mandated territory was defined by the Court's Opinion of 1950, and "it is in accordance with sound principles of interpretation that the Court should safeguard the operation of its Opinion of 11 July 1950 not merely with regard to its individual clauses but in relation to its major purpose" (separate opinion of Judge Sir Hersch Lauterpacht annexed to Opinion of 1 June 1956, *I.C.J. Reports 1956*, p. 45). It is in this spirit that enquiry must be made whether the

power of revocation of the Mandate was, either in the 1950 Opinion which is the broadest account of the principles governing the matter, or in the proceedings and arguments preceding that Opinion, regarded as being an element of the international status defined by the Court.

25. It will be recalled that the question put by point *(c)* of the request for opinion contained in the General Assembly resolution of 6 December 1949 ran as follows:

"Has the Union of South Africa the competence to modify the international status of the territory of South West Africa, or, in the event of a negative reply, where does competence rest to determine and modify the international status of the territory?"

This question was put in a sufficiently general way for it to have been possible, either in the Opinion of the Court, or in the separate and dissenting opinions, to raise the question of unilateral modification of the status of the Territory by the United Nations; competence "to determine and modify the status" is the widest kind of competence, since it enables the existing obligations both to be defined, and their limits stated, and also to be "modified". It is therefore important to observe that the only statement by the Court on point *(c)*, to be found in identical terms in the reasoning and in the reply itself, was:

"that competence to determine and modify the international status of South West Africa rests with the Union of South Africa acting with the consent of the United Nations".

While it is true that the Court's conclusion replied, at the time, to a claim by the Mandatory to modify the status of the Territory unilaterally, the formula used in the Opinion is absolute, and does not contain any suggestion of exceptions, as for example the case of unilateral revocation of the Mandate, or of any partial, less substantial, modification of the status by the United Nations. It must be recognized that neither the Court nor any judge who took part in the 1950 proceedings was ready to admit the existence of a power of revocation appertaining to the United Nations in case of violation of the Mandatory's obligations.

This was not, however, because the problem was not raised before the Court at the time. The written statement of the United States Government touched on the question (*I.C.J. Pleadings, International Status of South West Africa*, pp. 137-139) and the Secretary-General, in his oral statement, attributed sufficient importance to it to make it one of his conclusions:

> "Fourth, the possibility of revocation in the event of a serious breach of obligation by a mandatory was not completely precluded. It was suggested that in the event of an exceptional circumstance of this kind it would be for the Council or for the Permanent Court or for both to decide" (*ibid.*, p. 234).

Then the statement went on to discuss the notion of *"a solution agreed between the United Nations and the mandatory Power"*(*ibid.*, p. 236, italics in the original), which was to be confirmed by the Court in its reply to question *(c)*. On this point, the statement ended as follows:

> "Could not the International Court of Justice be put into a position to play a constructive role?" (for the interpretation and application of the Mandate) (*ibid.*, p. 237).

Without seeking to base a decisive argument on these facts, they do nevertheless make it impossible to advance the contrary argument that the reason why the question of unilateral revocation of the Mandate was not mentioned in the Court's reply to question *(c)* was because the problem had not been mentioned during the proceedings. As is apparent, it had been raised by the United States and by the Secretary-General.

26. As early as 14 December 1946, the General Assembly had adopted resolution 65 (I), inviting the Union of South Africa to propose a trusteeship agreement for the consideration of the General Assembly. And from that time on, invitations to negotiate followed each other; resolution 141 (II) of 1 November 1947, resolution of 26 November 1948, and so on up to the request for advisory opinion of 6 December 1949. After the Opinion of 11 July 1950, the General Assembly con-

tinued its efforts towards negotiation with the Union of South Africa (resolution 449 A (V) of 13 December 1950; resolution 570 A (VI) of 19 January 1952, in which the Assembly: "Appeals solemnly to the Government of South Africa to reconsider its position, and urges it to resume negotiations . . . for the purpose of concluding an agreement providing for the full implementation of the advisory opinion"; resolution 651 (VII) of 20 December 1952, which maintained the instructions to negotiate given to the *Ad Hoc* Committee of Five by resolution 570 A (VI) of 19 January 1952, resolution 749 A (VIII) of 28 November 1953, etc.). Up to the time of the Eleventh Session, in 1957, the General Assembly does not seem to have conceived of any other means of solution of the problem of South West Africa than that of negotiation, and it was only in resolution 1060 (XI) of 26 February 1957 that the Committee on South West Africa was instructed to examine the legal means at the disposal of the organs of the United Nations, the Members of the United Nations, or the former Members of the League of Nations; this was the source of the initiative of the two member States of the United Nations, who were also former Members of the League of Nations, which resulted in the Court's Judgments of 1962 and 1966. The question put to the Committee on South West Africa was:

> "What legal action is open to *the organs of the United Nations*, or to the Members of the United Nations, or to the former Members of the League of Nations . . . to ensure that the Union of South Africa fulfils the obligation assumed by it under the Mandate . . ." (emphasis supplied).

The general line followed by the United Nations was thus to obtain a South African commitment to negotiate a trusteeship agreement, with certain attempts to arrange an interim international status, as the Opinion recalls in paragraph 84.

27. It will be sufficient to observe that between 1950 and 1960, the date of the Applications filed by Ethiopia and Liberia, when it was a question of carrying on the work done by the Court in its Opinion of 11 July 1950, no one claimed that there existed a power of revocation of the mandate by the organs of the United Nations, or even a power to modify the provisions of the mandate by such unilateral means. The facts

169

THE CASE FOR SOUTH WEST AFRICA

afford the proof: it was known in 1960 that contentious proceedings before the Court would be lengthy and would involve some risk, whereas, according to the Court's present Opinion, a power of unilateral revocation of the Mandate by the General Assembly has always existed, ever since the refusal by South Africa to submit to supervision and present reports on its administration of the Territory. The least that can be said is that the General Assembly was certainly not aware in 1960 that it had such power, when it contented itself with commending Ethiopia and Liberia upon their initiative (resolution 1565 (XV) of 18 December 1960), and that the States which opposed the claims of South Africa were no better informed since, as became apparent in October 1966, it would have been infinitely more simple and rapid to "modify" the mandate by unilateral action in 1960, even after having consulted the Court on the means to be used, by a request for advisory opinion similar to that to which the Court has now replied *ex post facto*. But this was never contemplated at any time before the revocation declared in October 1966, so flimsy did the idea of a unilateral power to revoke the Mandate appear.

28. In 1955, at the time of the Opinion on *Voting Procedure on Questions Relating to Reports and Petitions Concerning the Territory of South West Africa* (Advisory Opinion of 7 June 1955, *I.C.J. Reports 1955*, pp. 67 ff.), Judge Lauterpacht gave exhaustive study to all the problems raised by the implementation of the Opinion of 11 July 1950, including that of the legal position of a mandatory which systematically refused to take account of the recommendations addressed to it (cf. his separate opinion at pp. 118, 120-121 and 122). It is important to note that, even when he supposes that the Mandatory had over-stepped "the imperceptible line between impropriety and illegality, between discretion and arbitrariness, between the exercise of the legal right to disregard the recommendation and abuse of that right" (p. 120), Judge Lauterpacht does not pronounce on the possible legal sanctions, and makes no mention of the idea of revocation for violation of the obligation of the Mandatory to act in good faith. The purpose of his argument is the affirmation of the legal nature of that obligation, the idea of sanction only being relied on as a confirmation thereof.

29. The conclusion to be drawn from the conduct of the United Nations and of the States most directly concerned by solution of the problem of South West Africa is that the power of revocation is not a feature of the mandates system as it was originally established. It is not consistent with any reasonable interpretation of the powers of the General Assembly in the field of mandates to discover today that it has had for 25 years what the Council of the League of Nations had never claimed, and thus has not merely means to revoke the Mandate, but also, merely by drawing attention to such power, the possibility of obliging the Mandatory to render account to it, which is an argument that was never employed.

30. The system described in the Opinion of 11 July 1950, which did not go so far as to affirm the existence of a legal obligation to negotiate a trusteeship agreement, did not entail, even implicitly, the concept of unilateral revocation, the accent being laid exclusively on the idea of negotiation between the United Nations and the Mandatory. As the Judgment of 21 December 1962 in the *South West Africa* cases subsequently explained, "the Council could not impose its own view on the mandatory . . . and the mandatory could continue to turn a deaf ear to the Council's admonitions" (*I.C.J. Reports 1962*, p. 337); the 1950 Advisory Opinion on the *International Status of South West Africa* had said that "the degree of supervision to be exercised by the General Assembly should not therefore exceed that which applied under the mandates system . . ." (*I.C.J. Reports 1950*, p. 138).

The existence in the mandates system of a power of revocation has not been proved.

31. The second justification presented to support the revocation of the Mandate refers to a special power of the United Nations to take a decision to revoke it, even if such power did not exist with regard to mandates originally, by a sort of transposition of a general rule relating to violation of treaties. It is sought to justify resolution 2145 (XXI), with regard to its effects, by an appeal to the general theory of the violation of treaty obligations, and by affirmation of the existence of a right for the United Nations, as a party to a treaty, namely the Mandate, to put an end to that treaty by way of sanction for the refusal of the other party, the Mandatory, to fulfil its obligations.

171

In the first place, the idea that the mandates system is a treaty or results from a treaty is not historically correct, as was recalled by Judge Basdevant:

"The Court has felt able to rely on what it recognizes as the treaty character of the Mandate established by the decision of the Council of the League of Nations of 17 December 1920. I do not subscribe to this interpretation. I adhere to the character of the instrument made by the Council of the League of Nations on 17 December 1920 . . . I have not found anything to indicate that *at that time* the particular character of the Council's instrument was disputed" (*I.C.J. Reports 1962*, p. 462; emphasis supplied).

It must be added that, even if one concedes that the Mandate is a treaty, there is no rule in the law of treaties enabling one party at its discretion to put an end to a treaty in a case in which it alleges that the other party has committed a violation of the treaty. An examination of the rival contentions is necessary, and the one cannot prevail over the other until there has been a decision of a third party, a conciliator, an arbitrator or a tribunal.

32. The mandates system having been established on the international level, it became binding subject to the conditions on which it was established, that is to say without the inclusion therein of any power of revocation. To modify any international status of an objective kind, there must be applied thereto the rules which are proper to it. The argument for the unilateral power of revocation of the mandate by the General Assembly has no basis but the idea of necessity, however it may be clothed. And, as Judge Koretsky recalled in 1962, the end does not justify the means (*I.C.J. Reports 1962*, p. 268). To say that a power is necessary, that it logically results from a certain situation, is to admit the non-existence of any legal justification. Necessity knows no law, it is said; and indeed to invoke necessity is to step outside the law.

33. In these circumstances, for me the problem of the legal consequences of resolution 2145 (XXI), and of the related resolutions of the Security Council, arises in a way very different from that adopted by the Court. As Judge Lauterpacht said in 1955, and as Judge Koretsky said in 1962, I consider that the recommendations of the General Assembly, "although

on proper occasions they provide a legal authorization for Members determined to act upon them individually or collectively, . . . do not create a legal obligation to comply with them" (*I.C.J. Reports 1955*, p. 115). In the present case, in the absence of a power of revocation in the mandates system, neither the General Assembly nor even the Security Council can cause such a power to come to birth *ex nihilo*. Thus we have here recommendations which are eminently worthy of respect, but which do not bind member States legally to any action, collective or individual. This classic view was laid before the Court by the representative of the USSR in the case concerning *Certain Expenses of the United Nations* (written statement, *I.C.J. Pleadings*, p. 273; oral statement, *ibid.*, pp. 411f.). In 1962 and in 1970, France also argued that the United Nations could not, by way of recommendation, legislate so as to bind member States (*I.C.J. Pleadings, Certain Expenses of the United Nations*, pp. 133 f.; written statement of France in the present case, *Pleadings*, Vol. I, pp. 365-368, with the reminder of frequently expressed reservations, *ibid.*, p. 368, note; see also the declaration of the United States Government on the attitude of certain States following the Opinion on *Certain Expenses of the United Nations*, in particular on the problem of the double standard obtaining among member States: UN doc. A/AC.121/SR.15.Corr.1).

Resolution 2145 (XXI) is a recommendation with considerable political impact, but the member States of the United Nations, even including those which voted for its adoption, are under no legal obligation to act in conformity with its provisions, and remain free to determine their own course of action.

34. There is still to be considered the argument that the Security Council has, if need be, "confirmed" resolution 2145 (XXI) (cf. the statements made in this sense on behalf of the United States Government by Mr. Stevenson, hearing of 9 March 1971). But how can an irregular act be rendered legitimate by an organ which has declared only to have "taken note" of it or "taken it into account"? To regularize an act connotes the power of doing oneself what the first organ could not properly do. And the Security Council has no more power to revoke the Mandate than the General Assembly, if no such power of revocation was embodied in the mandates system. Hence the problem remains.

As for the contention that the Security Council was entitled under Articles 24 and 25 of the Charter to intervene directly in the revocation of the Mandate and take decisions binding on States because the situation was being dealt with under the head of the maintenance of international peace and security, that is another attempt to modify the principles of the Charter as regards the powers vested by States in the organs they instituted. To assert that a matter may have a distant repercussion on the maintenance of peace is not enough to turn the Security Council into a world government. The Court has well defined the conditions of the Charter:

"That is not the same thing as saying that (the United Nations) is a State, which it certainly is not, or that its legal personality and rights and duties are the same as those of a State. Still less is it the same thing as saying that it is a 'super-State', whatever that expression may mean." (*I.C.J. Reports 1949,* p. 179.)

35. There is not a single example of a matter laid before the Security Council in which some member State could not have claimed that the continuance of a given situation represented an immediate or remote threat to the maintenance of peace. But the Charter was drawn up with too much precaution for the disturbance of its balance to be permitted. Here again the words used before the Court in 1962 by the Soviet representative are apposite:

"The opposing of the effectiveness of the United Nations Organization to the observance of the principles of the United Nations Charter is legally groundless and dangerous. It is clear to everyone that the observance of the principles of the United Nations Charter is the necessary condition of the effectiveness of the United Nations. The experience of the United Nations clearly shows that only on the basis of the strict observance of the principles of the United Nations Charter can the Organization become an effective instrument for the maintenance of international peace and security and the development of friendly relations among States." (*I.C.J. Pleadings, Certain Expenses of the United Nations (Article 17, paragraph 2, of the Charter),* pp. 411 f.; see also the French Government's written statement in the same case, *ibid.*, p. 134, and cf. the parliamentary statement of H.M. Government on the legal nature of obligations arising out of Security Council recommendations: *Hansard*, Vol. 812, No. 96, 3 March 1971, pp. 1763 ff.)

The same point was stressed by the delegates of several States in Security Council discussions of the matter with which the Court is now concerned. They pointed out that the only way of laying States under obligation would be for the Council to take a decision based on Chapter VII of the Charter after proceeding to effect the requisite determinations, a method which the Council chose not to adopt.

The degree of solidarity accepted in an international organization is fixed by its constitution. It cannot be subsequently modified through an interpretation based on purposes and principles which are always very broadly defined, such as international co-operation or the maintenance of peace. Otherwise an association of States created with a view to international co-operation would be indistinguishable from a federation. It would be precisely the "super-State" which the United Nations is not.

36. There are therefore no other consequences for States than the obligation of considering in good faith the implementation of the recommendations made by the General Assembly and the Security Council concerning the situation in Namibia (cf. oral statement on behalf of the United States, hearing of 9 March 1971, section IV *in fine*).

37. Nevertheless, considering the importance of the humanitarian interests at stake and of the question of principle raised before the Court for over 20 years, one cannot, I feel, merely record these legal findings and leave the matter there. It would be regrettable not to indicate means of pursuing what the Court established in 1950. It was in my view open to the Court to adopt towards the question put by the Security Council a different approach, one which would not only have been more in conformity with its traditions but also have offered the United Nations some prospects of a solution, instead of an impasse. However, as that approach was not adopted, I cannot do more than outline it.

What is essential in the case of a request for advisory opinion, as in that of a contentious application, is its actual subject, not the reasoning advanced in the course of the proceedings. A court seised of a matter must judge that matter and not another (cf. *Société Commerciale de Belgique, P.C.I.J., Series A/B, No. 78* p. 173; *Fisheries, I.C.J. Reports 1951,* p. 126 concerning *"Des elements qui . . . pourraient fournir les motifs de l'arrêt et non en constituer l'objet"*; similarly, in the *Minquiers and Ecrehos* Judgment, *I.C.J. Reports 1953,* p. 52, the Court distinguished between the reasons advanced and the requests made). The request made to the Court was that it should define the present legal status of Namibia, and the opposing contentions of States were no more than explanations proposed to the Court, some holding that the revocation of the Mandate was final, others that it was dubious or illegal. But this is veritably a request that the Court declare what has become of the Mandate and what are the legal consequences of various actions, whether on the part of the Mandatory or on the part of the United Nations. The Court was at liberty to reply to that request with reference to other reasons than those advanced before it, and by another system of argument, on one condition, that it did not reply to another request than that formulated and that it thus avoided transforming the case "into another dispute which is different in *character*"

38. The 1950 Advisory Opinion defines South West Africa as "a territory under the international Mandate assumed by the Union of South Africa on December 17th 1920" (*I.C.J. Reports 1950,* p. 143). Thus there exists an international mandatory regime which remains in force for so long as it has not been ended by a procedure legally opposable to all States concerned. The principle of the protection of peoples not yet fully capable of governing themselves, constituting "a sacred trust of civilization" concretized in the mandate status of 1920, still holds good. The Court had in 1950 shown the legal path to follow in order to modify and, if so desired, terminate that status. It was that path which ought to have been followed.

39. The Advisory Opinion of 11 July 1950 did not, to be sure, impose upon South Africa, as a legal obligation, the conclusion of a trusteeship agreement. The Court refrained from taking to its logical extreme the position of principle which it adopted in saying "To retain the rights derived from the Man-

date and to deny the obligations thereunder could not be justified" (*I.C.J. Reports 1950*, p. 133) and declined to say that the
Mandatory's obligations included that of converting the Mandate into a trusteeship agreement. But that is not the end of
the matter, as is shown by the suggestion of Judge De
Visscher made in subsequent writings supplementing the
views of his 1950 Opinion on the purport of the obligation to
negotiate (*I.C.J. Reports 1950*, pp. 186 ff.) and also the treatment of the problem by Judge Lauterpacht in 1955 (para. 28
above).

40. In my view the Court should in its present Opinion have
taken up and acted upon the observations made on this point
by the two judges mentioned. In its Judgment of 20 February
1969 (*North Sea Continental Shelf, I.C.J. Reports 1969*, p. 48)
it recalled the import of any obligation to negotiate, already
defined in the Advisory Opinion on *Railway Traffic between
Lithuania and Poland*: it is an obligation "not to enter into
negotiations but also to pursue them as far as possible with a
view to concluding agreements" (*P.C.I.J., Series A/B, No. 42*,
1931, p. 116). In 1969 the Court found that the negotiations
conducted prior to the *North Sea Continental Shelf* cases had
not satisfied that condition.

41. Let us briefly recall the position hereon of the South
African Government, which is to the effect that it was impossible for it to negotiate with the United Nations following the
Advisory Opinion of 11 July 1950. This contention is very
clearly argued in the South African Counter-Memorial and the
oral statement of 11 October 1962 (*I.C.J. Pleadings, South
West Africa*, Vol II, pp. 86-95, and Vol. VII, pp. 241-250).
According to that Government the *Ad Hoc* Committee set up
in 1950 and the Committee on South West Africa in 1953 had
been charged to seek ways and means of implementing the
Advisory Opinion; similarly, the Good Offices Committee set
up in 1957 was to seek an agreement whereby the Territory as
a whole would continue to have an international status consistent with the purposes of the United Nations. South Africa's
argument is based on these strict terms of reference and inden-
tifies them as the cause of the absence of any negotiations
with a view to the implementation of the 1950 Opinion. Thus
in 1959 South Africa offered "to enter into discussions with an
appropriate United Nations *ad hoc* body that might be

appointed after prior consultation with the South African Government and which would have a full opportunity to approach its task constructively, providing for fullest discussion of all possibilities", and this statement was repeated in identical terms in 1960 (*ibid.,* Vol. I, p. 83, Memorial of Ethiopia; and Vol. II, p. 91, Counter-Memorial).

42. Even before the 1950 Opinion the General Assembly, by successive resolutions in 1946, 1947 and 1948, had for its part thrice called upon South Africa to negotiate a trusteeship agreement. After the Court had found that South Africa was under no legal obligation to bring the Territory within the trusteeship system, the Assembly took many further initiatives to which paragraph 84 of the present Opinion alludes (see also para. 26 above).

43. The conflict of standpoints can be roughly summarized as follows: The aim of the United Nations was to arrive at the negotiation of a trusteeship agreement, whereas South Africa did not want to convert the Mandate into a trusteeship. It is necessary to determine which party has been misusing its legal position in this controversy on the extent of the obligation to negotiate. The difference in the appreciation of the legal problem as between 1950 and today bears solely on that point. In 1950 the Court was unable, in its Opinion, to envisage the hypothesis that difficulties might arise over the implementation of the obligation to observe a certain line of conduct which it found incumbent on South Africa in declaring that an agreement for the modification of the Mandate should be concluded; hence its silence on that point. But the general rules concerning the obligation to negotiate suffice. If negotiations had been begun in good faith and if, at a given juncture, it had been found impossible to reach agreement on certain precise, objectively debatable points, then it might be argued that the Opinion of 1950, finding as it had that there was no obligation to place the Territory under trusteeship prevented taking the matter further, inasmuch as the Mandatory's refusal to accept a draft trusteeship agreement could in that case reasonably be deemed justified: "No party can impose its terms on the other party" (*I.C.J. Reports 1950,* p. 139). But the facts are otherwise: negotiations for the conclusion of a trusteeship agreement never began, and for that South Africa was responsible. The rule of law infringed herein is the obligation to negotiate

in good faith. To assert that the United Nations ought to have accepted the negotiation of anything other than a trusteeship agreement on bases proposed by South Africa, that, coming from the Government of South Africa, is to interpret the 1950 Advisory Opinion contrary to its meaning and to misuse the position of being the party qualified to modify the Mandate. In seeking to impose on the United Nations its own conception of the object of the negotiations for the modification and transformation of the Mandate, South Africa has failed to comply with the obligation established by the 1950 Opinion to observe a certain line of conduct.

The United Nations, on the other hand, was by no means misusing its legal position when it refused to negotiate with any other end in view than the conclusion of a trusteeship agreement, for such indeed was the goal acknowledged by the 1950 Opinion and already envisaged by the League of Nations resolution of 18 April 1946. "It obviously was the intention to safeguard the rights of States and peoples under all circumstances and in all respects, until each territory should be placed under the Trusteeship System" (*I.C.J. Reports 1950*, p. 134). It would have been legitimate for the United Nations to have taken note of the deadlock and demanded South Africa's compliance with its obligations to negotiate.

44. This view is reinforced by South Africa's consistent interpretation of its own powers, whether it be its pretension to the incorporation of the Territory — something essentially incompatible with the mandate regime — or its contentions with regard to its legal titles apart from the Mandate. The legal position of Mandatory formally recognized by the Court in 1950 gave South Africa the right to negotiate the conditions for the transformation of the Mandate into a trusteeship; since 1950 that position has been used to obstruct the very principle of such transformation.

45. An analysis on these lines, if carried out by the Court and based on a judicial finding that there had been a breach of the obligation to transform the Mandate by negotiation as the 1950 Opinion prescribed, would have had legal consequences in respect of the continued presence of South Africa in the mandated territory. I consider that, in that context, the legal consequences concerned would have been founded upon solid legal reasons.

7

WORLD COURT ATTITUDES
ANALYZED

IN HIS INITIAL reaction to the South West Africa advisory opinion, the South African Prime Minister stated that the reasoning of the majority displayed the results of political manoeuvring rather than of objective adjudication. On this score, no impartial observer at The Hague could have been left in any doubt, and there have indeed been several independent comments to the same effect. This is the considered view of the South African legal team at The Hague.

Ample support for the Prime Minister's statement is provided throughout the lengthy record, partly in the historical background, partly in the actions of the majority of the court in the preliminary stages of the proceedings. This chapter confines itself to the support provided by the opinions themselves. The more closely the opinions are examined, the more apparent their essentially political nature becomes. This can briefly be demonstrated with reference to certain basic aspects.

Basically the court had to determine whether the United Nations organs had:

  (a) the legal power and if so,
  (b) the necessary justification for revoking South Africa's title to administer South West Africa.

Let us see first how the majority tried to cross the second one of these hurdles. The General Assembly, in purporting to revoke the mandate in 1966, stated that it found the justification in fundamental violation of the mandate by South Africa. The court therefore had to consider whether such violations had occurred. What were the majority's findings?

(i) In the first place it stated that . . . the revocation of the mandate could be justified by the admitted fact that South Africa had failed to submit to the supervision of the United Nations and to render reports to it (para 4). Facts concerning the merits of the South African administration, including a plebiscite, were accordingly not relevant and did not require consideration. As the Prime Minister correctly pointed out, this was not a ground relied upon by the General Assembly itself in its resolution 2145 of 1966. A study of the 1966 proceedings leaves no doubt that the General Assembly deliberately decided not to rely on this suggested ground. So the court in effect raises and convicts upon an accusation not made by the prosecutor!

(ii) Secondly, however, the court, having declared that it was not necessary to go into the facts concerning the quality of the South African administration nevertheless proceeded to do so and that in a most one-sided and uninformed manner.

It did so after rejecting South Africa's offers and requests to present a much more detailed and far-reaching investigation into the facts, including possibly inspections *in loco* and including in particular a plebiscite by which the inhabitants themselves could indicate whether they felt oppressed and wronged. The majority said all this was unnecessary, yet professed to know that South Africa's policies and actions were indeed so bad as to warrant a finding that they violated South Africa's obligations to the inhabitants! No wonder this action elicited from Sir Gerald Fitzmaurice the very strong protest that there were few, if any, mature systems of private law, the courts of which would have refused to hear such evidence.

At least one of the majority judges clearly felt uncomfortable about this aspect. Judge Dillard of the U.S.A. recognized that the merits of the policy of *apartheid* had "never been judicially determined and was not the object of adjudication in these proceedings". He accepted that it was not compatible with the court's judicial function to have determined this issue "in the absence of a full exposure of all relevant facts." He tried to explain why the court nevertheless did so, but his explanation, was, with respect, unintelligible.

As to the manner in which the majority judges dealt with the facts, it is hardly surprising to find that their statements are partial and lacking in objectivity. The following examples suffice: — Sir Zafrullah Khan devoted some pages of his individual declaration to this topic, stating *inter alia* that the policy of "a greater degree of ultimate independence for Bantu homelands" made little difference to the true nature of *apartheid* since "the main purpose of the policy . . . continued to be the domination of the white." From the vice-president, Judge Ammoun of the Lebanon, one learned that the "Namibian people . . . had itself asserted its international personality by taking up the struggle for freedom . . . Namibia has decided to fight".

From what has been stated above, it is abundantly clear that the Court wanted to have its cake and eat it too. The Court issued a strong condemnation of *apartheid*, but did not consider the facts and ascertained the true wishes of the inhabitants of South West Africa. Those facts and those wishes would have been freely available to the World Court, had it taken advantage of South Africa's offers.

The majority could indicate no basis in the Charter for the alleged power of the General Assembly to revoke the mandate. This was the main question in dispute and one which was argued at length in the proceedings. Yet the Court did not even attempt to answer it. All it said was that ". . . it would not be correct to assume that, because the General Assembly is in principle vested with recommendatory powers, it is debarred from adopting, in specific cases within the framework of its competence, resolutions which make determinations or have operative design". A host of vital questions are thereby left unanswered. What are the specific cases concerned? How can it make "determinations" which have binding force when its powers under the Charter are expressly confined to discussion and recommendation? What are the limits of its alleged power of binding determination?

183

In contrast to the Court's cavalier dismissal of this issue, Judge Sir Gerald Fitzmaurice in his dissenting opinion analysed it at length by reference to the provisions of the Charter and previous pronouncements of the Court. His conclusion was that with a few irrelevant exceptions there exists an "irrebuttable presumption" that the General Assembly has no executive or operative powers and that resolution 2145 (XXI) could have no higher status than that of a recommendation. And he points out that "the whole of this most important aspect of the matter, resulting from the Court's own jurisprudence as it was enunciated in the 1955 Voting Procedure case, is now completely ignored, and not even mentioned in the present Opinion of the Court — for the sufficient reason no doubt that there is no satisfactory answer that can be given to it".

The Court stated that Article 24 of the Charter vested the Security Council with powers to act as it did in the discharge of its function of maintaining international peace and security. In support of its statement, the Court did no more than refer to an opinion given to the council by the secretary general of the United Nations in 1947. Although the correctness of their opinion was one of the principal and most extensively debated issues in dispute in the proceedings, the court advanced not a word of reasoning for its acceptance of the opinion.

The provisions of Article 24, which actually limit the powers of the council, were said by the Court to extend them — and it placed no limits on these powers beyond the very wide purposes and principles of the United Nations set out in the Charter. It went on to state that under Article 25 the council's decisions are binding on all members of the United Nations. In his dissenting opinion Judge Gros of France pointed out that this was "another attempt to modify the principles of the Charter as regards the powers vested by States in the organs they instituted". And, he added, "to assert that a matter may have a distant repercussion on the maintenance of peace is not enough to turn the Security Council into a world government".

The implications which flow from the Court's attempt to attribute to the General Assembly and the Security Council implied powers which they clearly do not have under the Charter are enormous in their scope. Since they are mentioned elsewhere in this book they need not be repeated here. But it is interesting to note that the dangers inherent in the situation were foreseen by several members of the Court. Judge Gros, for example, pointed out that the constitution of an international organisation cannot be modified by purposes and principles which are always very broadly defined. "Otherwise," he said, "an association of States created with a view to international co-operation would be indistinguishable from a federation. It would be precisely the Super-State which the United Nations is not".

Judges Dillard of the U.S.A. and Onyeama of Nigeria were two others who obviously realised the danger to all members of the United Nations of attributing virtually unlimited powers to the General Assembly and the Security Council. But they sought to avoid the danger by attempting in their separate opinions to confine these powers to the particular case of South West Africa. The power of the Assembly to terminate the Mandate, they said, was a power *sui generis;* the situation was "very specific and unique". In other words there was one law for South Africa and another law for the other members of the United Nations. Needless to say, the judges concerned were unable to indicate any legal basis for the distinction they sought to draw.

The points of criticism mentioned above are by no means exhaustive, but they should suffice to indicate why Sir Gerald Fitzmaurice found it necessary to warn "those thinking of having recourse to the international judicial process at the present time" to "pay close attention" to the explanation of its attitudes which the Court gives in its opinion.

8

SOUTH AFRICA REJECTS
WORLD COURT OPINION

THE DECISION at The Hague prompted South Africa's Prime Minister, B. J. Vorster, to reply in a speech on June 21, 1971, in which he levelled a charge of "double standards" against the legal participants. Here is the text of his remarks.

I do not intend to embark this evening on a complete juridical analysis of the Advisory Opinion on South West Africa of the International Court of Justice. That would require more time. It is however already quite clear that the argument of the Court will not stand up to the test of juridical analysis and that all-too-familiar double standards are evident in the latest Opinion. Thus it is rather ironic that considerable emphasis is placed in the reasoning on the right of peoples to self-determination while South Africa's proposal to let the peoples of South West Africa have the opportunity of expressing their opinions is dismissed in a sentence or two. The Court rejected its own reasoning when it came to the exercise thereof by the peoples of South West Africa.

The pronouncement of the majority Opinion in The Hague this morning was the culmination of a systematic process of erosion of the authority and prestige of the International Court. This erosion process began as far back as 1966, soon after the Court delivered a verdict which was favourable to South Africa in respect of the earlier South West Africa case. Frustration reigned among the leaders of the anti-apartheid campaign and feelings ran high. This verdict, which was not merely an opinion, did not suit them at all and their anger knew no bounds.

In the United Nations some vied with one another to find the most abusive language for the Judges who found in South Africa's favour — Judges of the highest reputation internationally in the administration of justice. And let it now be stated in the clearest possible terms — that these Judges reached their verdict on no other basis than that of a sense of duty towards the judicial office to which they had been called and in doing so they upheld the highest traditions of that office. They did not seek international popularity. In other words, they realised that they would in all likelihood be jeopardised in their future careers as indeed was the case with a number of them. Nevertheless, they did not fail in their duty.

South Africa's enemies indicated in the United Nations that the Court would in future have to be packed with persons who would see to it that a verdict favourable to South Africa would not again be forthcoming from that quarter. A characteristic of today's Opinion is that the 1966 verdict was dismissed with contempt or was ignored — and with it the basic principles on which it rested — principles that had been built up through the long years of jurisprudence of the International Court and its predecessor, the Permanent Court.

I believe that no-one in the world can be so naiive as to think that this result was achieved by pure coincidence or by objective jurisprudence. I am waiting with interest to see how many States will in future have the necessary confidence to submit their disputes voluntarily for adjudication to the Court. South Africa's arguments are contained in thousands of pages of the Court records and will be available for all who are interested in studying them and forming their own opinion on the validity of the legal principles on which South Africa has built its case.

For the present, however, the essential question which each and everyone asks himself is: what is this all about? The answer to this question is that we are here concerned with a facet of the international political vendetta which has for many years now been waged against South Africa. The clearest evidence that most of our opponents are not concerned with the welfare of South West Africa is provided by the fact that they do not wish to test the standards of development reached by the peoples of South West Africa.

This naturally explains why our accusers have in the past always flinched from proposals that have contained the possibility of an inspection and have once again evaded a complete investigation into all the facts and circumstances and the testing of the wishes of the inhabitants of South West Africa themselves. The Advisory Opinion that the World Court has given today confirmed this fear of a thorough consideration of the hundreds of allegations of oppression. On the other hand, I see in this evasion of a thorough investigation of the facts a refusal by both the United Nations and the World Court to look facts in the face. They know that the facts of our administration of South West Africa will reveal the falsity of the gross accusations.

Considering the climate to which I have already referred, the pattern of events was not unpredictable. South Africa took part in the proceedings because it has nothing to hide and in order to show the world how strong the merits and justification of its case are. Its Legal Team succeeded outstandingly in doing so and I have already expressed my deep appreciation to them. Throughout it was not South Africa but its opponents who were on the defensive and on the retreat in regard to the merits of the case. From the time that the South African Legal Team arrived in The Hague in January for the preliminary aspects of the oral proceedings it was however clear that the majority of the Court had a steamroller approach which is foreign to a Court of Justice.

In the same way the participation in the proceedings of judges who had previously attacked South Africa in the United Nations in the most unrestrained language particularly with regard to policy and activity in South West Africa is unknown in civilized legal systems. The Court even continued to hear the case although the political pressure which the United Nations was putting on it obviously made it impossible to give an objective opinion. Although South Africa's request for the appointment of an *ad hoc* judge was refused, the O.A.U. was on the other hand allowed to take part in the proceedings in spite of the fact that three judges of its Member States served on the bench.

Against the background I have just sketched, it is not surprising that the opinions of the majority were clearly politically motivated however they tried to clothe them in legal language. The Court faced the problem of showing where the U.N. had acquired the competence to adopt binding resolutions on matters such as South Africa's right to administer South West Africa, for the Charter makes no provision for this. This aspect naturally has far-reaching implications for other countries as well, as they too may be affected in the future by the attribution of wide powers to U.N. organs. But the majority of the Court did not allow themselves to be put off in any way by this.

No provisions of the Charter were quoted to justify the action of the General Assembly and no bounds to the extent of its powers were indicated. The powers of the Security Council are according to the Court also virtually unlimited in spite of the clear wording of the Charter. If any value at all is to be attached to this Opinion it would set an extremely dangerous precedent for States in general. The question can be asked if the Court now wishes to turn the U.N. into a World Parliament. It is therefore not surprising that some judges tried to cover themselves by saying that the precedent is valid only for South Africa and not for other States.

I need scarcely add that they have not even tried to indicate a legal basis for such a distinction. But the majority opinions may be rejected not only on legal grounds. The majority can indicate no acceptable factual basis which would justify the termination of our right of administration. As chief justification for the decision the Court mentions our refusal to report on South West Africa to the U.N. But even the General Assembly has not relied on this in its resolution. And the further allegation in the majority opinions that we have failed in our duties towards the inhabitants of South West Africa is also without foundation.

The untenability of the majority opinions was underlined by the minority judges, Sir Gerald Fitzmaurice of Britain and Judge Gros of France. In the light of their analysis and findings it is clear that legal considerations were not a deciding factor for the majority. They even say so pertinently and have recorded their protest. Judge Fitzmaurice even warned States to study the reasoning of the majority carefully before they risk making use of the Court's jurisdiction in present circumstances. Indeed, the minority opinion shows not only disagreement but also the strong protest against the violation of law contained in the majority opinion.

It will be clear from what I have already said that the Government has no hesitation in rejecting the majority opinion. An Advisory Opinion by its very nature is of no binding force and in the present case is totally unconvincing. It is our duty to administer South West Africa so as to promote the well-being and progress of its inhabitants. We will carry out this duty with a view to self-determination for all population groups. We have guided and administered the peoples of South West Africa for more than half a century in a manner which has earned their wholehearted confidence. We have set them on the way of peace, prosperity and self-determination and we do not intend to fail that trust. We shall therefore proceed with our task and shall not neglect our responsibility towards South West Africa and its peoples.

G

A

GEOGRAPHICAL FEATURES OF SOUTH WEST AFRICA·

The Territory of South West Africa is situated in the south-western part of Africa, and is bounded by the Atlantic seaboard. The Tropic of Capricorn divides it into two nearly equal parts. The total area is 824,269 square kilometres (318,261 sq. miles) including the area of Walvis Bay (1,124 sq. kilometres or 434 sq. miles) which, although part of the Republic of South Africa, is administered, for the sake of convenience, as part of South West Africa. With a scant population of 526,004 in 1960 and estimated at 610,000 in 1966, this huge country has one of the lowest population densities in the world, less than one person per sq. kilometre, as compared with 12 in Liberia, 20 in the U.S.A. and 346 in the Netherlands, for example.

Topographically, South West Africa can be divided into three regions, the Namib, the Central Plateau and the Kalahari. The Namib is the western marginal area between the escarpment and the coast, a desolate strip of sand desert stretching along the entire coast-line and rising rapidly as one proceeds inland. It is 80 to 130 km. (50 to 80 miles) in width and constitutes rather over 15 per cent. of the total area of South West Africa. The Central Plateau lies immediately east of the Namib, and also stretches all the way from the northern to the southern boundary of the Territory. Varying in altitude from 1,000 to 2,000 metres (3,280 to 6,560 feet) it offers a diversified landscape of rugged mountains, rocky outcrops, sand-filled valleys and gently undulating plains. It covers rather more than 50 per cent of the Territory. Finally, there is the Kalahari which covers the eastern, north-eastern and northern areas of South West Africa. Its outstanding feature is its thick layers of terrestrial sands and limestone. Over the greater part of the area the main problem, and one which inhibits development, is a near-total lack of surface water. Moreover, ground water often occurs at such depth as to make it uneconomic to exploit. By contrast, floods occur annually in the eastern parts of Ovamboland and the Caprivi Strip, which are much better watered than the rest of the area.

A major problem in South West Africa is the sparseness, irregularity and, therefore, the ineffectiveness of the rainfall.

Practically the whole of the coastal area receives an average of less than 50 mm. (2 ins.) *per annum*, while the north-eastern part of the country receives over 400 mm. (16 ins.). The rainfall over the plateau area improves steadily from south-west to north-east. Only along the Okavango River in the north and in the Caprivi Strip can rainfall conditions — 600 mm. (24 ins.) — be regarded as favourable for the denser type of human occupation and fairly intensive agricultural exploitation.

Throughout the Territory, the effectiveness of the sparse rainfall is further reduced by its spasmodic distribution and a high rate of evaporation caused by the Territory being in the summer rainfall area, with high day temperatures. Low atmospheric pressure, due to high altitude, aggravates the effect. The distribution of rainfall throughout the year (or years) is such that, in effect, an average rainfall figure often represents the mean between the extremes of drought and flood conditions. Particularly is this true of the low rainfall areas. The north-eastern part of the Territory, however, has the combined advantages of a higher average rainfall, a longer rainy season and better distribution.

As a result of sporadic rainfall, all the inland rivers only flow intermittently, being in spate for a few brief periods during the rainy season and the river beds being dry for the rest of the year. The Fish River in the south is the only inland river with a fairly substantial number of permanent pools along its course, and during a good rainy season the river may actually flow for as many as four months of the year. A number of storage dams have been constructed on the rivers with intermittent flow, but serious difficulties arise as the result of the high silt content of the flood water and the high evaporation rate. In the northern area of Ovamboland, where the rainfall is normally sufficient to meet the water requirements of man and beast, recurrent periods of drought and consequent crop failure can nevertheless pose serious threats of famine. To combat this, the Administration has had built well over a hundred dams of different types and sizes.

The only permanent rivers in South West Africa rise outside its borders and, except for small sections flowing through the Territory, constitute part of the country's boundaries. In the south the Orange River flows in a 1,000 metre-deep gorge, and so possesses only a limited potential for irrigation. Along the northern boundary of the Territory two permanent rivers, the Kunene and the Okavango, offer the most reliable and accessible water supplies in South West Africa. Nevertheless, a number of obstacles must be overcome before their full potential can be exploited. In the case of the Kunene, owing to the slight gradient and brackish soils in Ovamboland, irrigation must be undertaken cautiously, and the most suitable crops and farming methods determined by experiment. Moreover, the tapping of the resources of the Kunene has been delayed by technical problems and because international agreement is required. Projects at present being implemented are dealt with later, in Appendix C. The Okavango River seems to offer better prospects for irrigation than the Kunene. It has been determined that from the best potential dam site on the Okavango some 50,000 to 60,000 hectares could be irrigated.

In some places in South West Africa underground water reaches the surface in springs, and many of the towns and Native settlements developed at such places. For the most part, however, underground water cannot be tapped without making use of boreholes. In the central and extreme southern parts, ground water in quantity is scarce, and drilling is often disappointing. Towards the east, conditions are more favourable, some boreholes frequently yielding more than 5 cubic metres an hour: but further eastwards the depth of the boreholes increases to about 300 metres which, together with a corresponding decline in the quality of the water, makes the cost of exploitation almost prohibitive.

The shortage and unreliability of water resources, as outlined above, naturally constitute a limiting factor in agricultural development. In 67.9 per cent of the Territory all dry-land cropping is completely out of the question; and only 1.1 per cent is really suitable for normal dry-land cropping. Stock farming is the predominant type of land usage, and, even with this, nature dictates, by means of such factors as vegetation and water supplies, the zoning of different types of stock — small stock in the arid southern areas, small and large mixed in the central areas, and large stock in the better watered north-ern and north-eastern Native areas.

Grazing land in the Territory has an extremely low carrying capacity. The southern areas support only one large-stock unit or six small-stock units on 30 to 45 hectares; but again the position improves progressively in a roughly north-eastern direction, to a maximum of about one large-stock unit per 6 hectares along the Okavango, Linyanti and Zambesi Rivers, the latter two flowing in the Eastern Caprivi Strip and along its boundary.

In view of the vastly superior potential of the northern and north-eastern parts of the Territory, it is not surprising to find the bulk of the population accumulated there, more particu-larly in Ovamboland, the Okavango and the Eastern Caprivi. This has traditionally been the situation; of their own volition the indigenous Obambo, Okavango and East Caprivi Peoples, jointly numbering over half the total population of the Terri-tory, settled in and confined themselves to these regions, which, though comprising a very small proportion of the total area of South West Africa, contain all the land suitable for normal cropping and the bulk of the best grazing. To this day the areas are reserved for the exclusive use and occupation of the groups concerned.

The mineral deposits of South West Africa display great variety, but only a few have proved of economic importance. There are concentrated occurrences of diamonds, mainly in the Southern Namib near Oranjemund, lead, zinc and copper, mainly at Tsumeb, and salt deposits; but for the rest the Terri-tory's mineral resources, as far as known at present are characterised by rich samples from small deposits scattered widely over the country. The Oranjemund and Tsumeb mines together account for about 96 per cent in value of the Terri-tory's total mineral output. The mining industry is reviewed in the Chapter on the Economy.

During the period following the Second World War, South West Africa has emerged as a fish-producing country of note, by exploiting her teeming marine life along an otherwise barren and inhospitable coast. Since South West Africa possesses no navigable waterways within the Territory, transportation depends mainly on roads and railways. Providing these has been, and still is, a major undertaking in the development of this vast and sparsely inhabited Territory. The only natural deep harbour along a long coastline is at Walvis Bay, which, as noted above, forms part of the Republic of South Africa.

B

POPULATION GROUPS IN SOUTH WEST AFRICA

The population of South West Africa is today, and has for centuries been, a heterogeneous one. The main population groups are the following (in the order in which it is proposed to discuss them below)—

(a)   The East Caprivi Peoples;
(b)   The Okavango Peoples;
(c)   The Ovambo;
(d)   The Bushmen;
(e)   The Dama (also known as Bergdama or Bergdamara or Damara of the Hills);
(f)   The Nama (also known as Khoi or Hottentots);
(g)   The Herero (also known as Cattle Damara or Damara of the Plains);
(h)   The Rehoboth Basters;
(i)   The European or White group (mainly of German and South African origin);
(j)   The Coloureds;
(k)   Others.

THE EAST CAPRIVI PEOPLES

The Caprivi Zipfel (or Caprivi Strip) became a part of South West Africa by a quirk of history. In an agreement of 1st July, 1890, the British Government recognized that the area in question (subsequently named after the German Chancellor, Count von Caprivi) would thenceforth fall within the German sphere of influence, so as to provide access from South West Africa to the Zambesi. In fact the Eastern part of the Caprivi is cut off from the rest of the Territory by large swamp areas. The Western part of the Strip is inhabited only by wandering bands of Bushmen. The inhabitants of the Eastern Caprivi are of Bantu stock, but are not ethnically related to any of the other Bantu clusters found in South West Africa, i.e., the Ovambo and the Okavango peoples or the Herero. Their ethnic relations extend in part northwards into Zambia and in part southwards into Botswana. The main population groups in the Eastern Caprivi are the Masubia and the Mafue. Together they constitute almost 88 per cent of the population, small numbers of the Mayeyi, Matotela, Mashi and Mbukushu tribes making up the rest. These small elements have in course of time become incorporated in the Mafue group.

At the head of each of the two main tribes is a Chief, advised and assisted by a Ngamlela, whose position resembles that of a prime minister, and by counsellor-headmen, representing particular areas. The people generally live in small villages, sometimes having as many as thirty or more habitations. Each tribe has its own vernacular, but all the people also know and speak Silozi (or, as it is also called, Sikololo) which has become the *lingua franca* and is used in the schools. It is a Bantu language, but quite different from the other Bantu languages spoken in South West Africa. By tradition, the East Caprivi Peoples are agriculturists and stock farmers, cultivating the land under a system of individual rights of occupation allocated by the tribal authorities. They augment their food supply by hunting, fishing and collecting wild fruits.

Like the other indigenous national groups, the people of the Eastern Caprivi have been influenced by processes of modernization and provision has been made for religious, educational and medical facilities. They are, however, very conservative, and their general way of life continues to follow the pattern of a subsistence economy. They can, nevertheless, find opportunities for employment in the Republic of South Africa as well as on the construction of public works in the Caprivi area itself. According to the 1960 census, the population was 15,840, representing 3.01 per cent of the total population of South West Africa. The estimated 1966 figure was 17,900 or 2.93 per cent of total population.

THE OKAVANGO PEOPLES

In 1960 the Okavango Peoples numbered 27,871 or 5.30 per cent of the total population of the Territory. The 1966 estimate was 31,500 or 5.18 per cent. They comprise five different tribes, namely the Kuangari, Bunja, Sambiu, Djiriku and Mbukushu, each of which inhabits an area of its own along the southern bank of the Okavango River. The Kuangali language is generally used by the Kuangari, Bunja, Sambiu and Djiriku with local dialectical versions, whereas the Mbukushu have a language of their own. The traditional economy along the Okavango is mixed agricultural and pastoral, with lands or gardens near the kraals (family villages). Stock consists of cattle and goats. Individual rights of occupation of land for cultivation are granted by the tribal authorities, but grazing is on a communal basis. Attempts have been and are being made to teach the Okavangos the principles of irrigation farming, which plays no role in their traditional way of life. This is elaborated later. Fish from the river provides a valuable addition to their diet.

Social organization is based on the matrilineal system, children belonging to the lineal group and clan of their mother. The custom is to live in family villages in which the family constitutes the most important socio-economic unit. The form of government consists of a hereditary chieftainship for each of the five tribes. The Chief, who may be a man or a woman, functions administratively in conjunction with counsellors and ward foremen and is also responsible for the administration of justice. Although each tribe is autonomous, matters of common interest are discussed by the Chiefs at joint meetings under the guidance of an administrative officer. In addition to utilizing employment opportunities created within the area, some Okavango men enter into employment for limited periods in the Southern part of the Territory.

THE OVAMBO

The Ovambo constitute the largest population group in South West Africa — according to the 1960 census they numbered 239,363 or approximately 45.5 per cent of the total population of the Territory (526,004). The 1966 estimate was 270,900 or 44.4 per cent of the total (610,100). There are eight Ovambo tribes, viz. Ndonga, Kuanyama, Kuambi, Ngandjera, Kualuthi, Mbalantu, Nkolonkati and Eunda, each living in its own area of Ovamboland. On account of its geographic isolation, being bordered on the south by vast uninhabited stretches, Ovamboland has had very little contact in the past with the groups living in other areas of South West Africa. However, the various Ovambo tribes were in the early days often at war with one another. Thus, on entering the Territory during World War I the South African forces found the Ovambo, in the words of General Smuts, "riddled with witchcraft and engaged in tribal forays in which there was no security for man or beast."

The social organization of the Ovambo peoples is based on the matrilineal system, and the mother's brother is an important person as far as authority and rules of inheritance are concerned. The tribes are subdivided into broad kinship groups or classes, membership of which is hereditary through the mother. The individual family is, however, the most important socioeconomic unit. The political organization of the Ovambo peoples is well developed, with hereditary chieftainships in the case of the Ndonga, Ngandjera and Kualuthi. Chiefs function together with elected headmen as Chiefs-in-Council. In the case of the other tribes, powers of government are exercised by elected Headmen-in-Council. Here, too, the Councils of the various tribes through the encouragement and guidance of South African officials have joint meetings from time to time in order to discuss matters of common interest.

The languages of the different Ovambo tribes belong to the Bantu language family. Although they differ to some extent, they are closely related to one another and are indeed inter-intelligible. The languages of the two largest tribes, the Ndonga and Kuanyama, have been developed into written languages. The Ovambo are both pastoralists and agriculturists. They live in family complexes consisting of a number of huts and cattle pens which are surrounded by the cultivated lands where millet, sorghum and beans form the main crops. The land belongs to the tribe, but individual rights of occupation of agricultural land are awarded to individuals for life against payment. Grazing is communal. Many Ovambo men accept employment in the southern part of the Territory for limited periods. Since 1870 the Ovambo have been strongly influenced by Christian Missionaries, particularly the Finnish Mission which has developed into an independent Ovambokavango Church, with adherents among the Okavango Peoples also.

THE BUSHMEN

In 1960 the Bushmen numbered 11,762 and constituted 2.24 per cent of the total population. The 1966 estimate was 13,300 or 2.18 per cent. They undoubtedly represent the most ancient section of the inhabitants of the Territory. They belong to the Khoisan peoples and are short in stature with a light yellowish-brown skin. In South West Africa the Bushmen consist predominantly of three groups: namely the Khung, Heikom and Mbarakwengo. The Bushmen are traditionally a hunting people who used to roam far and wide over the Territory in search of game and edible veld foods. The men did the hunting, for which purpose they mainly used bows with poisoned arrows, while the women looked after the gathering of plant foods.

The social organization of the Bushmen was very primitive and centred around small bands consisting predominantly of kinsfolk. Political organization was virtually non-existent. With the advent in South West Africa of more developed groups such as the Nama and Herero, the Bushmen came to be regarded as a danger to life and property (particularly cattle), and were accord-

ingly exterminated or driven away by the other groups
into the more inaccessible desert regions. Even in 1915,
General Smuts said, the South African occupation
forces found "the roving Bushmen still regarded as little
better than wild animals — human vermin of the veld."
The material culture of the Bushmen was a reflection of
their nomadic existence and simple economy. The roam-
ing Bushmen bands erected shelters of grass or branches
which were adequate for their needs while the food in
the vicinity lasted. When they moved on, these shelters
were abandoned and new ones erected elsewhere.

The Bushmen have a language of their own, which is
different from the Nama and Bantu languages, but
shares with the former the phonetic feature of clicks.
The South African authorities have made efforts to
induce the Bushmen to lead more settled lives so as to
facilitate the provision of services for them. In pursu-
ance of this policy, a settlement exists at Tsumkwe
where the Bushmen are initiated into the principles of
agriculture and animal husbandry. Moreover, a large
number of them are employed, at least sporadically, in
the modern economy, mainly on the farms. In this way
many have been adapted to a somewhat more settled
and developed way of life.

THE DAMA OR BERGDAMA

Physically, the Dama are a short-statured, negroid
type, quite distinct, on the one hand, from the light-
skinned Bushmen and Hottentots and, on the other,
from the Herero and Ovambo, who belong to the Bantu
branch. In 1960 they numbered 44,353 and constituted
8.43 per cent of the total population. The 1966 estimate
was 50,200 or 8.23 per cent. The Dama are also known
as the Bergdama or Bergdamara, and are given various
names, some with an uncomplimentary meaning, in certain of the native languages of South West Africa. Very
little is known of the origin or early history of the Dama.
They were first encountered in historical times as
fugitive bands eking out a miserable existence in the
more inaccessible areas of the Territory, or as slaves of
stronger groups, first the Nama, whose language the

Dama had adopted to the complete disappearance of their own, and later the Herero.

By reason of their servile or fugitive existence, the Dama originally possessed no significant political or social organization larger than the individual family, which was often polygamous. However, in 1870, on the urgent representations of missionaries, a tract of land was granted to a number of Bergdama at Okombahe in the Omaruru district. This was later confirmed by the German authorities, and has been maintained ever since. In the Okombahe area the Dama developed a central governing body consisting of a Chief and Councillors. Modernization has had a strong influence on the Dama. Many are engaged, mainly as employees, in the modern economy, and in the Okombahe area they engage in animal husbandry.

THE HOTTENTOTS OR NAMA

The Hottentots are a relatively short, yellowish brown-skinned people. They are probably of the same original stock as the Bushmen, whom they resemble somewhat in appearance. In 1960 they numbered 34,806 or 6.62 per cent of the population. The 1966 estimate was 39,400 or 6.46 per cent.

It is believed that the Hottentots lived originally somewhere in the region of the Great Lakes of East Africa. Probably as a result of pressure from the north by the Bantu, they gradually moved south-west across Central Africa until they reached the Atlantic. They then turned south, moving down the coast of Africa till well beyond the Cape of Good Hope. At different stages of this migration, sections of the people stayed behind, each of which developed into a separate tribe. Accordingly, there lived in the central and southern parts of South West Africa a number of Hottentot tribes, called Nama, after their language.

These Nama tribes were nomadic pastoralists, dependent on their herds of cattle, sheep and goats. No individual ownership of land existed. In their wanderings with their flocks, they exterminated, enslaved or drove away any Bushmen or Dama they encountered. The Nama speak one of the four closely related Hottentot languages which have no clear affinities with the other languages of the African Continent, although, as already mentioned, they share the peculiar feature of click sounds with the Bushmen.

The tribe was the major political unit among the Nama, with an hereditary Chief, assisted by a body of Councillors, at its head. During the first part of the nineteenth century, a number of Hottentot tribes, usually referred to as the Orlam Nama, moved back into South West Africa from the Cape Colony after having learnt the use of fire-arms and horses, a matter of some historical importance, as will be seen later. The further history of the Nama is interwoven with that of the Herero, and it will consequently be convenient, first, to say something about the latter.

THE HERERO

The Herero population of South West Africa is composed of various sections, known as Herero, Mbanderu, Tjimba and Himba. They belong to the southern group of the Bantu peoples, and in 1960 numbered 35,354 or 6.72 per cent of the total population. The 1966 estimate was 40,000 or 6.56 per cent. [1] They are, for the most part, of tall, slender build. According to Herero tradition, their forbears originally lived in the "land of fountains", west of Lake Tanganyika, whence they emigrated to the south. Eventually they reached the Kaokoveld in South West Africa where they remained for some time, probably till about the end of the eighteenth century. When they continued their southward movement, two sections, the Himba and Tjimba, remained behind in the Kaokoveld. They were later joined by a group of Herero who had returned from the South. The three sections together make up the population of the Kaokoveld which is reserved for them as a homeland.

---

[1] These figures do not include the Himba, Tjimba and Herero of the Kaokoveld, who are being dealt with below.

In 1960 the Kaokovelders numbered 9,234 or 1.75 per cent of the total population. The 1966 estimate was 10,500 or 1.72 per cent. They are mainly herdsmen who often trek with their stock from one watering place to another, leading an exceedingly conservative life, other cultures having made little impression on them. They seldom leave their home areas, and maintain, even in their dress, patterns of the distant past. Their traditional form of government is by headmen and councillors who represent various sections of the people. The Herero were exclusively pastoral nomads, and did not practise agriculture, their lives being built around their herds and flocks. Primarily they were interested in cattle although they kept sheep and goats as well. Land, which meant grazing, was regarded as belonging to the community.

The social organization of the Herero is unusual in that it is based on a system of double descent, an individual belonging to two social entities, namely, the *oruzo* of his father and the *eanda* of his mother. Both these groups have their rules and regulations. The Herero system of bilateral descent is unknown amongst the other ethnic groups of South West Africa and Southern Africa. It cannot be widened in scope, and it can only exceptionally be applied to a non-Herero. There is scarcely room for interlopers or new citizens, and so the Herero people can only regenerate itself from within. In this sense it is the perfect model of a "Chosen People": by immutable law, ordained from the beginning, all humanity consists only of Herero and Strangers.

The Herero language belongs to the Bantu family of languages, but differs substantially from other Bantu languages in South West Africa. The traditional religion of the Herero was closely bound up with ancestor worship, and centred round the holy fire which was always kept burning and could only be rekindled with sacred firesticks inherited from past generations. The Herero never developed a centralised political structure with a paramount authority. Hererodom meant a loose conglomeration of factions, each in itself independent and led by a Chief who was both leader and priest, and whose powers derived from his possession of the holy fire and from his wealth.

THE WARS BETWEEN THE HERERO AND THE NAMA

During 1829 and 1830, the southward movement of the Herero was accelerated by droughts, which forced them to move with thousands of head of cattle into territory claimed by the Nama. Clashes immediately followed, in which the Herero were initially victorious. Consequently the Nama sought the assistance of one Jonker Afrikaner, the Chief of a tribe of Orlam Nama, who was then living in the far south of the Territory. The possession of fire-arms and horses thereupon enabled the Nama to defeat the Herero decisively in a number of battles and minor clashes. In about 1840 Jonker Afrikaner established himself at Windhoek, and for the next twenty years dominated the central part of South West Africa. He kept the Herero in complete subjection. He also carried out successful raids against other Nama tribes and even against the Ovambo in the far north.

By 1860, however, the tide was turning. The Herero, while serving the Nama, had also come to learn the use of fire-arms. Jonker Afrikaner died in 1861, and shortly afterwards the Herero staged a successful revolution. The next nine years witnessed continual bloodshed as the Herero and various Nama tribes fought one another. In 1870 a peace treaty was signed, through the intervention of missionaries, who on the whole favoured the Herero. But in 1880 war flared up again, and after a number of bitter battles, the Herero succeeded in establishing themselves as the strongest force in the central parts of South West Africa. There were, however, a number of Nama bands who scoured the country, among them the remnant of the Afrikaner tribe. The introduction of German rule in South West Africa in 1884, did not of itself end hostilities in the Territory. As will be shown one of the most difficult tasks the German administration had to tackle was the pacification of the country. Hardly had this been accomplished than general uprisings broke out in the years 1903-1907, involving the Herero and most of the Nama tribes.

AFTERMATH OF THE WARS

Years of warfare had a catastrophic effect on the Natives of the southern and central areas of the Territory. The loss of life was immense, particularly among the Nama, Herero and

Dama, so that by the time peace had finally been established, these peoples were scattered, impoverished and demoralised. As will be explained below, after the inception of the Mandate the South African Administration tried to rehabilitate the tribes by providing reserves for them in which they could rebuild their traditional social and political structures. At the same time, they were assisted in various ways to improve their parlous economic plight, by opportunities for employment for them, improved water supplies and better stock, etc. At present the Nama and Herero live partly in their respective reserves, partly in the towns, and partly as employees on farms. Modern education has made considerable advances among them, particularly so in the case of the Nama.

THE BASTERS

During the latter half of the nineteenth century the Basters, persons of mixed Nama-European descent, left the northern Cape in South Africa and moved northwards into South West Africa. In 1870 they settled at Rehoboth, where they have lived ever since. They numbered in 1960, 11,257, representing 2.14 per cent of the total population. According to the 1966 estimate the figures were then 13,700 or 2.24 per cent. The Basters' language is predominantly Afrikaans and their way of life is similar to that of the Whites. In the Rehoboth Gebiet animal husbandry is the chief occupation, although a diversified economy has developed in the township of Rehoboth. Their form of government consists of a Chief and Councillors and they apply their old patriarchal laws.

THE WHITE GROUP

The inhabitants of European descent numbered 73,464 or 13.97 per cent of the total population in 1960. The 1966 estimate was 96,000 or 15.73 per cent. They first began to settle in South West Africa during the last century, even before the establishment of German authority. Most are of South African or German extraction, and speak Afrikaans, German or English. The European population practises a Western way of life. Its members are engaging in agriculture, commerce, industry and administration. The economy of the Territory and its administration depend largely on the knowledge and initiative of this population group. This was a major factor which induced first the German and, later, the South African authorities to encourage further settlement of Europeans in the under-populated central and southern parts of the Territory, as will be seen below.

COLOUREDS

The Coloureds numbered 12,708 in 1960, and constituted 2.42 per cent of the total population. The 1966 estimate was 15,400 or 2.52 per cent. For the most part they are relatively recent immigrants from the Republic of South Africa, and speak mainly Afrikaans. They are to be found predominantly in the larger towns such as Windhoek, Walvis Bay, Luderitz and Keetmanshoop, where they are employed in commerce or industry, or have their own businesses. Many are artisans in the building trade. A small proportion make a livelihood as stock-farmers.

OTHERS

Apart from the above main groups there is an established group of Tswana who live in the Aminuis area and are related to the Tswana peoples of Botswana. Together with various other smaller groups, most of whom speak Bantu languages but are not related to the groups mentioned above, they numbered 9,992 or 1.9 per cent of the total population in 1960. According to the 1966 estimate the figures were then 11,300 or 1.85 per cent.

POPULATION GROWTH

All earlier population figures for the indigenous groups were based on estimates and they cannot be relied upon with any measure of exactitude. Nevertheless, the general trends of those that are available reflect the catastrophic effects of the pre-Mandate violence and bloodshed amongst the groups in the central and southern areas, *vis-a-vis* the relatively settled conditions in the north. Thus the following figures show fairly sustained growth on the part of the Ovambo in the North:

1876	..	..	.. 98,000
1928	..	..	.. 147,600
1960	..	..	.. 239,363
1966	..	..	.. 270,900

To this may be contrasted the following table concerning the Herero, Dama and Nama groups in the South:

Since the inception of the Mandate, all population groups have shown sustained growth, as a result of the favourable conditions established. The general trend will already be apparent from the above figures in respect of the Ovambo, the Herero, the Nama and the Dama. Again figures available for 1921 are not considered reliable in respect of all groups. But the general trend is confirmed by reliable official figures as from 1951 onwards, based partly on census enumerations and partly on official estimates by modern methods. These show the following average annual rates of growth:

The figures for the White and Coloured groups were swelled by immigration and are therefore not strictly comparable to those for the indigenous groups. The 1960 and 1966 totals for each group have already been given in the text above, but are for convenience tabulated below:

Group	1874/1876	1912	1960	1966
Herero ...	90,000 (1874)	19,721	35,354	40,000
Dama ...	20,000 (1874)	19,581	44,353	50,200
Nama ...	16,850 (1876)	14,320	34,806	39,400

Group	1951-1960 & growth per annum	1960-1966: & growth per annum
White Group	4.2	4.2
Coloured Group	3.6	3.2
All Indigenous Groups	1.8	2.0

Ethnic Group	Total		1960-1966: Estimated growth per group of the population
	1960	1966	
Ovambos	239,363	270,900	31,537
Whites	73,464	96,000	22,536
Damaras	44,353	50,200	5,847
Hereros	35,354	40,000	4,646
Namas	34,806	39,400	4,594
Okavangos	27,871	31,500	3,629
East Caprivians	15,840	17,900	2,060
Coloureds	12,708	15,400	2,692
Basters	11,257	13,700	2,443
Bushmen	11,762	13,300	1,538
Tswanas and Other ...	9,992	11,300	1,308
Kaokovelders	9,234	10,500	1,266
TOTAL ALL GROUPS	526,004	610,100	84,096

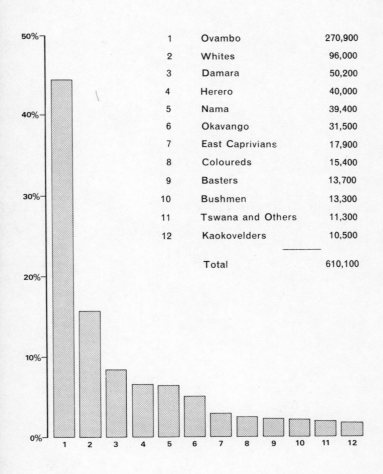

SOUTH WEST AFRICA POPULATION 1966 (ESTIMATED)

1	Ovambo	270,900
2	Whites	96,000
3	Damara	50,200
4	Herero	40,000
5	Nama	39,400
6	Okavango	31,500
7	East Caprivians	17,900
8	Coloureds	15,400
9	Basters	13,700
10	Bushmen	13,300
11	Tswana and Others	11,300
12	Kaokovelders	10,500
	Total	610,100

APPENDIX

C

SOUTH WEST AFRICA'S ECONOMIC BONDS WITH SOUTH AFRICA

by G. M. E. Leistner [1]

SOUTH WEST AFRICA is representative of Africa's most daunting development problems. The most formidable of these are the territory's harsh physical nature — consisting mostly of desert or semi-desert, the constant threats to the vital agricultural sector posed by drought and disease, its numerous small yet highly diverse peoples, the high rate of population increase, the striking contrasts between modern and traditional social and economic patterns, the dependence on sales of a few primary products to overseas markets — all these it has in common with much of the rest of this continent.

Few countries in the world are so sparsely inhabited — its 750,000 people are spread over 318,261 square miles, an area more than twice as large as California. New African countries are as susceptible to unpredictable economic and natural factors, and yet none has a social climate as free of tension as South West Africa. Not a single African country, including the Republic of South Africa, can boast a per capita Gross Domestic Product (GDP) exceeding South West Africa's 687 dollars in 1966. During the period 1963-69, total GDP rose by no less than 10.23 per cent p.a. and GDP per capita by 7.14 per cent p.a. at current prices.

---

1 The author is professor of Economics at the University of South Africa, Pretoria, and specialises in African development.

213

In this context, it must also be remembered that ever since the United Nations started functioning in January, 1946, its activities in respect of South West Africa have created uncertainty regarding the territory's continued stability — at least among outsiders. The South Westers themselves generally have shown little concern for the verbal battles fought over their destinies at the UN, the International Court of Justice and other international forums. With the odds stacked so heavily against social and economic progress, how could South West Africa advance as impressively as it has done, especially since World War II?

The three principal reasons — not necessarily in order of importance — appear to be the following:

1. The tenacity, skill and resourcefulness of the White population groups that have established modern economic activities under seemingly impossible conditions and are still sustaining these activities.

2. The close links between South West Africa and the Republic of South Africa — administrative, financial, commercial, technical and personal.

3. A competent and impartial administration adapted to the specific needs of the territory, and capable of maintaining the peace between peoples for whom the memory of the merciless wars in which their forefathers killed each other is still very much alive.

In the following outline, we shall be concerned only with the second of these three, scrutinising it from the viewpoint of economic development.

South West Africa's internal market is very small in terms of people and purchasing power. The whole population is about equal to that of a city like St. Louis, Mo., 10 years ago. Total GDP is less than the value of annual retail sales in the state of Alaska. No manufacturing industry of any consequence could produce profitably for a market of that size. Yet exports from South West Africa of manufactured as well as other goods are either impossible or at best difficult, because of a combination of factors that are all casually linked to the vast economic distances separating the productive activities from outside supplies (notably skilled labour, fuel, spare parts) and from consumers.

In the foreseeable future, therefore, the territory is bound to remain heavily dependent upon primary exports, in particular exports of the livestock, fishing and mining industries. Most African countries are faced with similar problems. To overcome them, the United Nations' Economic Commission for Africa is strongly advocating economic unions among several states in order to form the larger markets that are acknowledged to be indispensable to significant industrial development. The practical implementation of this crucial aim of regional economic unions has been woefully inadequate, and this is one reason why so many African states are anxious to establish the closest possible links with the economically powerful European Economic Community.

South West Africa need not look overseas for similar links. Being administered as an integral part of the Republic of South Africa, it has at its disposal the skilled manpower, the research facilities, the vast financial resources, and the entrepreneurial talent of a country which alone accounts for about one quarter of Africa's total GDP. Furthermore, South West Africa enjoys stable government, freedom from internal strife, protection against outside aggression, an able and dedicated civil service, a judicial system of unquestioned integrity, modern and expanding educational, health and other social services. These achievements still elude most other countries on this continent. These and other advantages are but different facets of the territory's close ties with South Africa. It is obvious even to the casual observer that South West Africa's prosperity, progress and stability can continue only for as long as these ties are maintained.

Without the heavily subsidised services of the South African Railways and Harbours Administration (SAR & H), the territory's economy could not have developed to the extent that it has. If these services were to be withdrawn, modern economic life would come to a standstill, with grave consequences for all inhabitants. The vast distances separating the few and generally small settlements, together with a serious shortage of water and the lack of local fuel, necessitate a disproportionately high capital investment and result in financial losses. Up to the end of March, 1970, the Railways had spent 292m. dollars on building up their present physical assets in South West Africa, and had accumulated a total loss of over

89m. dollars since they started operations in April, 1922. Both figures represent the sums of annual figures at prices prevailing at that time and would be very much higher at today's prices.

South West Africa's small and vulnerable economy could not possibly muster the financial, technical and human resources needed to operate this system. Yet on a per capita basis, South West Africa is far better equipped than any other African country. Its 23 miles of railway line per 10,000 inhabitants may be compared with 1.06 miles/10,000 in the United Arab Republic (UAR), 0.3 miles in Ethiopia, and 7.0 miles in the Republic of South Africa (data refer to 1964). Although large relative to the population, the South West African system constitutes only a small fraction of the total network operated by the SAR & H. Being run as an integral part of such a vast and efficiently managed organisation, the South West African System is spared the cost of research and many other essential technical, administrative and related services.

Staff is frequently interchanged between the territory and South Africa. Rolling stock, equipment, spares, etc., are freely interchangeable, and major repairs to locomotives and other rolling stock are carried out in South Africa. Similarly, the harbours of Walvis Bay (which is South African territory) and Luderitz are operated as part of the SAR & H. The road transport services of the SAR & H span the whole of South West Africa and are indispensable in conveying passengers, livestock and goods to and from outlying areas, notably Owambo. Regular flights by South African Airways connect Windhoek with Johannesburg and other major air routes in the Republic and overseas.

In post and telecommunication services, South West Africa is uncommonly well provided for, due to being treated as an integral part of South Africa's services. For every 10,000 inhabitants it had 422 telephones in 1968 as compared with 729 in South Africa, 115 in the UAR, 64 in Kenya and 15 in Ethiopia. In the same year, an average of 584 items of mail were sent or received by every 10,000 inhabitants of South West Africa as compared with 675 in South Africa, 95 in the UAR, 27 in Nigeria and 6 in Burundi. The value of telephone, telegraph and radio installations in the territory amounted to over 34m. dollars in March 1970. Whilst this is not as high as the corresponding figure for railway investment, figures such as these cannot measure the true economic significance of the facilities, or, for that matter, the costs and difficulties that would have to be faced in replacing them in the event of South Africa being forcibly compelled to relinquish administration of the territory.

The postal authorities have learned to deal with a variety of unusual technical and other problems over the years. Elephants uprooting telephones are not uncommon — besides the tribal people occasionally cut the wires to make copper ornaments. The drifting sand dunes of the Namib desert often cover their installations. The vast expanses of Owambo contain not a single stone for building and construction purposes, and in the rainy season the greater part of Owambo is under water. The research facilities and the experience of technical personnel in the Republic of South Africa are playing a vital role in maintaining and improving the intricate network of tele-communication services.

Inadequate water supplies is the foremost natural impediment to South West Africa's development. Until as recently as 1958/59, total expenditure on the improvement of the territory's water resources amounted to less than 1.4m. dollars annually, spent principally in respect of underground water and storage dams to retain part of the occasional run-off of the almost permanently dry river beds. Since then, large-scale projects aimed specifically at uplifting the non-white peoples, as well as road and other construction activities throughout South West Africa, have combined with new mining and industrial developments and together have resulted in ever higher levels of water consumption.

Total consumption is expected to rise to 865m. cubic metres in 1985 and 2,889m. cu. m. by the end of the century as compared with the 1970 figure of 334m. cu. m. The capital cost of providing the additional water which is estimated to be required by the year 2,000 will be about 3,760m. dollars. Preliminary estimates for the non-white homelands alone amount to 797m. dollars. The experts responsible for these estimates stress that they are conservative and merely an extrapolation of past tendencies, that is, they do not provide for unforeseen new industries, mines, etc.

217

Schemes of such magnitude are far beyond the financial and technical resources of South West Africa's small economy. Yet they must be carried out if natural population increase is not to lead to catastrophic pressure on the meagre resources of water and usable land. Due to the financial and technological strength of South Africa, it is a feasible proposition to implement large schemes to convey to the arid inland areas water from the Kunene and later from the other northern rivers. Work is presently under way on the first phase of a project to pump water from the Kunene River at Calueque in Angola, and to channel this water across the border into South West Africa.

Up to the year 1963/64, South West Africa was essentially dependent upon its territorial revenue to finance not only normal public administration but also capital expenditure on roads, dams, hospitals, etc. Only Whites were (and still are) paying income tax. The expansion of services and investment depended principally on the limited capacity of this population group, and was correspondingly slow.

At the end of 1963, the Commission of Enquiry into South West Africa Affairs (the Odendaal Commission) recommended a massive programme of capital works designed to provide the basis for significant social and economic advances by all population groups. For the first five years alone, the report envisaged capital expenditure amounting to at least 162m. dollars. At that time, the territory's total annual revenue amounted to a mere 47.4m. dollars, and it was clear that the proposed development schemes could only be implemented if the Republic were prepared to provide the funds. In fact, the Commission estimated that the South African Government, together with the SAR & H and other State undertakings would have to contribute a total of 220.5m. dollars over five years — a figure equivalent to roughly 388 dollars per head of South West Africa's population.

Up to March, 1969, 73m. dollars had been supplied by the Republic of South Africa in accordance with the Odendaal Commission's recommendations. Since then, an entirely new arrangement has come into force whereby the territory receives annually a specified percentage of the customs and excise revenue collected by the Republic, as well as other amounts from the South West Africa Account of the South

African Revenue Account (a total of 53.9m. dollars in 1970/71).

Thanks to this arrangement, South West Africa is no longer restrained by the relatively small and variable annual revenue available internally for financing essential social and economic development projects. The closer financial ties with South Africa allow needs and means to be matched far better than before. Being part of the rand currency area, South West Africa does not have to face the balance of payments problems that beset most developing economies, and furthermore it has ready access to capital markets in South Africa. The territory is well served by the large South African commercial banks, building and insurance societies, as well as by other financial institutions. The important modern agricultural economy could not survive without the backing of the Land Bank of South Africa.

Although mining is the principal source of public revenue in South West Africa (the 1970/71 estimates provide for 61.3m. dollars), the character of the economy is shaped by agriculture. The Republic is not only the principal market, but also a stable one for South West Africa's agricultural products. Roughly three-quarters of all cattle and about 70 per cent. of small stock marketed are sold in South Africa. Substantial amounts of butter and other dairy products are absorbed by South Africa in good years, whereas large quantities of butter are imported from South Africa in drought years.

Because of the cattle industry's high cost structure, all exports to overseas markets entail financial losses and the industry would collapse if the South African market for beef and dairy products were to be closed to it. A few years ago, about one half of South West Africa's total exports were estimated to be directed towards the Republic of South Africa whereas about 80 per cent. of the territory's imports were believed to come from South Africa.

In view of the efforts made in certain quarters to sever the territory from the Republic of South Africa, it is interesting to reflect on the wide variety of costly specialised services that would have to be built up starting anew if South West Africa were to become a state on its own.

At present the South African Police are maintaining law and order with a force whose size is insignificant relative to the

219

size of the country. Having regard to events in African countries even less ethnically diversified than South West Africa, it may be fairly assumed that a one-man-one-vote constitution imposed upon the territory would necessitate a police force many times as numerous as the present one, at a correspondingly higher cost. South West Africa is not militarised but the South Africa Defence Force would, of course, defend it against aggression from outside, and in the event of a South African withdrawal from the territory, this protection would fall away.

South West Africa's interests abroad are now represented by the Republic's Department of External Affairs, but should it become a separate state it would have to establish its own missions. In that event, South West Africa would also have to find the skilled personnel and the funds needed to promote its exports. The territory would have to look overseas for help in designing and executing highly complex water and power supply schemes. Outsiders lacking knowledge of local conditions would have to be called in to safeguard and promote natural resources such as fishing, mining, the soil, animal and plant life; to control the quality of canned fish and meat exports; to conduct research on soil mechanics, animal diseases, human nutrition, the supply of drinking water, and a host of other technical matters; to administer and expand such services as education, health, labour, the collection of revenue, and so forth.

At present, the wide range of specialised research, technical, financial, commercial and cultural services available in a modern industrial country such as South Africa, are at the disposal of the territory. And it has to be borne in mind that notwithstanding the international character of modern technology, the wide experience gained under the specific circumstances of Southern Africa is irreplaceable. Animal health, breeding, processing and marketing; animal and plant ecology; hydrology; mining technology; building and construction; human health and education — these and many other fields of specialised study are constantly being investigated in the territory, or else this is done on behalf of South West Africa by institutions such as the following:

The Onderstepoort Veterinary Research Institute
The Namib Desert Research Institute

The Weather Bureau
The National Institute for Water Research
The Fishing Industry Research Institute
The Animal and Dairy Science Research Institute
The Botanical Research Institute
The Horticultural Research Institute
The Plant Protection Research Institute
The South African Wool Textile Research Institute
The National Physical Research Laboratory
The National Building Research Institute
The National Institute for Road Research
The National Mechanical Engineering Research Institute
The South African Institute for Medical Research
The South African Bureau of Standards
The National Institute for Personnel Research.

In addition to these, there are the specialised research and information sections of the various State departments, as well as the services of private firms. The high standard of professional services enjoyed by the inhabitants of South West Africa in respect of health, education, architecture, engineering, accounting and so forth is due to the supervision by professional bodies such as the South African Medical and Dental Council, the Nursing Council and the Institute of South African Architects.

The natural preconditions for South West Africa's development, notably climate and physical structure, are unquestionably among the most difficult found anywhere in the world's less-developed regions. Yet, in the foreseeable future, few, if any, developing territories or States enjoy more propitious conditions for sustained economic growth and, hence, for social peace and progress. In view of the efforts being made by the United Nations and others to terminate South Africa's administration of South West Africa, it may be legitimate to speculate briefly about the possible consequences of a forced South African withdrawal.

Although the South African Government has never pronounced on the matter, it can reasonably be assumed that it would at least remove all locomotives, rolling stock, government motor vehicles, portable equipment and apparatus, as

221

H

well as records and files. All employees of the Government would presumably be ordered to return to the Republic of South Africa. Although exceptions would probably be made for humanitarian reasons, the above measures alone would inevitably lead to the complete standstill of all economic activities and administration, as well as the end of preventive and curative health services for people and animals.

The consequences are hard to imagine but even a little reflection will show that the termination of railway and tele-communication services alone must lead to great hardship in a country as vast and as dependent upon outside food and other essential supplies as South West Africa. Severe epidemics of malaria and other diseases are inevitable once there is an inter-ruption in the application of preventive health measures. Simil-arly, the territory's cattle industry would face ruin due to foot-and-mouth disease, and lung disease which are endemic in neighbouring areas.

What of the Non-White peoples whose well-being is presumably to be promoted by severing the territory's links with South Africa? Apart from the consequences of introduc-ing a Westminster type of democracy in a country such as South West Africa with its ethnically highly diverse inhabi-tants, the Non-Whites would also be hard hit by loss of employment. The termination of the extensive development projects currently being established in respect of water, power, education, health, etc., as well as the deteriorating posi-tion in respect of food, health, education, etc., referred to above, would inevitably lead to suffering for the peoples of South West Africa.

At present, well over 80,000 Bantu men alone are gainfully employed in South West Africa, besides Bantu women and other ethnic groups. There is no doubt that a substantial portion would lose their jobs as the result of the standstill — and possibly the collapse — of the modern economy and admi-nistration that would result from a South African withdrawal. And obviously this would not be merely a brief interval fol-lowed by still faster growth rates.

It is difficult to imagine how a UN controlling authority could replace the well over 5,000 white administrative officers, engineers, technicians, teachers, etc., that are now employed by the Government. Furthermore, it can be assumed that a large proportion of professional men, businessmen, clerical and other employees in the private sector, including Coloureds and Bantu, would prefer to return to South Africa where they would readily find employment.

Whereas this departure of skilled people would in itself suffice to disrupt the economy seriously, it is doubtful that a UN administration could find the necessary funds to meet the annual recurrent budget (about 162m. dollars p.a.), let alone the very large sums for essential capital developments (notably water). Obviously, the economic upsets sketched above would significantly affect the territory's internal revenue. Even assuming that the diamond and other mines, which at present directly contribute approximately 61m. dollars to public revenue annually, were to continue functioning without interruption, there would still remain a shortfall of over 100m. dollars to be covered, mostly from outside the territory (on the optimistic assumption that current expenditure as well as rates of taxation and duties would remain unchanged).

Enough has probably been said to show that the economic ties between South West Africa and the Republic of South Africa are crucial if progress and stability in the territory are to continue. It would be interesting to learn how those seeking to sever these bonds propose to promote the economic well-being of *all* indigenous people, be they Owambo, White, Damara, Nama, Kavango, Herero, Coloured, Bushman, Tswana, Baster or other.

(e) There is a need for statesmanship to prevent an impasse. A wise and proper solution would take into account the wishes of the inhabitants. So long as South Africa continues in administration of South West Africa, whether legally or not, her co-operation is necessary for the ascertaining of those wishes. In the context of the Court proceedings South Africa offered its co-operation in making its plebiscite proposal. And the possibilities of reaching agreement about a fair and practicable testing of the wishes of the inhabitants, independently of the context of the Court Proceedings, ought at least to be explored before any other action is decided upon.[f]

However, whereas South Africa was in principle favourable to an impartial supervision of the suggested plebiscite, and herself proposed the very thing, United Nations supervision would certainly not in her view qualify as impartial, regard being had to so much past experience. Meanwhile no better evidence can be provided of the irrational, illogical and unrealistic position of the majority of the World Court than the fact that, had South Africa heeded this Opinion (and moved out of South West Africa immediately, closing its borders and its harbour of Walvis Bay) then even in the few short months between the Opinion and the publication of this book hospitals would have closed, trains would have ceased to run and no longer would there have been any telephone or telex connection with the World.

The coal which South Africa provides for the generation of power would soon have been used up, and the pumps which bring water to man and beast in this barren desert-like country would long since have stopped. People would either have fled the territory, or else have been dying of thirst in their thousands. Whether the Court would have wished it or not, all over South West Africa the lights would by now have been out.

f See e.g. the article by George F. Kennan, former U.S. Ambassador to Moscow, in the January 1971 issue of *Foreign Affairs*, and Appendix C in which Professor Eric Leistner deals with the ties between South Africa and South West Africa.

APPENDIX
D

RESPONSE TO AWAKENING
POLITICAL ASPIRÁTIONS
Special Survey

SOUTH AFRICA'S POLICY for South West Africa has always been governed by the need to distinguish between the various population groups, which differ so markedly in ethnic origin, culture, language and level of development. There are no less than eight major non-White groups who consider themselves as separate peoples and who clearly wish to remain so. At the inauguration of the South African mandate in 1920, their history of internecine was still a recent memory. In the economic sphere reciprocal protection was imperative in order to eliminate friction which would seriously have hampered progress.

For example, the indigenous groups had to be protected against the private enterprise of the White man, whose capital, skills and business expertise the underdeveloped man could not match. The latter's homelands therefore needed protection, and their ownership, occupation and use had to be reserved for the particular groups in question. The White man might try to buy the land. Other non-White groups might attempt to take it by force in the traditional manner.

In South West Africa, the various groups had, within their respective domains, adopted different forms of self-government appropriate to their situation. On the one hand, there was the White group, used to Western democratic procedures and the testing of public opinion by means of the ballot box. At the other end of the scale were primitive people, such

as Bushmen, whose organization was based on the maintenance of an efficient and mobile band of hunters. Between
these two extremes were others differing greatly from one
another in the type of governmental organization each required
and had evolved for itself.

South Africa was well versed in this kind of situation and
unhesitatingly applied a policy of differentiation in the administrative sphere — as, indeed, other powers were doing in
other parts of Africa — by recognizing the indigenous political
and administrative institutions she found in South West Africa
and encouraging them to operate more efficiently. After the
Second World War nationalistic movements arose in Africa
and subject peoples clamoured for 'freedom' while 'colonialism' and 'empire' came to be regarded as unethical concepts.

Up to the middle 1950s colonial and trusteeship powers
were stressing that adequate educational advancement and
economic self-sufficiency were essential if independence were
to be granted. But the anti-colonialists began to insist that political advances must always take precedence over economic
and educational considerations. Although in Southern Africa
circumstances differed in certain respects from those further
north, a similar need arose to accelerate the tempo of advance
and to devise ways and means of satisfying the awakening political aspirations of the under-developed peoples. The problem
was how to do this in a way that would do justice to all concerned and would avoid catastrophic upheavals, particularly in
view of such wide ethnic diversity.

The problem was thrown into focus by events in other countries where ethnic differences existed. In many such situations
there were indications that certain peoples and groups were
unable to assimilate because of their unwillingness to do so. In
many cases, such groups were incapable of jointly governing a
country in a manner fair and acceptable to all, the underlying
reason being, not that one group was superior or inferior to
another, but simply that the differences between them were
too great. On the African continent, many new states became
independent under constitutions providing for national governments elected by a majority vote, ethnic differences being
either disregarded or not adequately provided for. This often

led to bloodshed, refugeeism and the undermining of the economy.

If South Africa had bowed to the pressure to weld South West Africa into one integrated political entity, to be ruled on the basis of one man one vote for the entire population, the prospect would immediately have arisen of domination by the Ovambo, who constitute 45 per cent of the total population, or by persons exploiting this group's numerical preponderance. Under such integration, the groups faced with subordination would include the most highly developed ones, so important to the whole economy, as well as the weakest and least developed, who have the greatest need for protection. For all the minority groups it would mean the denial of their self-determination, indeed subjugation, a prospect likely to evoke the strongest forces of resistance. It was not difficult to foresee likely chain reactions of violence, the collapse of the economy and the breaking down of so much that had been built up, the sufferers being all the inhabitants.

This conclusion has received very weighty support from a number of quarters, among them the findings of the 1962-63 Commission of Enquiry into South West Africa Affairs, usually known as the Odendaal Commission. It consisted of experts of the highest order in the fields of government and administration, economic development, medical services, ethnology and agriculture. The Commission was appointed by the South African Government to conduct a thorough enquiry and to make recommendations, including a five-year plan, on co-ordinated and accelerated development in all spheres of life for all the inhabitants of South West Africa, 'and more particularly its non-White inhabitants.'

After extensive investigations, the Commission came to the firm conclusion, based on careful reasoning, that the aim of self-determination for the various groups would not be furthered by 'one mixed central authority for the whole Territory.'

Overwhelming support for this was provided by the statements of a number of expert witnesses of exceptional standing in their evidence before the International Court of Justice at The Hague. Some of them came from countries outside South

Africa; others — from inside the Republic — had spent most of their lives serving the diverse peoples of South Africa in a variety of spheres — education, the church, the press, the social sciences, economics and agriculture. Their testimony was uncontradicted, and its basic contentions went unchallenged in cross-examination.

Further very significant support for the South African Government's views of the situation has come from the various non-White groups themselves. What, then, was the alternative, bearing in mind the need for accelerated development towards emancipation and self-realization? In South Africa's view the only feasible course was a broad, flexible general approach, seeking as far as practicable the separate development of each group towards self-determination and self-realization — or turning them 'into self-respecting and self-governing organic entities.'

Experience elsewhere had amply shown that there was no practicable middle course. Every policy which suggested the granting of limited rights to the various groups inside one political structure, had the prospect of one man one vote as an unavoidable end result, with its easily predictable consequences. This would inevitably evoke rising tensions between the groups and a struggle for supremacy.

The South African Government has, therefore, resolved upon the broad approach of separate development as the best means of hastening emancipation. In the political sphere this entails developing institutions of self-government for each of the peoples concerned. Then, when they reach a stage where they are able to control their own destiny, they may negotiate with others on a basis of equality, and decide with whom, on what terms and in what manner — politically, economically, etc. — they wish to co-operate for the common interest.

In the economic sphere the objective is to create increased opportunities for each national group, protecting them against others in so far as that may be necessary. Therefore, accelerated economic development in the homelands of the indigenous groups is a first priority, and education on sound lines, attuned to their needs and developing at the correct pace, must go hand in hand with this.

The policy of separate development is essentially dynamic and flexible, designed to cope with ever-changing circumstances and needs. The growing autonomy of the various peoples should not be construed as an effort to maintain them for all time as totally distinct and isolated units too small to maintain a viable economy in the modern sense. On the contrary, it is hoped and can be confidently expected that the closest economic co-operation will come about between them, on the basis of agreement between equals. This already occurs to a large extent today and must increase in the future as a necessary corollary to economic advance; and since economics and politics defy efforts to contain them separately in watertight compartments, but of necessity must interact, increasing opportunity for profitable political co-operation will arise.

This means that groups which today insist on remaining apart, in their own interests, will most probably at a later date wish to come together in certain respects, to pursue what have by then become common interests. It is a form of economic and political evolution which has occurred in many parts of the world and is proceeding, even today, in Europe in the form of the Common Market. Indeed, a common market may well prove the most suitable form for co-operation to take between the disparate groups in South West Africa — and, perhaps, not only there, but over a far larger area of the Continent, if the nature of present economic developments is any indication.

Another important consideration is that as the political and economic organs and institutions develop among the non-White peoples, the importance of contact and consultation between them and the central governing authority must necessarily grow, and in increasing measure their wishes will have to be taken into account on matters of mutual concern. However, at this stage it is impossible to foresee with any degree of accuracy the ultimate interactions of the various population groups. Circumstances will alter radically.

What is considered anathema today may well become sound practical politics tomorrow, and vice versa. Nor is it necessary to embark on speculation as to what the ultimate future political pattern will be — i.e. whether and to what extent there may be amalgamations or unions of some kind, federations, commonwealth or common market arrangements, etc. The peoples themselves will ultimately decide. Meanwhile, South Africa's task and solemn duty is to help the diverse peoples of the Territory to advance economically, socially and politically, to the stage when they themselves will be able to decide their own future wisely; protecting, guiding and helping them, in a spirit of trusteeship, until their emancipation has been attained.

The South African Government has set itself the task of leading the main population groups of South West Africa in an increasing measure to self-government. The two major population groups, the Ovambo and the White groups, amounting to about 60 per cent of the total, are already self-governing. Ovamboland is situated in the far northern sector of the Territory and is bordered on the south by vast uninhabited stretches. Consequently it has had very little contact with the groups living in other areas. Some trade was carried on to obtain copper and iron, but few Ovambo ever left their tribal territory.

The Ovambos were little affected by the German rule of South West Africa and when South African Administration began, the various Ovambo tribes had for a very long time functioned as separate political entities, each with its own system of rule. The South African Government stationed representatives in Ovamboland and set in motion a process leading to a more modern and effective system of self-government for the region. In 1967 the responsible South African Cabinet Minister announced to a representative meeting of the seven Ovambo tribes that the way was open to them to advance to self-government in accordance with their own wishes. But he recommended that they should include elected representatives in addition to the traditional leaders or chiefs in their system of self-government, in a manner to be determined by themselves.

The Minister assured his audience that the Government intended to continue its assistance on a basis of consultation and co-operation, and envisaged further development in Ovamboland, more buildings, more efficient hospitalization, increased school facilities, more and better roads, extended water services, expansion of business and so forth. He announced a comprehensive plan for expenditure in Ovamboland over the next five years, of about £17m. by one Department alone, on various development projects. The reaction of the Ovambo nation to the Government's offer to grant them self-government was one of unanimous and enthusiastic approval.

As in many societies in Africa, the traditional institutions of the Ovambo people allow the expression of public opinion in a strikingly democratic way. For months various processes of consultation and deliberation took place individually in each tribal group. The other Native nations of South West Africa were also consulted and as a result, enabling legislation under the title 'Development of Self Government for Native Nations in South West Africa Act' was passed by the South African Parliament in 1968. This allowed for specific constitutional arrangements for the developing nations, according to the wishes of each nation.

There is nothing rigid in this legislation and it largely confirms historical facts and circumstances as they exist in South West Africa. Should any population group wish to introduce elected members into their system of government, it would, in terms of the legislation, be free to do so. The type of franchise could be universal, or qualified adult franchise, or a mixture of systems. The Act confirmed the basic right of self-determination of each of the groups. Proclamations issued by the State President in October 1968 established a Legislative Council and an Executive Council in Ovamboland. Jurisdiction over departmental administrative affairs was transferred from the White Native Affairs Commissioners to the Executive Council. The proclamation also laid down rules of procedures and financial regulations.

In accordance with the wishes of a general assembly of delegates from all the Ovambo tribes, which had met in September, 1968, it was provided that the Legislative Council would function on a federal basis, each of seven communities corresponding with the various tribal groups to be represented by six representatives. Each community nominates one member to the Executive Council, which therefore comprises

231

seven members, each of whom is responsible for the control and administration of one or more government departments. The Legislative Council elects the Chief Councillor, who is the head of the executive government, from among the seven Councillors. The Government departments initially established were those of Authority Affairs and Finance, Community Affairs, Works, Education and Culture, Economic Affairs, Justice and Agriculture.

All the posts in the Ovamboland public service are designed to be filled as soon as possible by Ovambos, but in the initial stages, the South African Government will second officials where trained Ovambos are not yet available. The first session of the Ovamboland Legislative Council was opened in October 1968. From the inception of the mandate the White population in the Territory was at a stage of development which justified a form of self-government of a parliamentary nature. This was granted by the South West Africa Constitution Act of 1925 which made provision for the establishment of a Legislative Assembly, an Executive Committee and an Advisory Council. It gave the White group considerable control of its own affairs. But Native Affairs have at all times been excluded from the competence of the South West African Legislative Assembly, and retained by the South African Government.

In bringing education to South West Africa's indigenous groups, the authorities had to contend with a number of problems not usually encountered in such acute forms in other parts of the world. These were the scattered nature of the population, the vast distances, the parents' discouraging attitude to education, the lack of employment opportunities and the diversity of the population. Against this background the Government has done well by increasing school enrolment from 15 per cent of the Native children of school age in 1922-24 to 68 per cent in 1969.

In 1960, when school attendance for these developing groups in the Territory was 40 per cent, the comparative figure was 35 per cent for Kenya, 28 per cent for Ghana, 25 per cent for Nigeria, 14 per cent for Tanganyika, 13 per cent for Ethiopia and 12 per cent for Liberia. A UNESCO document reveals

232

that for the African states as a whole only 16 per cent of the children of school age were enrolled in 1961.

In the period 1960-65, the growth in enrolment amongst South West Africa's non-White groups was particularly impressive. For the Coloured group the increase was 180 per cent against an estimated population increase of 23 per cent. For the Bantu groups the increases were 75 and 14 per cent respectively. The total number of 113,495 pupils of all groups at school in 1968 received instruction from 3,408 teachers. Adult literacy is estimated at being 56 per cent. Through the gradual conversion of mission schools to community schools, parents have been given an opportunity of playing an active part in education services for their children.

The new Augustineum near Windhoek which was completed in 1968 at a cost of £900,000, provides teacher training and secondary, academic, commercial and technical education to the developing nations. At Onguediva in Ovamboland, a similar but more elaborate project will be completed this year at an estimated cost of more than £3m. Two agricultural schools are being established at a total cost of almost £900,000. The total cost of new educational premises to be erected in the next three years amounts to about £14m. University education is supplied in South Africa, and the Administration provides financial assistance for candidates with the necessary qualifications.

Rapid strides are being made in expanding health services for the different population groups of South West Africa. More than £3m. in capital was spent from 1962 to 1969 in creating new facilities, while running expenses totalled £13m. over the same period. Of the total expended on capital costs, 86.1 per cent was devoted to facilities for the developing and Coloured population groups, as against 13.9 per cent for the White group, who constitute about 16 per cent of the total population.

Further extensions to hospital facilities now on the drawing boards for the indigenous and Coloured groups will cost an estimated £23m. over the next five years. There are at present 155 hospitals and clinics in the Territory. Of these 117 are for the non-White groups, 21 render services to all population groups and 19 serve the White population group. Hospital fees for Whites are assessed according to income, but for non-Whites the fees are normally 10 cents (1/2) for admission, and in-patients 50 cents (5/10), irrespective of the duration of treatment, but only if they are able to pay.

There are now 114 medical practitioners and 16 specialists in South West Africa, which works out at 4,500 inhabitants per physician. Except for South Africa, there is no country south of the Sahara with a more favourable distribution of physicians to population. The ratio of about 10 hospital beds per 1,000 of the non-White population groups compares with 1.89 for Tanzania, 0.54 for Nigeria and 1.37 for Liberia.

Growth — that is the watchword of booming South West Africa today. Once one of the undeveloped countries of Southern Africa, the last decade has seen the territory emerge into the light of a new and promising future. The results are to be seen throughout the territory — giant irrigation projects, power schemes, roadworks, mining ventures, housing plans, health service projects, and transport facilities.

South West Africa's 1969 budget of £80m. made up of allocations by the Administration and the South African Government, is twice that of Rhodesia and no less than ten times that of neighbouring Botswana — figures which point the way to sustained growth on a scale unprecedented in the history of the territory. Gross national product last year was £200m. — and this from a population of only 610,000. Estimates are of a steady 5 to 6 per cent rise in G.N.P. annually, in future.

South West Africa's indigenous population has derived appreciable benefits from the establishment and growth of a modern economy. The wages of workers from the indigenous nations in South West Africa are considerably higher than in other African countries. Particularly is this true of unskilled labourers, who make up the bulk of wage earners in all these states. Apart from wages, the immediate supplementary benefits of employment in the modern sector of the economy are obvious and important: better housing, food and clothing; improved health; a generally higher standard of living and a more secure existence.

On their return home to the traditional subsistence economy, they carry with them goods and ideas from the new one, thus spreading fresh ways of thinking which are gradually permeating and changing the old order in the homeland. The desire for a wider range of consumer goods stimulates the quest for gainful employment which, in turn, leads to a better appreciation of the value of education and the benefits of increased production.

It is in this climate that the Government is introducing measures to stimulate material progress. The signs are, therefore, promising, for in the first instance economic development means human development. Progress had reached the point some two or three years ago where the infusion of capital and the application of years of patient research work could begin to bear fruit. The conditions for accelerated development have, therefore, been established which justify the expenditure of large funds which South Africa and the Territorial revenue are supplying for a variety of essential projects.

At present the Government is engaged on a five-year development plan for South West Africa which will entail an estimated direct expenditure of £87m. A hydro-electric project on the Kunene River in Ovamboland is to be commenced at a preliminary cost of £34m. This scheme also provides for the supply and distribution of water by canals which will extend for a distance of 165 miles. The total cost of the project will amount to £137m. It will involve the construction of at least six power stations, which will serve all the main centres by means of an extensive grid network.

An irrigation project for Ovamboland will involve capital expenditure on waterworks alone of about £20m. divided into four five-year development phases. Similar water plans are also being prepared for the other homelands. Hereroland is high on the list of priorities. Discussions are also taking place with neighbouring governments on the use for mutual benefit of the Okavango and Kwando Rivers, in which the Okavango, Caprivi, Herero and Bushmen peoples have a special interest.

Vast areas will be added to the existing homelands to provide a sound basis for development. Developed farm land to an extent of 3,076,155 hectares and valued at more than £13m. has already been purchased by the Government for this purpose. Such additions, consisting as they do of fully developed White farms, are a particularly valuable form of aid, in that the indigenous groups will derive immediate benefit from good water supplies, fencing and the like.

APPENDIX

E

SYNOPTIC TABLE

SIR GERALD FITZMAURICE'S DISSENT

MAIN SECTIONS

DETAILS

237

In general, the areas of the indigenous peoples enjoy climatic conditions and water resources vastly superior to those in the White farming areas. In agriculture, stock diseases have been successfully controlled, and traditional subsistence farming methods are being replaced by more modern techniques. About one million hectares of farmland are now in the process of being rehabilitated. The South African Bantu Investment Corporation is playing an increasingly important role in the economic development of the homelands of South West Africa by promoting the growth of commerce and manufacturing industry. An amount of more than £10m. was recently earmarked for a new five-year plan to be carried out in the Territory.

There are already about 36,000 miles of road in the Territory and at least £12m. will be spent annually to expand the network of tarred roads alone, linking centres as far north as Grootfontein and Tsumeb with the central system. In spite of its small population South West Africa has some 1,500 miles of rail links. Telephone and telex links are being extended, and Windhoek will shortly receive one of the most up-to-date microwave telephone systems available. The total expenditure on development projects for the years 1963-64 to 1966-67 in respect of the indigenous groups alone amounted to £45m.

BIBLIOGRAPHY ON SOUTH WEST AFRICA

1) Bruwer, J. P.: *South West Africa — The Disputed Land* (Cape Town, Nasionale Boekhandel) 1966.

2) Giniewski, P.: *Livre Noir, Livre Blanc — Dosier du Sudouest Africain* (Paris, Berger-Lerrault) 1966.

3) International Court of Justice. South West Africa Cases 1960-1966:
    Counter-Memorial filed by the Government of the Republic of South Africa.

4) International Court of Justice. South West Africa Cases 1960-1966:
    Rejoinder filed by the Government of the Republic of South Africa.

5) International Court of Justice: South West Africa Cases. *Pleadings, Oral Arguments, Documents.*
    1962-1966.

6) International Court of Justice: *Verbatim Record (CR71/1 and on) South West Africa Pleadings, The Hague, 1971.*

243

7) International Court of Justice: *Reports of Judgments, Advisory Opinions and Orders: Advisory Opinion of 21.6.1971.* (The Hague No. 352) 1971.

7a) Molnar, Thomas: *South West Africa* (New York, Fleet Publishing Co.) 1966.

8) Republic of South Africa. Commission of Enquiry into South West Africa Affairs 1962-1963. *Report.* Pretoria, Government Printer, 1964. (R.P. 12/1964).

9) Republic of South Africa. Department of Foreign Affairs. *South West Africa Survey 1967.* Pretoria, Government Printer.

10) Republic of South Africa. Department of Foreign Affairs. *South West Africa. South Africa's Reply to the Secretary-General of the United Nations (Security Council Resolution 269 of 1969).* Pretoria, Government Printer, 1969.

11) Republic of South Africa. Controller and Auditor-General. *Report on the Appropriation Accounts and Miscellaneous Accounts of the South West Africa Administration.*

12) Republic of South Africa. *Estimate of the Expenditure to be Defrayed from South West Africa Account.*

13) Republic of South Africa: *Ethiopia and Liberia versus South Africa* (Official account of the proceedings on South West Africa before the International Court of Justice at The Hague, 1960-1966). Pretoria, Department of Information, 1967.

14) Rhoodie, E. M.: *South West: The Last Frontier in Africa* (New York, Twin Circle Publishers) 1967.

15) South African Embassy: *Report from South Africa,* special Survey on South West Africa (London) 1971.

16) South West Africa Territory. *Estimates of the Revenue to be Collected and Expenditure to be Defrayed from Revenue Funds and Loan Account and Estimates of Expenditure from the Territorial Development and Reserve Fund and Roads Fund.* Windhoek.